The Other Side of Glamour

Global Film Studios
Series Editor: Homer B. Pettey

This series examines European, North American, South American, African, and Asian film studios and their global influence. Taking a multifaceted analysis, each volume addresses several studios representing an era, a regional intersection of production, a national cinema or a particular genre.

edinburghuniversitypress.com/series/gfs

The Other Side of Glamour

The Left-wing Studio Network in Hong Kong Cinema in the Cold War Era and Beyond

Vivian P. Y. Lee

EDINBURGH
University Press

Edinburgh University Press is one of the leading university presses in the UK. We publish academic books and journals in our selected subject areas across the humanities and social sciences, combining cutting-edge scholarship with high editorial and production values to produce academic works of lasting importance. For more information visit our website: edinburghuniversitypress.com

Edinburgh University Press Ltd.
The Tun—Holyrood Road
12 (2f) Jackson's Entry
Edinburgh EH8 8PJ

First published in hardback by Edinburgh University Press 2020

Typeset in 12/14 Arno and Myriad by
IDSUK (Dataconnection) Ltd,
and printed and bound by CPI Group (UK) Ltd, Croydon, CR0 4YY

A CIP record for this book is available from the British Library

ISBN 978 1 4744 2462 2 (hardback)
ISBN 978 1 4744 9470 0 (paperback)
ISBN 978 1 4744 2463 9 (webready PDF)
ISBN 978 1 4744 2464 6 (epub)

Contents

Figures

Acknowledgments

This book was completed at one of the most tumultuous times in the history of Hong Kong, as the city was going through wave after wave of mass protests of a scale and proportion unrivaled by any other metropolitan city in the world. During the final months of writing, the upheavals and controversies streaming through the news channels sounded like distant echoes to the momentous events of a bygone era. The uncanny resonances between past and present, perhaps, can engender new ways of engaging with history itself.

I owe a debt of gratitude to the many people who have been the greatest friends and colleagues in my professional and nonprofessional life. The anonymous reviewers and editorial board members of the Edinburgh University Press offered valuable guidance at different stages of preparing the manuscript. Special thanks are due to Professor Homer B. Pettey, founding editor of the Global Film Studios series, for his invaluable advice and support throughout the process of writing this book. A team of committed research assistants has contributed to the archival research on Cold War–era Hong Kong cinema. I am especially grateful to Dr. Pedith Chan, Dr. Vivian Ting, and Dr. Hyuk-chan Kwon for their friendship and moral support during the most difficult times. Dr. Benglan Goh, my long-time friend and mentor, has always been a source of inspiration. The witty dialogues and generous sharing of academic and non-academic friends are always a blessing to me.

This project was supported by research grants from the Research Grant Council of the Hong Kong SAR (Project No. 9002312; 9002742). Versions of selected chapters have been presented at academic conferences in Hong Kong and overseas, including the International Symposium on

Rethinking Chinese Language Film History (Hong Kong Education University, 2018), the International Conference on Global Cities: The Networks of Connectivity in East Asia, Southeast Asia and the Pacific Region, 1850–1950 (City University of Hong Kong, 2018), and the 4th Annual Conference on the Film Histories of Taiwan and Asia (National Taiwan University of the Arts, 2019). As always, any misspellings and errors that the reader may find in this book are mine.

I dedicate this book to my family, for always being there for me.

A note on the timeline

The reader will find that certain historical figures and events are cross-referenced in different parts of this book. Due to the complexity of the sociopolitical landscape in post-World War II Hong Kong and the intertwined nature of the subject matters in question, close examination of any segment of time will not be effective without due awareness of the larger context that very often exceeds the scope of a single chapter. As a quick-reference tool to navigate the flow of events, a timeline has been compiled to offer an at-a-glance overview of important events and persons involved in the development of the left-wing cinema in Hong Kong. In-text references to the timeline appear in the chapters to avoid redundancy in factual details.

In compiling the timeline, a considerable number of primary and secondary sources have been consulted to clarify discrepancies in dates, spellings, and other factual details. Where possible, information from primary sources, such as newspaper reports and press statements, is adopted. In the absence of first-hand materials, available secondary sources are compared to verify factual accuracy based on their cited references and other contextual details pertaining to the subject in question. Where conflicting understandings are noted in different accounts or reports and the means of verification have been exhausted without yielding a convincing conclusion, no entry is made in the timeline. Additional explanatory details, where appropriate, are given in the footnotes of the respective chapters.

Timeline

1934
- Tianyi (Unique) Film Company establishes operations in Hong Kong.

1935
- The First Cantonese Cinema Clean-up Campaign is launched by the Hong Kong Overseas Chinese Education Committee.
- Grandview Film Company Limited, founded by Chiu Shu-sun and Kwan Man-ching in San Francisco, moves to Hong Kong.

1937
- Tianyi Film Company is reorganized into Nanyang Film Company under Shaw Rende.
- The Central Film Censorship Committee proposes a ban on dialect film to be implemented on 1 July. The South China Film Association sends a delegation to Nanjing to petition against the ban. Delegates include Lee Fa, Chiu Shu-sun, Chuk Ching-yin, Ko Lei-hen, and Chan Kwan-chiu. The central government agrees to a three-year deferral of the ban.
- The ban is disrupted by the outbreak of the War of Resistance against Japanese Aggression on 7 July.

1938
- The Second Cantonese Cinema Clean-up Campaign is launched by Lo Ming-yau, Lai Man-wai, and Ho Ming-wah, etc.

1941
- Japanese occupation of Hong Kong begins when Sir Mark Young, then governor of Hong Kong, surrenders the colony to Japan on 25 December.

1945

- End of Japanese occupation on 15 August.
- Resumption of the civil war between the Nationalist Party (KMT) and the Chinese Communist Party (CCP).

1946

- Great China Film Company is founded by Jiang Boying in partnership with Shaw Runde.

1947

- Yung Hwa Film Company is founded by Zhang Shankun and Li Zuyong.

1948

- A group of left-wing filmmakers, including Yang Hanseng, Cai Chusheng, and Shi Dongshan, arrive in Hong Kong. Plans are soon underway to establish a progressive film company (Nanguo; see 1949).

1949

- The Third Cantonese Cinema Clean-up Campaign is launched by a group of left-wing filmmakers. A joint statement is published in local newspapers, including *Ta Kung Pao*, *Wah Kiu Yat Po*, and the *Kung Sheung Daily News*, on 8 April.
- The Nanguo Film Company is founded on 5 May. In partnership with the Hysan Lee family, who own the Lee Theatre in Hong Kong, the deal is facilitated by Yuen Yiu-hung, film producer and general manager of the Lee Theatre.
- Zhang Shankun establishes the Great Wall Pictures Corporation (also known as the Old Great Wall) on 3 July.
- South China Film Industry Workers' Union is established on 10 July.
- The People's Republic of China is founded on 1 October.

1950

- The Nanyang Film Company is renamed as Shaw and Sons Ltd. The Nanyang Studio is also renamed as the Shaw Studio.
- Fifties Film Company is established by a group of former Yong Hwa filmmakers in the midst of Yong Hwa's financial difficulties. Co-founders include Bai Chen, Sima Wensen, Liu Qiong, Hu Xiaofeng, Li Lihua, Shu Shi, and Sun Jinglu.
- Shipping industry tycoon Lui Kin-hong takes over the Great Wall Pictures Corporation on 25 January and renames it as the Great Wall Movie Enterprises Limited (the "New Great Wall"). Yuan Yang'an becomes general manager.

- Dragon-Horse Films is founded by Fei Mu and Zhu Shilin on 22 February with financial backing from Wu Xingcai, a studio owner and entrepreneur from Shanghai.
- In May, the Southern Film Company Limited is founded with a mission to distribute Soviet and Mainland Chinese productions in Hong Kong. The company is the sole distributor of Hong Kong progressive films in Mainland China and Southeast Asia.
- The Korean War breaks out in June. The US imposes a total trade embargo on China. Supply of raw materials for film production from the US is suspended.

1951

- The Hong Kong government revises the *Places of Public Entertainment Ordinance* to expand the scope of "public entertainment" to include exhibition of images, photography, books, and other kinds of performances.
- The Hong Kong government announces the setting up of Frontier Closed Areas along the northern border of Hong Kong in May.
- Taiwan announces a ban on Chinese-language films (戡亂時期國產影片處理辦法) involving left-wing production companies, stars, directors, and scriptwriters on 7 September.

1952

- The Liberty Film Company is founded by Huang Cho-han.
- Eight left-wing filmmakers—Liu Qiong, Shen Ji, Shu Shi and Sima Wensen, Qi Wenshao, Yang Hua, Ma Kwok-leung, and Di Fan—are deported to Mainland China on 9–10 January. Other left-wing filmmakers, including Bai Chen and Jiang Weixiang, are deported to Mainland China later in the same month.
- Sun Luen Film Company is established on 29 February. Co-founders include Lo Duen, Chan Man, Lee Hok-wah, and Tse Chai-chi.
- The Feng Huang Motion Picture Company is founded by Zhu Shilin in October. Its precursors are Dragon-Horse Films and Fifties Film Company.
- Union Film Enterprise Ltd. is established on 16 November. Among its twenty-one co-founders are Ng Cho-fan, Cheung Ying, Chun Kim, Tsi Lo-lin, and Lee Sun-fung.

1953

- Singaporean entrepreneur Loke Wan Tho's Cathay Organization dispatches Albert Odell to Hong Kong to establish the International Films Distribution Agency. The company also finances Yung Hwa's productions.

- Hong Kong and Kowloon Union of Free Workers in the Film Industry is established on 27 March. (The Union was renamed in the 1950s and 1990s to include theater workers; see below.)
- Asia Pictures is established by Chang Kuo-sin in July with the financial support of the US-sponsored Asia Foundation.
- The Hong Kong Government's Film Censorship Regulations (under the *Places of Public Entertainment Ordinance*) is announced in November. All films, including local and imported films, had to be submitted to the censorship committee for approval for public release. Submissions should include film posters, advertisements, and visual and textual materials used for publicity. An appeal mechanism is introduced with the establishment of the Board of Review to deliberate on challenges to the decisions of the panel of censors.

1955

- Loke Wan Tho's International Films takes over Yung Hwa.
- Shaw establishes its Cantonese film unit.
- On 23 February, the KMT government announces a set of regulations (附匪電影事業及附匪電影從業人員審定辦法) to tighten the procedure of deliberation on left-wing film companies and filmmaking personnel.
- Kong Ngee Motion Pictures Production Company is founded by Union director Chun Kim on 1 August with the support of Ho Khee-yong, owner of Kong Ngee (Singapore).

1956

- In March, International Films merges with Yung Hwa to form a new company, Motion Pictures and General Investment Co. Ltd. (MP&GI). Loke Wan Tho recruits Robert Chung, who trained at Twentieth Century Fox in the US, as general manager, and Stephen Soong, a renowned writer and translator, as production manager.
- Wah Kiu Film Company is founded by Cheung Ying and Tse Yik-chi with the financial backing of Macau tycoon Ho Yin in August.

1957

- The Hong Kong and Kowloon Union of Free Workers in the Film Industry is renamed as the Hong Kong and Kowloon Cinema & Theatrical Enterprise Free General Association ("Free Association").
- Run Run Shaw establishes the Shaw Brothers (HK) Co. Ltd. and acquires land to build the 650,000-square-foot Shaw Movie Town in Clear Water Bay, Kowloon.

1958

- The Great Leap Forward, an ambitious five-year campaign to transform China's agrarian society into a modern industrial society, begins in Mainland China.

1959

- Lan Kwong Film Company is founded by Huang Cho-han with the financial support of Kong Ngee. Lan Kwong specializes in Cantonese film production. Its precursor is Liberty Film Company (1952–1958), a Mandarin film studio.

1962

- Sun Ngee is established by Chun Kim to strengthen the Cantonese production capacity of the Kong Ngee group. Chiu Ngee Motion Pictures, a member company specializing in Chiuchow (Chaozhou) dialect films, is also established.

1963

- Yuet Ngee, a Kong Ngee group studio, is established, specializing in martial arts films.
- Loke Wan Tho announces the establishment of Taiwan International Film Company as MP&GI's overseas branch to expand into Taiwan's film market.

1964

- MP&GI President Loke Wan Tho dies in a plane crash on 20 June after attending the Asian Film Festival in Taiwan. The accident also claims the lives of Loke's wife and accompanying MP&GI staff.
- MP&GI is reorganized into the Cathay Organisation (HK) Ltd. in July.

1966

- A solo hunger strike to protest against the Star Ferry fee increase escalates into large-scale protests and labor strikes in April.
- The Great Proletariat Cultural Revolution (1966–1976) breaks out in Mainland China in May.

1967

- *Wenhui Bao* publishes an article from a Beijing magazine, *Red Flag*, by Yao Wenyuan (a member of the Gang of Four), in which a Hong Kong left-wing film, *Sorrows of The Forbidden City*, is severely criticized. Zhu Shilin, the film's director, is reported to have died of a stroke after hearing the news on 5 January.

- The Hong Kong government imposes a curfew after a labor strike at a plastic flower factory in San Po Kong triggers large scale riots in May.
- Two prominent left-wing stars, Shek Hwei and Fu Chi, are arrested for participating in the anti-British riots in July.
- In September, Great Wall's leading female star Hsia Moon leaves Hong Kong.
- Sun Luen's general manager, Liu Yat-yuen, is arrested. Liu was a member of the Executive Committee of the All-Circle Struggle Committee during the 1967 anti-British riots in November.
- Union Film Enterprise Ltd. closed down, three years after it ceased production in 1964.

1970
- Golden Harvest Group is founded by Raymond Chow, Leonard Ho Koon-cheung, and Leung Fung.
- In May, production and management personnel at Sun Luen, Feng Huang, and Great Wall are ordered back to Guangzhou to attend thought education sessions and to work in the factories. During this time, film production at the three studios is suspended. Sun Luen ceases production between 1970 and 1971.

1971
- Cathay's film production unit is closed down after the release of its last film, *From the Highway*, in February 1970. The company sells its studio to Golden Harvest while retaining its distribution and exhibition business.

1972
- US President Richard Nixon begins his seven-day visit to Mainland China on 21 February. The historical trip signals a normalization of diplomatic relations between the US and the PRC.

1980
- Cinema City and Films Co. Ltd. is founded by actors Raymond Wong, Karl Maka, and Dean Shek. Its precursor is Warrior Films (founded in 1979).

1982
- British Prime Minister Margaret Thatcher visits Beijing in September.
- Feng Huang, Sun Luen, Great Wall, and Southern Film Corporation are consolidated into Sil-Metropole Organization Ltd. in November.

1984

- Hong Kong businessman Dickson Poon and kung fu star Sammo Hung found D&B Films.
- The Sino-British Joint Declaration is signed between Britain and China. This historical document stipulates the return of sovereignty of Hong Kong to the PRC on 1 July 1997.

1987

- *The Film Censorship Ordinance* (1987) introduces a three-tier classification system by age categories: Suitable for All Ages; Not Suitable for Children; Persons Aged 18 or above only. In 1995, Category II is further divided into II(a): Not Suitable for Children and II(b): Not Suitable for Young Persons and Children.

1996

- The Hong Kong and Kowloon Cinema & Theatrical Enterprise Free General Association is renamed the Hong Kong Cinema & Theatrical Enterprise Association Ltd. It is subsequently renamed the Hong Kong & Macao Cinema & Theatrical Enterprise Association Ltd. in 1999.

1997

- Hong Kong officially reverts to Chinese sovereignty on 1 July, ending 156 years of British rule.

For J. Lee

Introduction

As a contribution to the Global Studios series, this book is the first book-length study in English dedicated to Hong Kong's left-wing film studios as a network of individual and corporate agents serving a common ideological course under the auspice of the Communist Party (CCP). Critical discourse on the Hong Kong left-wing cinema has emphasized the progressive filmmakers as primarily an ethical force caught in a left–right divide and an advocate of social and cultural reform through the cinematic medium. While this ethical-reformist bent of the cinematic left is central to the aesthetic vision and public image of the progressive film community, the analysis presented in this study pays attention to the institutional and corporate character of the left-wing film apparatus and their strategic self-positioning in the mainstream film industry during the 1950s and 1960s. This understanding of the left-wing's praxis will have a bearing on production and exhibition strategies of film studios, as well as the continuation of the left-wing film network in the post-Cold War, post-Cultural Revolution era. Considering the change in industrial status and sociopolitical prominence of the reconstituted left-wing film network since Hong Kong's return to Chinese rule in 1997, the temporal stretch to the post-handover period is deemed necessary for an overall evaluation of the historical trajectory of the left-wing film establishment in Hong Kong, in particular in relation to China's cultural policy toward Hong Kong since the mid-twentieth century. In addition to elucidating the historical trajectories and representative figures and films of the major studios, the inquiry into the cinematic left in Hong Kong in this study is informed by the following questions:

- How did the left-wing studios and filmmakers position themselves and their productions in colonial Hong Kong vis-à-vis their right-wing counterparts and other commercial studios at the time?

- Apart from studio labels, what qualities would identify a film as "left-wing" that would differentiate it from non-left-wing (or "right-wing") films?
- Is there a consistent intellectual-political orientation in left-wing studio productions? If so, how did the studio management and production crew negotiate perceived conflicts between art, ideology, and entertainment?
- To what extent has the left-wing studios completed their historical mission since the consolidation and restructuring of the four major studios into a more commercially driven enterprise, Sil Metropole (Hong Kong), in the early 1980s?
- What is the historical significance of the left-wing cinema before the 1980s, and how does it contribute to our understanding of Hong Kong's film culture past and present, and more broadly the relationship between film and society in Hong Kong?
- Does the cinematic left have an "afterlife" in Hong Kong cinema since its decline in the late 1960s, and where can we find its traces today?

Since its inception more than a century ago, Hong Kong cinema has been a preeminent form of local entertainment and a site of ideological contentions propelled by colonial, national, and international politics at different historical junctures until today. Whether seen as "quasi-national," diasporic, or *bentu* (local),[1] Hong Kong cinema in the last century was never far from the epicenter of major political earthquakes that had shaken the foundations of national and international orders. Operating a film studio in a colonial city that was virtually defenseless against the regional economic and political torrents sweeping up its shores, therefore, was no small feat. Oftentimes, artistic vision and idealism had to be guided by shrewd entrepreneurship and astute political sensibility to steer an uncharted course in a small capitalist colonial enclave where trade and commerce were its founding principles.[2] Covering a time span of six decades since the end of World War II, this book traces the historical development of the left-wing film establishment in Hong Kong, which came into being between 1949 and 1952, developed in full swing for about fifteen years, and then went into decline by the end of the 1960s. In the early 1980s, the "classical" left-wing studios were refashioned into a state-owned film and media enterprise that would play a pivotal role in the integration of the Hong Kong and Mainland film industries.

The inquiry begins with the interplay between the macropolitics of the Cold War and the micropolitics of a regionalized/localized ideological warfare between the Nationalist Party (KMT) in Taiwan, the CCP in Mainland China, the British colonial government in Hong Kong, and US intelligence and propaganda agencies. This historical context lends itself to a critical mapping of the general contours of the "cultural Cold War" between the KMT and the CCP as it materialized in the so-called "left–right divide" in the filmmaking world. Indeed, the local film industry was as much a product of the colonial administration's laissez-faire policy as a site of ideological and political contest. While the major studios are the main axis of analysis, the historical trajectory and later transformation of the left-wing cinema in Hong Kong cannot be fully understood without tracing the footprints of their subunits and other cultural agents (who may or may not be a member of the organized "left"), the totality of which made up the left-wing film apparatus, or the left-wing film network, in Hong Kong. This understanding of the cinematic left sheds light not only on the left-wing's engagement with the art and politics of filmmaking, but also on their institutional character and corporate strategies to claim a place in the commercial mainstream. This understanding of the left-wing film network, in turn, illuminates their nuanced legacy in Hong Kong cinema today.

Equally deserving readers' attention, especially those who are better versed in the Western left-wing traditions, are the political forces that conditioned the development of Hong Kong's "left-wing," which was essentially a product of the political rivalry between the KMT and the CCP, whose strategy of "making full use of Hong Kong in the interest of long-term planning"[3] had remained a guiding principle for the party's activities in the British colony throughout the latter half of the twentieth century. In Hong Kong, the "left" is a political entity commonly known as *zuo pai* (lit. the "leftist camp"), which in the Cold War era implicated its opponent, the "right-wing" or *you pai* (lit. the "rightist camp"). As such, the left-wing consisted of a multilayered and sophisticated network of social and cultural organizations, businesses, and schools that formed the CCP's "united front" in Hong Kong.[4] To avoid being politically explicit, the cinematic left identified themselves as "progressive filmmakers" (hence "progressive films") to distinguish their work from commercially oriented and right-wing (pro-Taiwan) films. Instead of being a self-constituted intellectual-cum-workers movement with an anti-establishment bent, the left-wing was an extension of the influence of the CCP in Hong Kong characterized by a patriotic and anti-imperialist outlook. The left-wing cultural front consisted of schools, newspapers, publishing companies, and film studios directly or indirectly sponsored by the Chinese government. As Ching Cheong has cogently argued, the political left in Hong Kong consisted of (and still does) individuals and groups from all levels of society. It is "a unique community distinguished by their support of the Chinese Communist Party and the People's Republic of China."[5] As such, the terms "leftist" and "left-wing" as they have been understood in the West cannot be assumed to be equally valid in the context of pre- and post-World War II Hong Kong. In this book, the term "left-wing" is used to refer to filmmakers, studios, and related organizations directly or indirectly under the supervision of the CCP, as well as left-leaning individuals affiliated with the "official" left-wing establishment.

The film industry in postwar Hong Kong

From the 1930s to the outbreak of World War II, Hong Kong became the center of Cantonese film production with a growing demand in southern China and the Chinese diaspora. Following a hiatus during the Japanese occupation (1941–1945), the reshuffling of the global political and economic order in the second half of the twentieth century increased the leverage of the Hong Kong film industry to develop into a Cantonese film production metropolis in the world. While Hong Kong was gestating toward a regional Cantonese film culture with a transnational distribution network, Mandarin film studios continued to maintain a healthy supply of Mandarin films to the local and overseas Chinese audience throughout the 1940s. Successive waves of immigration from Mainland China in the first-half of the twentieth century had encouraged the development of Mandarin and Cantonese films as two distinctive and transnationally popular Chinese-language cinemas, while other dialect films were also produced on a smaller scale.[6] The parallel hegemonies of Mandarin and Cantonese cinemas were also visible in the major left-wing studios, which roughly observed the division of labor in their respective language specialization with occasional crossovers. At the same time, the local film scene was also animated by the blossoming of acting and filmmaking talents. Studio-owned magazines, too, became a popular pastime among local as well as overseas Chinese audiences.[7]

Hong Kong cinema transformed itself from a complementary production base for the film industry in Shanghai into what Chu Yingchi calls a "quasi-national" cinema with its own distinctive artistic and production practices.[8] This incubation period saw the introduction of sound film in the 1930s and the consolidation of the political boundary between British Hong Kong and Communist China shortly after 1949. These two events would have a lasting impact on the local film industry in the latter half of the century. The first Cantonese talkies have been dated back to around 1933. Among the contenders for the "first Cantonese talkie" title are *White Gold Dragan / Bai jin long* (1933), *Blossom Time / Genü qingchao* (1933), and *The Idiot's Wedding Night / Shazai dongfang* (1933).[9] *Blossom Time* was the debut film of Grandview, a major Cantonese film studio with bases in the US and Hong Kong. Produced by Tianyi (Unique) in Shanghai, the success of *White Gold Dragon* prompted Shanghai-based studios to set up filming facilities in Hong Kong to expand Cantonese sound film production. However, the first Cantonese talkie made in Hong Kong was *The Idiot's Wedding Night / Shazai dong fang* (1933). Since then, Cantonese-language films continued to grow in popularity in southern China and the Chinese diasporas across Southeast Asia and North America.[10] While sound films usually had a greater appeal to the local audience and therefore made good business sense, linguistic affiliation would also strengthen regional distinction, a noncommercial by-product with more far-reaching repercussions in national identity politics. This "language issue" gradually snowballed into keener market competition between Mandarin- and Cantonese-language films (the biggest dialect cinema in the Chinese-speaking world), and no less a political concern of the Nationalist government at a time when a single national language (*guoyu*) was deemed essential to unify a country besieged by external and internal threats. Under the banner of the "New Life Campaign," the Chiang Kai-shek regime was especially hostile to Cantonese films and a ban was proposed in 1937. The KMT authorities softened its stance after a collective lobbying by filmmakers, who stressed the propagandistic value of local dialect films.[11]

The politics of filmmaking in Hong Kong was indexical to the larger picture of a new global order emerging in the wake of World War II and successive waves of decolonization and nation-building in former European colonies. At a historical juncture where international axes of power were defined by Cold War politics, Hong Kong's status as a British colonial city at the southern border of the People's Republic of

China (PRC) with a predominantly Chinese-speaking population was a political and cultural pedigree that would cast a long shadow over its successive governments and no less the people who came to be known as "Hongkongers." Before the PRC closed its doors to the world on the eve of the Great Proletariat Cultural Revolution (1966–1976), cross-border commute between Hong Kong and Mainland China had been frequent and relatively hindrance-free.[12] This explains why the local film industry had been maintaining a close relationship with film studios and personnel in the Mainland, whether cooperating or competing in film ventures. The career of Lai Man-wai, remembered as the "father of Chinese cinema," reflects this two-way traffic between Hong Kong and Shanghai as well as the transnational character of Hong Kong cinema. Lai's filmmaking ventures straddled Shanghai and Hong Kong. He set up his first studio, Minxin, in Hong Kong in 1923, followed by a Shanghai branch in 1926, when film production in Hong Kong was interrupted by a prolonged labor strike.[13] Among his business partners were influential tycoons among the Chinese elite in the British colony. One of Lai's cross-cultural ventures was his collaboration with Brodsky in 1913 in the production of a feature film, *Zhuangzi shiqi* (Zhuangzi Tests His Wife), which was released in Los Angeles in 1917.

Political events such as the US trade embargo and the imposition of political and trade barriers between Hong Kong and Mainland China significantly altered the landscape of film production in Hong Kong. Prior to the founding of the new socialist regime in 1949, the political struggle between the Nationalist and Communist camps and the civil war that ensued after 1945 had already driven thousands of refugees to Hong Kong. Apart from a chronic housing crisis and the shortage of social infrastructure to cater to the postwar population boom, the economic and cultural capital that came with these "southbound" migrants also made possible a speedy economic rehabilitation, when both Taiwan and Mainland China were engrossed in internal chaos and a bitter ideological struggle as both claimed to be the legitimate government of China. Comparatively, Hong Kong was able to maintain a greater degree of political stability. As a laissez-faire economic zone located at an intersection of the socialist and capitalist blocs, the colonial city was also an ideal gateway for espionage and other covert forms of political infiltration. Leveraging their bargaining power with the British colonial administration, the KMT, CCP, and

US intelligence and propaganda units channeled financial and human resources into local cultural and social organizations to pursue their political interests. It was under these circumstances that Cold War politics penetrated the cultural scene and social life of the Hong Kong society, where the "left–right" politics in Hong Kong cinema began to take shape.

The origins of the left-wing film establishment in Hong Kong can be traced back to the left-wing film movement in Mainland China in the 1930s.[14] In the late 1940s, a number of left-wing filmmakers supported by the Communist Party came to Hong Kong to start film production in the territory. Driven by intellectual idealism, social mission, and ideological conviction, these filmmakers displayed a close affinity with the south-bound intellectuals from Mainland China, an émigré community that had maintained a strong emotional connection to their home country.[15] They had to reinvent themselves as a "progressive" cultural force with a reformist agenda while competing with the more established commercial counterparts who had close business ties with Nationalist Taiwan. Their effort to reform Cantonese cinema (considered to be corrupt and decadent) resulted in the Third Cantonese Cinema Clean-up Campaign in 1949,[16] the same year that saw the founding of the People's Republic. The 1950s was a decade of exploration and consolidation of progressive filmmaking in Hong Kong, with the establishment of four major left-wing studios and the formation of a left-wing film network that encompassed production, distribution, and exhibition facilities. Compared to the "revolutionary films" in Mainland China, the left-wing cinema in Hong Kong continued in more diverse and localized forms. Acting on the party's instruction to stay close to the taste and interest of the local people, filmmakers steered away from explicit political messages and propaganda, producing works that would meet the dual objectives of moral education and entertainment.

This left–right divide did not preclude indirect forms of collaboration across the rivalling camps in the film industry. In some cases, it was politically imposed on filmmakers and stars who were obliged to either take sides or jeopardize their careers. The historical footprints of the left-wing studios therefore frequently crossed paths with their right-wing counterparts as a result of the entwined political, cultural, and economic forces in Hong Kong. Against this complex historical backdrop, the political and cinematic identity of the "left-wing" was created, negotiated, defined, and redefined.

The left-wing studios

As a precursor to the subsequent chapters, where readers will see more detailed discussion on studio history, style, and production and exhibition strategies, it would be helpful to highlight a few features of the respective studios in the context of the cultural and filmmaking environment in the 1950s and 1960s, a period that marked the blossoming and decline of the "classical" left-wing cinema in Hong Kong. The focus here is on the film industry and filmgoing culture in Hong Kong in the 1950s, the founding principles of the left-wing studios, their self-positioning in the Hong Kong film market, and major turning points in the fortunes of left-wing films that would make their eventual decline and consolidation inevitable. To better serve the purpose of this introduction and the rest of this book, the discussion below consists of historical snapshots serving as indexes to the following chapters, where the respective themes and arguments are further elaborated.

The relocation of the film industries from Shanghai to Hong Kong since World War II had fostered an émigré cinema that distinguished the studio productions in the 1950s and 1960s, when Hong Kong–made films became popular cultural products across many parts of Southeast Asia. Meanwhile, the local population made up of both recent migrants from Mainland China (mostly Mandarin-speaking) and fellow Cantonese-speaking residents who may or may not be "natives" but had longer and deeper roots in the territory. The Mandarin-Cantonese split was further complicated by the presence of other dialect groups of Fujian, Chaozhou, and Hakka origins, to name a few. As far as the local cinema was concerned, Mandarin and Cantonese films were predominant as they accounted for the largest market shares. Political stability, reliance on overseas markets, and a complex and versatile demographic makeup contributed to the special character of Hong Kong cinema in the mid-twentieth century. The impression, and to some extent reality, of being a "rootless" society, ironically, became a fertile field for different forms of ideological interventions and cultural self-inventions.

When the Communist Party set up its filmmaking apparatus in Hong Kong, the agenda was to establish a stronghold for socialist film production and distribution outside Mainland China. Meanwhile, a cluster of "southbound" intellectuals, many of whom were nurtured by the progressive thoughts of the 1920s and 1930s, found themselves embittered by the capitalist system under British rule, where they saw ordinary folks suffering from glaring social inequality, class exploitation, and aggravating social problems. It was also a time when labor movements began to take on more organized forms, sometimes escalating into large-scale strikes and conflicts.[17] A mixture of political idealism and patriotism prompted these filmmakers and writers to launch a concerted effort in reforming the "decadent" and unhealthy film culture of Hong Kong, their city of exile.

Besieged by intensifying political tensions arising from the US anti-Communist campaign in the region and local skirmishes sponsored by the KMT and the CCP, the British administration in Hong Kong had been hard-pressed to maintain its political neutrality while keeping a wary eye on the versatile situation in Mainland China. The localized Cold War in Hong Kong had an immediate and material impact on the colonial government's cultural policy. The most obvious effect on the film industry was the segmentation of film studios according to their professed ideological allegiance. Indeed, the left, right, and middle positioning resulted from both personal convictions and more pragmatic concerns. Research on film censorship has shown how the colonial administration had exercised tacit political monitoring of the circulation of both local and foreign films with unwelcome political overtones that might affect its relationship with neighboring countries.[18] This politicized film production environment had an instrumental role to play in filmmaking, industry structure, market differentiation, and competition between film studios.

Union and Sun Luen were the two major left-wing studios specializing in Cantonese films. Both studios were distinguished by their unambiguous progressive outlooks and mission statements, which the founders and production teams put into practice in earnest. Sun Luen and Union's productions can be defined by their creative adaptation of the aesthetic taste and preferences of the so-called south-bound artists to appeal to the local audience and to make their films contextually relevant. Committed to a cinema of high social and artistic value, Union and Sun Luen became the labels of many Cantonese film classics that contributed to the distinctive "look" of Cantonese cinema of the time. Equally noteworthy was the doubling up of on- and offscreen roles of leading actors and actresses at Union (and Sun Luen in the first few years): film stars and directors were co-founders of the studios who also played executive and decision-making roles in the studios' management. Such a "democratic" culture was unusual in commercial operations but worked to the advantage of both the stars and the left-wing studios in navigating an alternative course in an otherwise intensely competitive film market. The serious social drama films aside, Union and Sun Luen also produced lighter entertainment films to capture a wider spectrum of audience. This popular turn bespeaks the dilemma and complexity of "being left-wing" in an unfavorable social and political environment. One can say that the genre films reflected the reality and nature of the cinematic left in Hong Kong, and more importantly a humanistic vision that mediated the filmmakers' ideological prerogatives.

Great Wall and Feng Huang (also known as Phoenix) were the left-wing's Mandarin studios. Great Wall's precursor was Great Wall Pictures Corporation (also known as the Old Great Wall). First established in 1949 by Zhang Shankun, a veteran film producer from Shanghai, the company ran into a financial crisis in 1950 that led to Zhang's departure. Great Wall was soon restructured (later known as the "new Great Wall") under its top executive, Yuan Yang'an, in 1950 (see timeline). The predominance of progressive filmmakers who remained at Great Wall led to a strategic repositioning of Great Wall, which started production of progressive films with a view to fostering a "healthy film culture" and social atmosphere.[19] Great Wall's new management, however, was not immune to market demands. Within the first year of its operation, the company managed to roll out a number of commercially successful costume and historical dramas. High production values and star power firmly established Great Wall as a leading left-wing studio in Hong Kong in the 1950s. Founded in 1952, Feng Huang was supported by the new government in China. Like Union and Sun Luen, Great Wall and Feng Huang had a synergetic relationship in staff deployment and resource sharing. This aspect of the left-wing's business model is further explored in Chapter 2. The four left-wing studios also worked with their Mainland counterparts in (co-)producing feature and documentary films that took advantage of the exotic scenery in China that was not available in Hong Kong. Sun Luen was among the most proactive forerunners in film co-production. A memorable example is *House of 72 Tenants* (1963; dir. Wong Wai-yat), a co-production with the Pearl River Studio.[20] Applauded as a ground-breaking film at the time, *House of 72 Tenants* was later remade by Chor Yuen in a TVB-Shaw production in 1973. Other more recent imitations and adaptations of the film include Stephen Chow's *Kung Fu Hustle* (2004) and *72 Tenants of Prosperity* (Eric Tsang, Chung Shu-kai, and Patrick Kong, 2010).

As Hong Kong fell victim to the whirlwind of ultra-leftist politics in Mainland China, (which materialized in the 1967 Hong Kong Riots),[21] left-wing film production began to take a downturn. Shocked and confused by the capricious course of events sweeping through the country, left-wing filmmakers found their work being condemned as "poisonous weed." At the peak of the Cultural Revolution, party representatives in charge of resource allocation and political guidance in Hong Kong then demanded the studios to strictly follow the latest political prerogatives. The result was an about-turn toward formulaic propagandistic films divorced from local reality. At the same time, left-wing studios were facing tough competitions from their commercial rivals, Shaw and MP&GI, who continued to roll out star-studded blockbusters sold through their local and regional distribution networks. Feng Huang, Great Wall, and Sun Luen thus were hard-pressed for solutions to stay in business, while Union had already folded by 1967 due to the retirement or departure of acting talents. From the mid-1960s and throughout the 1970s, the left-wing studios in Hong Kong struggled to survive the damage done during the Cultural Revolution. In 1983, the "big three" decided to experiment with joint production. Their first joint venture was *Shaolin Temple*, which was also the debut film that started the career of Jet Li as the new generation kung fu superstar after Bruce Lee. *Shaolin Temple* thus paved the way for the consolidation of Feng Huang, Great Wall, and Sun Luen into what came to be known as Sil-Metropole (Hong Kong). The establishment of Sil-Metropole can be seen as a landmark in the history of left-wing studios in Hong Kong, and ironically also a signal of further marketization and commercialization of left-wing studio productions in Hong Kong. Sil-Metropole offers an insightful case study of the historical transformation of left-wing film studios in Hong Kong. More importantly, its arrival and evolution coincided with China's Reform and Opening Up era, which kicked in a new phase of globalization of Chinese cinema with deep repercussions in the film industries and film cultures of Taiwan, Hong Kong, and Mainland China in the following decades. The decline of left-wing studios during the Cultural Revolution and their subsequent consolidation into a more market-oriented conglomerate can be seen as the end of the golden age of the "classical" left-wing cinema in Hong Kong. This said, the ethos of the left-wing was taken up, albeit in nuanced articulations, by directors committed to the social realist aesthetic. The legacy of the left-wing cinema can be observed in less politically driven productions in the post-Cultural Revolution era, when China began in earnest a new phase of economic modernization laid out in Deng Xiaoping's Reform and Opening Up policy. In Hong Kong, the film industry was going through a structural transition, with the reorientation of Shaw from film production to television broadcasting and the phasing out of the major studios. The continuation of a socially engaged cinema within a commercial mainstream dominated by popular genre films would prove to be vital to the nurturing of the new auteurs associated with the Hong Kong New Wave.

A recurrent question raised in this study is the multifaceted meaning of "being on the left" in Hong Kong at different historical moments. As Christine Loh (2018) has argued for a reevaluation of the left from being an "underground front" in the colonial era to a new hegemonic force that ironically has to keep the ruling party "underground" in the postcolonial present,[22] the historical trajectory of the left-wing film network in Hong Kong speaks volumes about the under-articulated dilemmas and anxieties of being left, right, and middle in Hong Kong, which has remained an existential condition of the ex-colony at large. It is hoped that this book will contribute toward shortening the perceptual distance between the heyday of the left-wing studios and contemporary realities of the Hong Kong film industry, for reasons partially laid out above and further examined in the rest of this book.

Critical discourse on the left-wing cinema: points of departures

Over the years, vast amounts of historical sources have been discovered and archived by researchers inside and outside Hong Kong. The Hong Kong Film Archive (HKFA) has published filmmakers' memoirs and collections of essays of various lengths and depths showcasing important figures, studios, trends, and events of the earlier decades of the local film industry. In addition to two volumes on the Shaw Brothers and MP&GI, edited volumes on the left-wing studios and filmmakers' memoirs and interviews have been published, including *One for All: The Union Film Spirit* (2011), *Artistic Mission: An Exploration of Sun Luen Film Company* (2011), *Cold War and Hong Kong Cinema* (2009), and *Age of Idealism: Great Wall and Feng Huang Days*.[23] The collection, consolidation, and organization of primary and secondary sources that are otherwise scattered, damaged, or lost in time is indispensable to further research on the left-wing cinema since the early 1950s. To a certain extent, these publications have shaped the direction of critical discourse on the left-wing cinema in Hong Kong. Emerging from this body of literature is a general impression that the left-wing cinema was a patriotic and progressive cultural force struggling under an unfriendly and politically biased colonial regime known to be an ally of the US. A favorite metaphor of the left-wing's "in-betweenness" is the word *"jiafeng,"* literally meaning a crack, fissure, or rupture.[24] In this discourse, the left-wing inhabited this ruptured space and found itself caught in the political schism created by the rivalry between the KMT and the CCP. Another common expression frequently invoked is "All for One, One for All," a quote from a left-wing film in the 1950s that has been popularized by commentators to represent the left-wing's ethos. This phrase not only underscores the "spirit" of left-wing films, but has also found its way into later interpretations on the historical and social significance of the left-wing cinema.[25] In this discourse, the left-wing is also characterized as a "new cultural elite" dedicated to the course of social and cultural reform.[26] A common thread that runs through these accounts is the political backdrop of the localized Cold War in Hong Kong and the unfavorable cultural environment under British colonial rule. Evidence of systemic bias against the progressive film circle ranges from censorship, surveillance, market access control to arrests and prosecutions. Against this background, the left-wing film community emerges as an ethical force on a mission of artistic and cultural reform. Patriotic and anti-imperialist in outlook, the left-wing film community was committed to raising the artistic and moral benchmarks of Hong Kong cinema.

A more complex picture than a one-sided bias against pro-CCP groups is revealed in historical research on Hong Kong during the Cold War period. The British colonial administration's balancing acts of political censorship and monitoring did not spare KMT saboteurs, and colonial governors were not necessarily acquiescing toward the US intelligence when internal security was at stake.[27] Not to be neglected in this truncated relationship was the institutional nature of the left-wing film establishment: as a constituent of the PRC's "cultural brigade" (*wenhua jundui*) in Hong Kong,[28] it was the outcome of long-term strategic planning of the state whose ultimate purpose was political in nature.

While the left-wing studios' institutional nature has been widely acknowledged, the deeper implications of its political origins are usually relegated to the back seat in an ethical-idealist critique. Not that this portrayal is incorrect, but the complexity and ambivalence of the cinematic left's status as the CCP's film production apparatus in Hong Kong, hence a member of the state's cultural brigade among other party-affiliated agencies stationed in the British colony, is sometimes obscured in a narrative informed by the idealist, aspirational, and patriotic qualities of the left-wing cinema. While one should not overlook the marginalization of non-US/KMT friendly individuals and organizations in colonial Hong Kong, there is evidence that the colonial administration was equally troubled by the KMT's sabotage activities and the US's overexertion of its political influence through its intelligence and propaganda networks in the region (cf. Chapter 1). Studies on film censorship, surveillance, and the US's intelligence activities have shown how the British colonial government had tried to keep conflicting parties on a delicate balance instead of adhering to a rigid anti-Communist Cold War mentality.[29] According to a recent study on film censorship in Hong Kong from the 1940s to the 1970s, censorship on films from the Mainland were actually more relaxed than those from Taiwan by rate of pass in the 1950s, and a gradual relaxation was observed from the mid-1960s onward.[30] What Priscilla Roberts calls "the acrobatics of multiple balancing"[31] that characterizes the colonial administration's approach to the localized Cold War in Hong Kong should be a more accurate description of the complex realities faced by both the government and the Hong Kong society at large. What's more, such balancing was not exclusively the duty call of the colonial government but was also an indispensable survival skill by which individuals and organizations, left or right, navigate the stormy waters of Cold War politics in postwar Hong Kong. It is also in this critical light that the historical trajectory of the left-wing film network is reconsidered in the following chapters.

Chapter synopsis

The main historical timeframe of the book corresponds to the Cold War era, which also coincided with the early history of the People's Republic of China (PRC) since its founding in 1949. Chapter 1 offers an overview of the political and filmmaking landscape of post-World War II Hong Kong. Specific emphasis is placed on the local manifestations of Cold War politics against which the left-wing film apparatus was constituted as a member of the CCP's cultural brigade in the British colony. To the left-wing filmmakers, being "popular" served both ideological and commercial ends. Their films therefore had to be popular cultural products in the first place before they could be an effective means of ideological persuasion. In this light, the corporate strategies in the "making of" a popular left-wing cinema in Hong Kong deserves closer attention. Chapter 2 introduces the four major left-wing studios, namely Great Wall, Feng Huang, Sun Luen, and Union, to shed light on the production and exhibition strategies that enabled the left-wing film establishment to compete with their much better resourced right-wing counterparts in the local and overseas markets. Very often, the line between the "left" and the "right" was more fluid than fixed, as both camps were struggling for survival in a highly politicized market environment where political credentials may not make good business sense at all times. What, then, did it mean to be "on the left" under the peculiar circumstances of Hong Kong's localized Cold War? This question informs the inquiry into the ecology of film production and exhibition in Chapter 2. The next two chapters zoom in on the aesthetics and politics of left-wing films. As far as left-wing Cantonese films are concerned, critical discourse has tended to focus on a number of well-known classics, while relatively less attention has been paid to the left-wing's engagement with popular genres to balance their aesthetic, ideological, and commercial objectives in the making of "spiritually and morally uplifting films" that appeal to the tastes and interests of the local audience. In this light, Chapter 3 examines a cluster of genre films in greater depth to shed light on the left-wing's quest for popularity in the commercial mainstream. Gender politics takes the front seat in the discussion of the left-wing's critical intervention in the cinematic imagination of modernity in Hong Kong cinema in Chapter 4. While images of the "fallen woman" and the "modern girl" have been the most important tropes in critical discourse on the literary and cinematic imagination of Chinese modernity since the 1930s, they have remained understudied subjects as far as the Hong Kong left-wing cinema is concerned. In this chapter, these figures of modern femininity in left-wing films are discussed in comparison with their right-wing counterparts to make a case for the left-wing's reinvention of these gendered metaphors of capitalist modernity through a critical engagement with popular film genres.

While the havoc of the Great Proletariat Cultural Revolution (henceforth Cultural Revolution) in Mainland China (1966–1976) was undeniably attributable to the left-wing studio's decline,[32] the left-wing cinema in Hong Kong is certainly not to be regarded as passé. The end of the Cultural Revolution brought in a new era of economic reform and rapid modernization in Mainland China. Beginning from the 1980s, a corresponding adjustment in the state's cultural policy was noticeable in the gradual opening up of China's cultural market to foreign imports and investments. Aware of the structural damage done to its film production base in Hong Kong, the Chinese government moved quickly to revive the left-wing film establishment once public order was restored in China.[33] Chapter 5 looks at the corporate history of the left-wing establishment since the early 1980s, when China began a new and ambitious modernization project under the leadership of Deng Xiaoping. This period also witnessed the transformation of Hong Kong's left-wing film apparatus into a modern film and media conglomerate, Sil-Metropole (Hong Kong). While the left-wing studios were thrown into an operational disarray during the peak of the Cultural Revolution, the local film industry was also going through a critical transition that prefigured the arrival of the so-called "golden age" in Hong Kong cinema in the 1980s. As a state-owned film and media enterprise in Hong Kong, Sil-Metropole's corporate repositioning in the local and regional film markets before and after the change of sovereignty in 1997 would transform it into a major cultural broker between the Hong Kong and Mainland film industries.

The "afterlife" of the left-wing cinema outside its institutional bounds can be traced in the work of non-left-wing filmmakers. Chapter 6 considers the work of two non-left-wing directors, Patrick Lung Kong and Cecile Tang Shu-shuen, whose diverging intellectual and aesthetic temperaments make a case for the nuanced, and sometimes controversial, legacies of the conventional left-wing, which has so far remained an understudied subject. As critical transitions, Long and Tang's careers expose the still haphazard film production and reception environment in the late 1960s and 1970s, when Hong Kong society was finding its way out of the political conundrums of the previous decades. As argued throughout this book, the left-wing film apparatus in Hong Kong can better be understood as a network of a diversity of cultural agents, from acting and production personnel to studio managers, theater operators, and their financial partners. The final chapter (Chapter 7), therefore, is devoted to lesser known members, that is, the satellite studios, of the left-wing film network and how these smaller units served the interest of the reconfigured left-wing film production and China's investment in national soft power in the age of media globalization. Surviving in an intensely politicized environment prompted both film studios and filmmakers to adopt a dynamic and flexible approach to survive in a capricious political climate. What has emerged from this scenario is the active cultivation of a "middle ground" by different parties as a temporary relief from the straitjacket of left–right politics.

Notes

1. See Chu, *Hong Kong Cinema: Coloniser, Motherland, and Self*, xviii–xxi.
2. Instead of enlightenment and evangelism, such as in the case of the older colonies, Wang argues that when the British came to Hong Kong, trade and commerce had become the exclusive objective. Wang, *Anglo-Chinese Encounters since 1800*.
3. Mao Zedong's dictum had guided the Chinese government's policy toward Hong Kong, which was briefly interrupted by the radical forces during the 1967 anti-British riots. See Tsang, *A Modern History of Hong Kong*, 153; and Loh, *Underground Front: The Chinese Communist Party in Hong Kong*, 125.
4. For an in-depth analysis of the CCP's "underground front" in Hong Kong, see Loh, *Underground Front: The Chinese Communist Party in Hong Kong*.
5. Ching, *The Origins of the Hong Kong Riots*, 9.
6. Xiamen (Amoy) and Chaozhou dialect films were also produced on a small scale. See Ng, *Chaozhou-dialect Films in Hong Kong Cinema*; and Ng, *Amoy-dialect Films in Hong Kong Cinema*.
7. Studio-owned magazines were distributed internationally with regular updates on screen icons, new projects, and publicity events. The most popular of these publications are the *Great Wall Pictorial* (Great Wall), *Union Pictorial* (Union), *International Screen* (MP & GI), *Southern Screen* (Shaw), and *Hong Kong Movie News* (Shaw).
8. Chu, *Hong Kong Cinema: Coloniser, Motherland, and Self*, xi–xxi.
9. Although *White Gold Dragon* is the mostly cited "first Cantonese talkie," evidence from other sources suggests that both *Blossom Time* and *The Idiot's Wedding* were produced/released in the same year. *The Idiot's Wedding* is also considered to be the first Cantonese talkie made in Hong Kong. See Chung, *100 Years of the Hong Kong Film Industry*, 80–91.
10. Fu, *Between Shanghai and Hong Kong*, 56; Law and Bren, *Hong Kong Cinema: A Cross-cultural View*, 120.
11. The South China Film Association sent a delegation to Nanjing to petition against the ban. Delegates included Lee Fa, Chiu Shu-sun, Chuk Ching-yin, Ko Lei-hen, and Chan Kwan-chiu. The central government agreed to a three-year deferral of the ban. Cf. timeline.
12. As a free port, the British colonial administration had encouraged migration of labor from former British colonies such as India and Pakistan while maintaining an elite British profile at top-level policy- and decision-making roles.
13. Lai negotiated a deal with Brodsky in 1913 to create special effects for the film. See Zhang, *Chinese National Cinema*, 31.

14. On the left-wing film movement in Mainland China in the 1930s, see Pang, *Building a New China in Cinema*.
15. The term "south-bound" itself implied both migration and the geopolitics of a notional north-south divide, where the "north" designates the so-called "Central Plain" or "China proper," a privileged term in relation to the less civilized "south," the peripheral southern region that is historically and metaphorically inferior to the north. Emotionally attached to the home country, their work very often expresses a sense of displacement and homesickness, which usually was accented by a self-perceived marginality living in a British colony cut off from the Chinese cultural tradition.
16. The third of its kind since the late 1930s, the 1949 campaign was initiated by progressive filmmakers who later founded the left-wing's Cantonese film studios, Union and Sun Luen. This is discussed in more detail in Chapter 1.
17. The intensification of workers' discontent prompted leftist labor unions to mount large-scale protests that culminated in the 1967 anti-British riots. The connection between the Hong Kong riots and the Cultural Revolution is explained in Ching, *The Origins of the Hong Kong Riots*, and Cheung, *Hong Kong's Watershed the 1967 Riots*. Cf. Chapters 1 and 2.
18. Ng, "Inhibition vs. Exhibition: Political Censorship"; Yip, "Closely Watched Films: Surveillance and Postwar Hong Kong Leftist Cinema"; Du, "Censorship, Regulations, and the Cinematic Cold War in Hong Kong," 117–151.
19. Making educational and morally uplifting films was repeatedly emphasized in party officials' advice to left-wing filmmakers in Hong Kong. See Ho, *Artistic Mission: An Exploration of Sun Luen Film Company*, 24–25; and Lo, "Reflections on the Left-wing Cinema," 86.
20. The Hong Kong production company was Hungtu (1959–1965), a subunit of Sun Luen specializing in Chaozhou dialect films. Of the twelve films credited to Hungtu, four were co-produced with the Pearl River Studio.
21. A spinoff of the Cultural Revolution, the 1967 anti-British riots lasted for eight months and resulted in numerous deaths and hundreds of injuries. Different interpretations of the origins of the disturbance and course of events have been offered by various political camps and researchers. See Ching, *The Origins of the Hong Kong Riots*; and Cheung, *Hong Kong's Watershed the 1967 Riots*. Cf. Chapter 2.
22. Loh, *Underground Front: The Chinese Communist Party in Hong Kong*.
23. The HKFA's publications are mostly in Chinese. Some titles are available in English translation. A full catalogue is available at https:// www.filmarchive.gov.hk/en_US/web/hkfa/publications_souvenirs/pub.html (last accessed 18 May 2018).
24. *Jiafeng* is frequently used to characterize the existential condition of the left-wing cinema. See Zhang, *Studies on Hong Kong Leftist Films*; Lee, "The Best of Both Worlds: Hong Kong Film Industry during the Cold War Era," 90; and Chung, "A Film Industry In-between Two Political Powers," 175–177.
25. This ethical approach pervades several volumes of the HKFA's publications, including the titles cited in this chapter.
26. See, for example, Chang, *Screening Communities: Negotiating Narratives of Empire, Nation, and the Cold War in Hong Kong Cinema*, 75–101; and Zhou, "Hong Kong's Leftist Cinema during the Cold War Era," 21–34.

27. Lombardo, "A Mission of Espionage, Intelligence and Psychological Operations," 64–81; Tsang, "Strategy for Survival: The Cold War and Hong Kong's Policy," 294–317. See Chapter 1 on the colonial government's handling of the left–right rivalry.

28. Ho, *Artistic Mission: An Exploration of Sun Luen Film Company*, 23.

29. Leary, "The Most Careful Arrangements for a Careful Fiction," 548; Lombardo, "A Mission of Espionage, Intelligence and Psychological Operations," 64–81; Ng, "Inhibition vs. Exhibition: Political Censorship of Chinese and Foreign Cinemas in Postwar Hong Kong," 23–35; Yip, "Closely Watched Films: Surveillance and Postwar Hong Kong Leftist Cinema," 35–59; and Tsang, "Target Zhou Enlai: The 'Kashmir Princess' Incident of 1955," 766–782.

30. Du, "Censorship, Regulations, and the Cinematic Cold War in Hong Kong," 126–130. According to Du, "There was not necessarily more room granted to anti-Communist USIS films for exploitation than to Communist films of the Mainland during this period, if the films were of an overtly propagandist character" (142).

31. Roberts, "Cold War Hong Kong: Juggling Opposing Forces and Identities," 35.

32. Zhang, *Studies on Hong Kong Leftist Films*, Chapter 4.

33. A meeting with Hong Kong's left-wing filmmakers was held in Beijing in January 1979 to reassure them of the Party's full support in reviving Hong Kong's "patriotic" film production. See Chapters 6 and 7.

Chapter 1

The left-wing film apparatus in postwar Hong Kong

Between 1949 and 1952, the left-wing film community in Hong Kong was reconstituted into a consolidated network, which in the next few years was further expanded through horizontal and vertical integration to become an integrated corporate entity ready to claim a place in the mainstream cinema. The formation and consolidation the left-wing film apparatus in Hong Kong coincided with the foundation of the People's Republic of China and increasingly proactive steps undertaken by the US and Taiwan governments in strengthening their positions in the cultural Cold War in Hong Kong. Beginning with an overview of the cultural landscape against the backdrop of intensifying KMT–CCP rivalry, this chapter will bring to light the systematic efforts of the CCP in mobilizing the left-wing film community in Hong Kong as a branch of the Party's "cultural brigade." The formation and further extension of this network alongside the local and regional advancement of the right-wing's film and cultural enterprises would have a far-reaching impact on the structure and practices of the Hong Kong film industry in years to come.

Hong Kong's status as a British colony was an amalgamation of mixed blessings and ironies. On the one hand, the colonial city was sheltered from the renewed conflicts between Nationalist Taiwan and the Communist China since the end of the Second World War. Political neutrality also helped diffuse the tension and conflicts arising from the interstate rivalry during the Cold War. As both the US and the PRC relied on Hong Kong as a base for their intelligence operations, taking over the British colony was not on the agenda of Beijing after 1949, whose policy of "making full use of Hong Kong in the interest of long-term planning" had been a guiding principle since the founding of "New China."[1] On the other hand, as a politically neutral contact zone, the colonial city was a fertile ground of intelligence and propagandistic activities that, at times, necessitated more proactive acts of deterrence on the part of the British to maintain its "fiction of political neutrality."[2] The delicate balance of power also created a space for contending political forces and interests to advance their courses through this city-port as an intelligence and trading hub.[3] Where the British colonial government found itself in dire straits to maintain political stability, and no less its legitimacy over the last piece of jewel on the British crown, political adroitness enabled the administration to steer a course of relative peace and stability over the precarious waters of Cold War politics in the region.

While the larger picture of the Cold War was defined by the political tug-of-war between the US-led capitalist countries (the "free world") and the USSR and its Communist bloc allies, Hong Kong's status as a British colony geographically, linguistically, and politically caught between two competing Chinese regimes added some intriguing qualities to the already tense and versatile Cold War balance of power, especially in the realm of culture. A tacit understanding between these different powers to observe a non-military interference principle, therefore, had shaped the cultural character of the localized Cold War in Hong Kong.[4] Commentators sometimes use the term "mini-Cold War" to characterize the state of affairs in Hong Kong during the 1950s and 1960s.[5] In Hong Kong, the mini-Cold War refers to the covert and overt political machinations and ideological manipulations employed by various political interests from Nationalist Taiwan, Communist China, the US, and the British colonial government through various cultural, social, and economic channels. A KMT-CCP power struggle on the surface, the situation was further complicated by the active behind-the-scene maneuvers of the United States, which extended its own intelligence and propaganda artilleries into the British colony as a vanguard against the spread of Communism in Asia. It is a known fact that the US was behind the KMT's anti-Communist activities through its information service (USIS) and the American Consulate to forestall PRC-backed Communist infiltration in Hong Kong,[6] whose status as a free port made it an ideal international information and intelligence center. In the eyes of the CCP, Hong Kong's strategic value as a "watch tower" and "beachhead" to "break the embargo by [the] US-led Western camp" on China served as a disincentive to territorial claims.[7]

The importance of film as a propagandistic medium need not be further emphasized. Throughout the 1930s and during the War of Resistance Against Japanese Aggression (1937–1945), the control of film production had been a great concern to both the Nationalist government and the Japanese authorities in the occupied areas.[8] The Communist Party was also actively increasing its own film production capacity to spread revolutionary thought across the country. Well before the defeat of the KMT in the civil war in 1949, left-wing filmmakers supported by the CCP had already started to set up film production units in Hong Kong, whose accessibility to other Chinese-speaking communities in the region made it an ideal location for a film production and distribution base outside Mainland China. Left-wing film production in Hong Kong continued after the founding of the PRC (and the retreat of the KMT government to Taiwan) with the foundation laid by these pioneers. Their successors were intellectuals and cultural workers who came to Hong Kong during and after the Japanese occupation. (It is worth mentioning here that members of the CCP's cultural front from other media agencies would also play strategic roles in the formation of the left-wing film establishment in the early 1950s; cf. Chapter 2.) Witnesses of the havoc of foreign invasion and well exposed to the progressive intellectual culture of the 1920s and 1930s, these individuals were embittered by British colonial rule in Hong Kong, where glaring social inequality and class exploitation were rampant. A mixture of political idealism and nationalistic sentiment prompted these filmmakers and writers to mount a concerted effort in reforming the "decadent" and "shameful" film culture of Hong Kong, their city of exile.[9] These early attempts later materialized in an active agenda of the left-wing studios to develop a "progressive cinema" (*jinbu dianying*) in Hong Kong.

Ideals and politics aside, the influx of filmmaking personnel and capital from Shanghai to Hong Kong to escape the ravage of the civil war fostered an émigré cinema that distinguished the commercial mainstream in the 1950s and 1960s. The commercial films, especially those produced by the two leading Mandarin film studios, the Shaw Brothers and MP&GI (Cathay), are characterized by strong emotional connections to an imaginary "China" that had fallen, a lost homeland that inspired the imagination of south-bound directors and writers.[10] Founded by Chinese entrepreneurs from Singapore, both Shaw and MP&GI were transnational film companies with established networks in Southeast Asia, where a lucrative market existed for Mandarin, Cantonese, and other dialect films. In Hong Kong, the local population was made up of both recent migrants from Mainland China (speaking Mandarin and a variety of Chinese dialects) and a Cantonese-speaking majority and other dialect groups of Fujian, Chaozhou, and Hakka origins who may or may not be "natives" but had longer and deeper roots in the territory. As far as the local cinema was concerned, Mandarin and Cantonese films were predominant as they accounted for the largest market shares. Political stability, reliance on overseas markets, and a complex demographic and linguistic makeup therefore contributed to the special character of Hong Kong cinema in the mid-twentieth century. The impression, and to a certain extent reality, of being a "rootless" immigrant society, ironically, made Hong Kong an ideal place for different forms of ideological interventions and cultural self-expression.

It can be said that the subsequent left-wing film network had its foundation laid in the preceding decades. The rest of this chapter offers a critical overview of the conditions of film production in postwar Hong Kong. It outlines the main activities of the major corporate and individual players to leverage their power and influence in the territory. It is believed a critical introduction to this important phase in Hong Kong's film history will serve the interest of a reexamination of the institutional and corporate character of the left-wing studio network that took shape in the early 1950s. As of the time of writing this book, a majority of published work on Hong Kong cinema during the Cold War era is in Chinese, spanning a wide spectrum of genres, approaches, and depths, from anecdotal recollections, oral histories, and topical research articles to archival and curatorial writings.[11] As noted in the Introduction, this critical discourse tends to emphasize the left-wing's precarious position as a community of progressive (pro-CCP) filmmakers closely watched over by a suspicious and unfriendly colonial regime that also happened to be an ally of the US.[12] While there is a substantial body of work in English on the complex sociopolitical landscape of Hong Kong during the Cold War, the extent to which the left-wing cinema had participated in the "cultural cold war" in Hong Kong and its longer-term implications has not yet been adequately addressed in all its complexity in published work on the subject, which is mostly available in Chinese (cf. Introduction). A topic that has attracted critical spotlight is film censorship and surveillance in the context of the KMT-CCP rivalry in Hong Kong.[13] Drawing upon a diverse range of primary and secondary sources, this chapter attempts to offer a topographical mapping of the cultural space of left-wing film production under the influence of Cold War politics, on which the thematic analysis of the history of left-wing film studios in the following chapters is based. The discussion below prioritizes those aspects of the Cold War that had material impact, directly or indirectly, on the cultural politics in the local society to illuminate the analysis in rest of this book. As such, it is intended to be a tool to unpack the discourse and practices of the left-wing film network in Hong Kong cinema since its incubation and heyday, before we turn to its more nuanced legacies in the post-Cold War era, when both the Hong Kong and Mainland Chinese film industries felt the need to reinvent themselves to catch up on regional and global realities.[14]

Cinema and the politics of culture in post-World War II Hong Kong

The Cold War era was also a time when the world witnessed the disintegration of European empires and the rapid decolonization of former colonies on a world scale. At the same time, the new Communist regime founded upon the ruins of the pro-US Nationalist government in Mainland China in 1949 drew the curtain of a new political drama in British Hong Kong. If the military and diplomatic rivalry between the Cold War power blocs determined the macropolitical climate of postwar Hong Kong, the more localized struggle for legitimacy and influence between Nationalist Taiwan and Communist China had turned the British colony into an ideological battleground with material repercussions in the social, political, and cultural realms. While Britain was a close ally with the United States, geopolitics dictated that the interests of British Hong Kong would be best served by maintaining political neutrality, at least at the level of diplomatic self-positioning vis-à-vis both the "free world" and its Communist counterparts. Meanwhile, the colonial government had to keep a close and anxious watch over its formidable neighbor up north, and no less the anti-Communist machinations by the US and Taiwan that occasionally became a source of headache to the colonial administration. Indeed, the ruling elite had been continuously monitoring the potential threat to internal security posed by sporadic border incidents, especially when there was a possibility of provoking anti-British sentiments and labor disputes among disgruntled workers in the territory.[15] Devoid of sustainable natural resources and heavily reliant on imported supply of necessities (including staple food and fresh water from Mainland China), Hong Kong was a city besieged by contending interests of both macro- and micropolitical origins. As far as the relationship between the colonial administration and its London headquarters was concerned, the lived realities of the colony occasionally compelled the local officials to take a different, if not deliberately ambivalent, approach in handling situations where perceptions between the center and the periphery differed. While the protection of British interests in Hong Kong was always the first priority of colonial governance, occasional tension and misalignments were inevitable at the level of local policymaking and implementation.[16]

Amidst escalating military and diplomatic tensions on a regional and global scale and periodic domestic crises throughout the 1950s and 1960s, Hong Kong society nonetheless enjoyed relative stability that allowed trade and commerce to continue with minimal disruption. Political neutrality also guaranteed greater freedom of expression and more liberal policies toward social and cultural organizations, from publishing houses, news agencies, film studios, and charity organizations to labor unions and schools. This said, the colony's political neutrality rested on the delicate balance of power between multiple players. Stability and the smooth-running of society, therefore, were never taken for granted. Sometimes, the colonial administration had to invent a role that may not sit well with American prerogatives or the general direction of British diplomacy at the time. Numerous accounts have pointed out how at critical moments the colonial administration in Hong Kong attempted to fend off aggressive US interference in local affairs to avoid confrontations with the PRC.[17] Keeping the aggressive moves of various "warring states" at bay, thus, was the best way to serve British interests in Hong Kong.

One can say that the Hong Kong cultural scene was benefiting from the turmoil that had ravaged other parts of Greater China, as intellectuals, cultural workers, and capitalists escaping the war-inflicted areas took refuge in the British colonial enclave. Elsewhere in Asia, the US had been using its influence to mount an aggressive anti-Communist campaign. Singapore, for instance, implemented a series of policies to prohibit pro-Communist activities in education and the press. In 1958, a blacklist of publishers based in Hong Kong and China was drawn up for accelerated surveillance and censorship.[18] Meanwhile, the ruling parties in Taiwan and Mainland China were still preoccupied with postwar rehabilitation and consolidation of state power. When all parties were exercising self-restraint to avoid armed conflict, the KMT-CCP struggle for political legitimacy was displaced into the notionally neutral British colony, a Chinese-speaking city well connected to the global Chinese diaspora. In the eyes of the CCP, Hong Kong by now had become an important conduit of socialist ideology toward overseas Chinese communities.

It was under these circumstances that the ideological machines of the powers in conflict began to establish their footholds in the colonial city by direct and indirect means. Apart from setting up financial and commercial enterprises, both the Nationalist and Communist parties were actively investing in education, social welfare, and the mass media. These organizations came to be known as either "rightist" (pro-Taiwan) or "leftist" (pro-China) schools and organizations depending on their political affiliation and source of funding. The mainstream educational system, on the other hand, was dominated by schools directly administered by the government, and those founded by the Protestant and Catholic churches, NGOs, as well as other local religious (mainly Buddhist and Daoist) organizations. While the colonial system privileged an English-medium education,[19] the importance of Hong Kong as an ideological battlefield was noted by the American, British, and Chinese governments. As one scholar observes, Hong Kong offered "a more neutral platform for Chinese-medium education, one that would help to counter the attractions of Communist-run mainland universities among young people in Hong Kong and beyond while avoiding the ideological rigidities of Nationalist-administered Taiwan institutions."[20] Meanwhile, the leftist schools were important bases not only for patriotic thought education in the British colony, but also for the recruitment and training of future ideologues and political leaders of the pro-Beijing camp in Hong Kong in years to come.[21] The CCP was more proactive in engaging the locals through workers' unions, welfare centers, and clinics, all being effective means for mass mobilization. Labor organizations, leftist newspapers, and schools played an important role in organizing strikes and mass protests during the anti-British riots in 1967 (also known as the Hong Kong Riots), when ripples of the Cultural Revolution (1966–1976) in China began to spread over the China–Hong Kong border.[22]

The most visible signs of the political struggle between Taiwan and China were found in the mass media. At a time when the television set was not yet a common household item, newspapers were the primary means to shape public opinion and perceptions of domestic and international affairs. Also pertinent to the discussion here is the role of newspaper and magazine columns as the basis of ideological persuasion and debates under the guise of "culture." It is a well-known fact that the KMT prided itself as the true heir of the Chinese cultural tradition founded upon Confucian ethics while projecting an outlook of a modern capitalist nation and a member of the "free world." The CCP, on the other hand, cultivated a progressive image, posing itself as a champion of social equality and enlightened egalitarian values against a decadent, exploitative, and corrupt capitalist society that Hong Kong presumably had become under British rule. Patriotism, anti-imperialism, and anti-feudalism, hence, were the guiding principles of the CCP's cultural front in Hong Kong. Given the extent of infiltration by the KMT and the CCP in the social and cultural life of the colony, the propagandistic work of the leftist and rightist camps resulted in a bifurcated mediascape. The US, through the Asia Foundation, was indirectly supporting an anti-Communist campaign in the mass media. Its effort was matched by the left-wing in almost equal terms. Not to be overlooked is the fact that the state of affairs in the cultural realm was also a by-product of the British colonial policy of "indirect rule" in Hong Kong. First articulated by colonial administrator Fredrick Lugard, who left Nigeria to assume governorship in Hong Kong (1907–1912), the concrete manifestation of this principle was the grooming of a select group of native elites to oversee the day-to-day management of local affairs from social welfare to dispute resolution among the Chinese.[23]

As the powers at stake had precluded any realistic expectations of a political takeover of the territory either by the Nationalists or the Communists, the battle for legitimacy and popularity between the left and the right was fought in the realm of culture. While the print media might be more explicit in demarcating ideological boundaries in the contest for public opinion leadership, the film industry was subject to both overt and covert forms of (self-)censorship and scrutiny. Toward the late 1960s, the intensification of the Cultural Revolution in Mainland China resulted in the loss of the China market and the growing importance of the Taiwan market, where Mandarin films had an absolute advantage (cf. Chapter 2). While a division of labor between Mandarin and Cantonese films was observable among the major film studios, as far as the commercial mainstream was concerned, Mandarin films were better resourced under the support of a sophisticated distribution and exhibition network in Hong Kong and Southeast Asia. The Cantonese film sector, on the other hand, was less structured and output quality was uneven, while countless numbers of Cantonese films were credited to short-lived production companies, many of which simply folded after a single release.

The discrepancy in employment conditions, financial stability, production strategy, and more generally business culture between the Cantonese and Mandarin clusters was a hard fact in the filmmaking world, while the general perception that Cantonese films were products of a much lower order in need of a major shake-up was widespread among educators and cultural workers in Hong Kong since the 1930s.

The haphazard working conditions and uneven output quality turned out to be an opportunity for left-wing filmmakers to launch a more rigorous campaign against the "unhealthy" practices in Cantonese cinema and thereby transform the local film culture through a socially engaged cinema of higher educational and artistic value. The urgency to "clean up" the Cantonese film scene was shared and expressed by leading figures from the progressive camp on numerous public occasions, culminating in the Third Cantonese Cinema Clean-up Campaign in 1949, in which film workers were called upon to take stringent measures to improve the content, subject matter, and artistic quality of Cantonese films. In a passionate and patriotically worded statement, the signatories declared battle on what they called "poisonous films." The filmmakers' nationalistic sentiments nonetheless ran through their call to arms directed against what they saw as an unhealthy and morally degenerated film culture (discussed below).

Even though patriotism and anti-imperialism were quite openly embraced, the filmmakers cautiously stayed within the bounds of their professed cultural mission. Consistent with the CCP's "making full use of Hong Kong in the interest of long-term planning" strategy, patriotism and anti-imperialism had to be translated into softer moral lessons and social messages that appealed to the underprivileged and the working class, who constituted a significant proportion of the local population in mid-twentieth century Hong Kong.[24] From published records of the speeches and correspondences of party officials in charge of Hong Kong affairs, overt political mobilization was not a preferred strategy of the Chinese government. Until the decision-making center in the PRC was overtaken by the extreme left (*ji zuo*) on the eve of the Cultural Revolution, party leaders would prefer a non-radical form of progressive cinema that would more effectively appeal to the local audience while avoiding direct confrontations with the colonial government.[25]

To some extent, this relatively flexible policy toward left-wing film-making in Hong Kong reflected the party leaders' understanding of the special status of Hong Kong in the CCP's united front strategy, which concerned not only the new regime's political claim of sovereignty over KMT-ruled Taiwan in the long run, but also its emotional claim of nationhood in the eyes of overseas Chinese. Shouldering the responsibility of local and overseas audience cultivation, Hong Kong's brand of left-wing cinema had to strike a balance between its artistic, political, and commercial objectives. The productions of the left-wing studios during the 1950s and 1960s therefore exhibited a much greater diversity in subject matter, style, and genre types than their Mainland counterparts. This said, such an approach would also make room for ideological persuasion by adapting the language and style of the popular cinema (Chapters 3 and 4). As some researchers have pointed out, socially engaged films with a patriotic bent were regularly distributed in Southeast Asia by the two leading right-wing Mandarin studios when good business took a priority seat over political admonitions.[26] As discussed further in the next chapter, the shifting left–right boundaries are also reflected in more subtle patterns of negotiation and adaptation in production and exhibition strategies to survive market versatilities. After all, the left-wing's counter-hegemonic mission could only be accomplished through gaining a foothold in the mainstream cinema. The filmmakers' oppositional politics vis-à-vis prevailing commercial practices, as vocally expressed in the 1949 Clean-up Campaign, was buttressed by their entrepreneurial acumen and adaptability compatible to their right-wing counterparts.

The three Cantonese Cinema Clean-up Campaigns: ethics, ethos, and politics

Between the mid-1930s to 1949, the Hong Kong film industry had undergone three high-profile campaigns to "clean up" malpractices and unhealthy elements in the Cantonese cinema. As Teo observes, Cantonese cinema of this period suffered from an "inferiority complex" thanks to the general perception that a film's aesthetic quality and value was inseparable from its educational and social function, an influence of the left-wing film tradition among émigré filmmakers and intellectuals from Shanghai.[27] The First Clean-up Campaign took place in 1935, when Ho Yim, a local educator and chairman of the Overseas Chinese Education Association, called for a reform of the degenerated Cantonese cinema, which was found to be saturated by low-quality films of supernatural and erotic content. The 1935 campaign targeted students and the educational sector with a view to reinforcing national identity, scientific knowledge, and humanistic values. Launched at the beginning of Japan's invasion of China, the Second Clean-up Campaign (1938) emphasized the social function of film and the cinema's mission to contribute to national survival.[28] Supported by local Christian groups, the conveners were senior members of the film industry, among whom were Luo Mingyou, founder of one of the biggest studios in Shanghai, and the "father of Chinese cinema," Lai Man-wai. Compared to its predecessor, the rigor of the second campaign created a platform for like-minded filmmakers to further their efforts in improving the conditions and quality of Cantonese film production.[29]

The nature of the Third Clean-up campaign was slightly different from the first two in terms of scale, involvement of local filmmakers, effort put into the implementation of the action plan, and long-term impact. On 8 April 1949, a joint statement by over one hundred and fifty left-wing filmmakers, including directors and leading stars from the progressive film circle, was published on local Chinese newspapers, including the CCP's official mouthpiece, *Ta Kung Pao* (Figure 1.1), and two non-left-wing newspapers, *The Kung Sheung Daily News* (Figure 1.2) and *Wah Kiu Yat Po* (Figure 1.3). In this strongly worded statement, the signatories expressed their indignation and the urgent need to get rid of "poisonous films" in Cantonese cinema. In view of

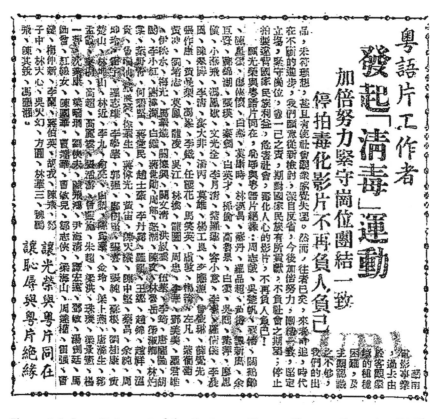

Figure 1.1 Press Statement of the Cantonese Cinema Clean-up Campaign (1949), *Ta Kung Pao* (8 April 1949, p. 4).

Figure 1.2 Press Statement of the Cantonese Cinema Clean-up Campaign (1949), *Kung Sheung Daily News* (8 April 1949, p. 5).

Figure 1.3 Press Statement of the Cantonese Cinema Clean-up Campaign (1949), *Wah Kiu Yat Po* (8 April 1949, p. 7).

the "shameful" practices that had pervaded the local film industry, the filmmakers called on the Hong Kong film community to support the course of nation-building and social advancement:

> South China's film industry has been constrained by both external difficulties and a lack of understanding by its practitioners. Regretfully, the films we make are a disappointment. As filmmakers we must unite and stand firm against making films that would endanger our society and betray the interest of the nation and its people. Together, we must engage in critical self-reflection and work harder to contribute to our country. Let's bid farewell to humiliation … May glory be with Cantonese cinema! (*Ta Kung Pao*, 8 April 1949, author's translation)

On 15 April, two articles on *Ta Kung Pao* gave enthusiastic support to the campaign, followed by at least two more column commentaries on 29 April and 6 May. In the following month, a proposal was drawn up to advocate a co-op mode of film production to achieve the goals of the campaign.[30] A series of new developments followed the initial call to arms: the South China Film Industry Workers' Union (SCFU) was established in July 1949 as a networking platform for progressive filmmakers. In 1950, two left-wing film companies, Fifties and Dragon-Horse, were founded. In January 1950, the Great Wall Pictures Corporation was renamed as Great Wall Movies Enterprise Ltd. after a takeover by shipping tycoon Lui Kin-hong. The deal was facilitated by Fei Yimin, general manager of *Ta Kung Pao* and the brother of renowned left-wing film director Fei Mu (founder of the Dragon-Horse Films).[31] Four months later, the Southern Film Corporation, the PRC's sole distribution agent in Hong Kong, was established. These initial steps taken by the left-wing film community were obvious signs of a systematic effort to consolidate the progressive filmmaking foundation in Hong Kong. The year 1950 was also an eventful year in international politics. It marked the beginning of the Korean War and the US embargo on China (which also included Hong Kong). In the following year, the KMT government in Taiwan announced a ban on Chinese-language films involving left-wing companies as well as acting and production personnel. While a direct connection cannot be established, three major left-wing studios, Sun Luen, Union, and Feng Huang, came into being within the same year of the deportation of senior film personnel at Fifties and Dragon-Horse in January 1952. By the end of 1952, the left-wing film network in Hong Kong was firmly in place.

It is worth noting that between the 1949 manifesto and the founding of Union and Sun Luen (the left-wing's two Cantonese studios) in 1952, the Cantonese film industry was plagued by sluggish box office performance, short-lived profit-taking speculations, and widespread unemployment. The prolonged industry-wide recession was attributed to several factors, including the US trade embargo, low quality productions, and political uncertainties in the region.[32] It was therefore more than a coincidence that Sun Luen and Union were established with a mission to carry out a comprehensive reform of Cantonese cinema. While Union prided itself as a bottom-up initiative by leading filmmakers and screen icons, the studio's aesthetic principles and social vision were aligned with the three major left-wing studios directly under the auspice of party officials. Great Wall and Feng Huang (which came into being after the closing of Dragon-Horse) became the Mandarin production units of the left-wing film network. These left-wing studios would play an important role in reshaping the contours of Hong Kong cinema in the next fifteen years.

The 1949 campaign was a landmark event frequently referenced by researchers in recounting the history of the left-wing cinema, if not Cantonese cinema as a whole. Indeed, the campaign's impact was not just limited to Cantonese-language films because it was a collective reform movement joined by progressive filmmakers from both the Cantonese and Mandarin-speaking clusters. Compared to its two predecessors, the 1949 campaign was more an orchestrated effort by the progressive film community. The campaign's conveners and signatories consisted of prominent actors, directors, and producers who later founded the Union and Sun Luen studios as a first step to claim a space in the mainstream cinema. These studios would become the Cantonese stream of the left-wing film network with affiliated theater circuits supported directly and indirectly by the CCP. The close relationship between the left-wing studios and other branches of the CCP's cultural front in Hong Kong can be gauged through the management structure of Sun Luen and Great Wall: Sun Luen's overseer, Liu Yat-yuen, was head of *Wenhui Bao* (another CCP news agency in Hong Kong); Fei Yimin, head of *Ta Kung Pao*, became general manager of the reconstituted Great Wall. According to Lo Duen, Liu Yat-yuen was the chief architect of the left-wing studios until the late 1960s (cf. Chapters 2 and 5).[33]

Consolidation and extension of the left-wing film network

Since the late 1940s, the CCP had been actively grooming its film production personnel in Hong Kong as part of its cultural united front to serve the long-term interest of the new regime in Mainland China. As previously mentioned, the left-wing film apparatus in Hong Kong was consolidated between 1949 and 1952, a critical juncture that saw the establishment of the People's Republic of China, the emergence of a more vocal progressive film community in Hong Kong, and the organized effort of this community to reform the local film culture. Meanwhile, the KMT government was stepping up its effort to align pro-Taiwan filmmakers and tighten its political censorship of Chinese-language films. The co-existence of two rival Chinese regimes gave form and substance to the mini-Cold War in Hong Kong, a historical turning point that would have a lasting impact on society and culture in years to come. By 1952, the "core" of the left-wing film network was completed. It consisted of four film studios with a clear division of labor in the production of Mandarin and Cantonese films, and one distribution agency overseeing both import and export of left-wing films. In addition to the four major studios, the left-wing's Cantonese stream was further extended through the establishment of Wah Kiu Film Company (1963–1967), a studio founded by Cheung Ying, a prominent actor at Union with the financial support of a business tycoon based in Macau (Chapter 2) and a cluster of short-lived sub-units or satellite studios (Chapter 7). Active in engaging like-minded non-left-wing investors, Sun Luen facilitated the establishment of the Hong Kong branch of a Singaporean film company, Kong Ngee, in 1955.[34] While not explicitly espousing a progressive agenda, Kong Ngee (Hong Kong) was under the direction of Chun Kim, one of the co-founders of Union who would become the mentor of a younger director, Lung Kong, who harbored a very different ideological outlook and yet remained committed to the ethos of a socially committed cinema (Chapter 6). The partnership with Kong Ngee also included distribution of left-wing productions in Singapore. By the mid-1950s, the left-wing cinema had formed a network consisting of four core studios, subsidiary studios, a distribution agency, and a non-left-wing partner with overseas connections. This network would further extend its reach to film exhibition through setting up theater circuits, a subject explored in the next chapter. As such, the cinematic left was well set to further their reformist agenda and make an impact on the local film industry. Sun Luen, Union, Wah Kiu, and Kong Ngee would soon become known as the "big four" Cantonese film companies in Hong Kong. For the first time in the history of Hong Kong cinema, Cantonese film production entered a new phase with the arrival of the "big four" whose working culture and corporate practice distinguished themselves from the hit-and-run mode of their peers. This phase of the development of the left-wing cinema also recalls an early remark by a senior party official, Liu Shaoqi, that "only Cantonese films can take roots in Hong Kong," in his advice on the direction of progressive filmmaking in the British colony.[35] The diversified production labels also facilitated the incubation of a more dynamic progressive film culture that differentiated itself from the didactic and doctrinaire revolutionary films in Mainland China. Unlike the intense competition between the commercial studios, the left-wing film studios exhibited a complementarity in personnel deployment and resource sharing that would enable them to compete with their much stronger rivals. These and other aspects of the left-wing film network are discussed in greater depths in Chapter 2.

Notes

1. Loh, *Underground Front: The Chinese Communist Party in Hong Kong*, 125; Mark, *Hong Kong and the Cold War*, 26–30.
2. Leary, "The Most Careful Arrangements for a Careful Fiction," 548.
3. On the colonial government's efforts to rein in US-backed Nationalist activities in Hong Kong, see Tsang, "Strategy for Survival: The Cold War and Hong Kong's Policy," 294–317.
4. Roberts, "Cold War Hong Kong: Juggling Opposing Forces and Identities," 42–46.
5. Lee and Wong, "Introduction," 5; Fauve, "On Growing Up in the 1960s," 14–15.
6. Lombardo, "A Mission of Espionage, Intelligence and Psychological Operations," 64–81; Du, "Censorship, Regulations, and the Cinematic Cold War in Hong Kong," 138–143.
7. Lu, qtd. in Roberts, "Cold War Hong Kong: Juggling Opposing Forces and Identities," 32.
8. On the Japanese military's policy toward film production in the occupied region, see Fu, *Between Shanghai and Hong Kong: The Politics of Chinese Cinemas*, 93–132; Zhou and Li, *The Early History of Hong Kong Cinema*, 251–254.
9. This sense of outrage and shame was expressed in a strongly worded announcement of the third Cantonese Cinema Clean-up Campaign. Cf. Chapter 2.
10. Hong Kong International Film Festival, *China Factor in Hong Kong Cinema*.
11. Characterizing the left-wing filmmakers as "cultural elites" on their way to creating a "Confucian cultural universe" by left-leaning Cantonese film directors, Chang

(*Screening Communities: Negotiating Narratives of Empire, Nation, and the Cold War in Hong Kong Cinema*) examines the role of postwar Hong Kong cinema in shaping a sense of local community with reference to specific film genres, i.e., official documentary, melodrama, and the youth film during the 1950s.

12. This perspective runs through numerous historical and critical accounts on the subject. See, for example, Wong and Lee, *Cold War and Hong Kong Cinema*; Ho, *Artistic Mission: An Exploration of Sun Luen Film Company*; Ng, *One for All: The Union Film Spirit*; and Zhang, *Studies on Hong Kong Leftist Films*.

13. See Ng, "Inhibition vs. Exhibition: Political Censorship of Chinese and Foreign Cinemas in Postwar Hong Kong," 23–35; Yip, "Closely Watched Films: Surveillance and Postwar Hong Kong Leftist Cinema," 35–59; Van den Troost, "Under Western Eyes," 89–112; and Du, "Censorship, Regulations, and the Cinematic Cold War in Hong Kong," 117–151.

14. Readers can also refer to the timeline for a chronological order of the key events and historical figures cross-referenced in the following account.

15. Large scale labor movements that resulted in temporary shut-downs of trade and services included the Seamen's Strike (1922) and the Guangdong–Hong Kong Strike-Boycott (1925–26). See Loh, *Underground Front: The Chinese Communist Party in Hong Kong*, 44–52.

16. The British government in London tended to be more conciliatory toward the US at the expense of Mainland China, but as Nationalist sabotage and operations against Communist China became more intense in the 1950s, the colonial administration began to take stauncher actions against the saboteurs. See Roberts, "Cold War Hong Kong: Juggling Opposing Forces and Identities," 40–41.

17. Ibid., 35–36; Mark, *Hong Kong and the Cold War*, 182–183, 185–194.

18. "Prohibition of Importation, Circulation or Sale of Communist and Other Prejudicial Publication," 15 August 1958, Research Unit, Special Branch, Singapore; this document's Appendix A and B contain the lists of prohibited publishing societies and authors.

19. Law, *Collaborative Colonial Power: The Making of the Hong Kong Chinese*, 31–56, 57–76.

20. Roberts, "Cold War Hong Kong: Juggling Opposing Forces and Identities," 46.

21. A good example is the Pui Kiu Secondary School, which was active in recruiting students to the leftist course. Tsang Yuk-sing, co-founder and former president of the biggest pro-China political party in Hong Kong—the Democratic Alliance for the Betterment of Hong Kong (DAB)—taught at Pui Kiu and became its principal before he began his full-time political career. His brother, Tsang Tak-shing, was jailed for two years for distributing inflammatory publications during the anti-British riots in 1967. Witness accounts on the riots can be found in a recent documentary film, *The Vanished Records* (dir. Lo Yan Wai Connie, 2017).

22. According to Ching, *The Origins of the Hong Kong Riots*, the 1967–68 Hong Kong Riots was a sub-stream of the Cultural Revolution. Ching's argument is based on a close analysis of previously undisclosed notes and diaries of CCP leaders and archival research on British and Chinese policies during the Cultural Revolution. Cheung, *Hong Kong's Watershed: The 1967 Riots*, offers a similar account,

substantiated by first-person interviews with retired core personnel of the CCP's cultural front in Hong Kong.

23. British Nigeria was regarded as a "model for indirect rule." The system was "rigorously modernized" under the governorship of Lugard. Crowder, "Indirect Rule: French and British Style," 197–198.

24. Among the domestic crises faced by the colonial government were rampant corruption and class exploitation, two "internal factors" that historians attributed to the outbreak of the 1967 riots. See Ching, *The Origins of the Hong Kong Riots*, 14–15.

25. Ho, *Artistic Mission: An Exploration of Sun Luen Film Company*, 22; Liao, "On the Work on Hong Kong Cinema," 451–458.

26. See Mak, *Hong Kong Cinema and Singapore: A Cultural Ring between Two Cities*, 13; and Lee, "The Best of Both Worlds: Hong Kong Film Industry during the Cold War Era," 86.

27. See Teo, *Hong Kong Cinema: The Extra Dimensions*, 3–28.

28. Ibid.

29. The immediate impact can be seen in the reduction of the so-called *shenguai* films, a localized genre label for low-budget formulaic supernatural and fantasy films that had come under strong criticism by the progressive camp. See Yu, *The History of Hong Kong Cinema II*, 188–189.

30. Su Yi, "A Recommendation," *Ta Kung Pao*, 6 May 1949.

31. Sil-Metropole Organisation, *Sixty Years of Sil-Metropole*, 30, 62.

32. The SCFU reported on the adverse market situation due to both internal and external factors; see *Wah Kiu Yat Po*, 9 July 1952. Local News Section, 2.

33. Liu Yat-yuen was also a member of the Executive Committee of the All-Circles Struggle Committee during the 1967 anti-British riots. His involvement in the riots resulted in his arrest by the Hong Kong police in late 1967. Liu, in a recent documentary on the 1967 Riots (*Vanished Archives* [2017]), revealed that the Executive Committee was actually not the decision-making body.

34. The establishment of Kong Ngee and its sister studio, Sun Ngee (1962), also led to the draining of acting talents at Union, which ceased production in 1964 and formally closed in 1967. Cf. timeline.

35. Ho, *Artistic Mission: An Exploration of Sun Luen Film Company*, 22.

Chapter 2

Left in the right way: corporate strategy and the making of a popular left-wing

Chapter 1 has delineated the multidimensional power dynamics that characterized Cold War politics in British Hong Kong and the film production environment under the conditions of the ideological tug-of-war between Taiwan and Mainland China since 1949. Apart from the 1967 anti-British riots and sporadic disturbances to the social and economic status quo caused by union strikes that preceded it,[1] the most enduring battle was fought in the realm of culture. The local film industry, too, was subject to distinctive forms of cultural politics as studios and practitioners at all levels were drawn into a polarized ideological warfare that soon materialized into more overt forms of institutional interference. While this period of Hong Kong's film history has been discussed in numerous accounts, the task here is not so much a panoramic scanning of events as a perspectival mapping of the filmmaking world in post-World War II Hong Kong. Drawing upon existing sources on the subject, this chapter addresses questions of thematic importance to the present study: What does it mean to be the left, right, and middle in the film industry during the 1950s and 1960s? What was it like to be on the "left" side of the filmmaking world under the peculiar circumstances of the mini–Cold War? To what extent had the left-wing filmmakers established their own industrial apparatus that would allow them to compete with the major commercial (right-wing) studios in terms of financing, production, and popularity? How successful were these models? This chapter therefore is concerned with the left-wing film apparatus as a corporate entity and their strategic self-positioning in the competitive film market. From this perspective, it is essential to consider exhibition practices of theater circuits to shed light on how the left–right dynamics was played out in the formation and realignment of theater circuits. "How left is the left?"—the concluding question of this chapter—attempts to bring into sharper focus the "middle ground" cultivated by cultural agents on both sides as an ad hoc backdoor to seek temporary relief from the tightrope of Cold War politics. The reflections here complement the closer examination of studio history, film styles, and genres in Chapters 3 and 4 to raise questions about a cinematic legacy of the left-wing in the later decades.

Locating the left, right, and middle in the film industry

As noted in the Introduction, the meaning of "leftist" or "left-wing" in Hong Kong is a matter of political loyalty and patriotism among pro-CCP groups at different levels of society. While filmmakers commonly identify themselves as "progressive film workers," left-wing or leftist cinema is a term widely adopted in critical literature to distinguish a field of analysis. The invocation of "left-wing" or "leftist" in such a context would also imply an indirect reference, if not a form of address, to a corresponding "right-wing," who were also called "freedom filmmakers." In short, a set of context-specific political vocabularies had emerged in postwar Hong Kong that would define the nature of left–right cultural politics with a direct bearing on the actual practices of film production and exhibition. As we shall see, as far as the film industry was concerned, considerations of business survival quite often superseded political demarcations. Regardless of ideological affiliations, there always existed an interstitial space or "middle ground" mediating the interests and aspirations of individuals. Not surprisingly, despite the left-wing's strong sense of social responsibility and anti-capitalist convictions, the left–right rivalry was also defined by the rules of the film market. The competition for popularity, inevitably, was always a weighted objective in production strategies as well as exhibition and distribution practices, while collaboration between the two rival camps for mutual benefits was still possible. Positioning the "big four" left-wing studios in the filmmaking world, therefore, should not lose sight of the "non-left."

The postwar film industry boom in Hong Kong and Southeast Asia prompted into being a large number of short-lived or "one film studios" that folded after a single venture. What can be immediately observed here is that the left-wing studios were more eager to set up satellite companies to increase production capacity (cf. Chapter 7). Union and Sun Luen were operating on a co-op mode, which means films were made on a project-by-project basis (discussed below). While this allowed the studios to maintain a minimum overhead with maximum flexibility in manpower deployment, the studios' stringent quality control resulted in longer production cycles, hence limiting revenue and cash flow. Feng Huang and Great Wall were also aware of the problem of insufficient output to capture greater market shares in Hong Kong and overseas.[2] Shaw and MP&GI, in contrast, were closer to the industrial model of Hollywood, with well-resourced and integrated production, distribution, and exhibition units in Hong Kong and Southeast Asia. The increasing demand for high quality Chinese-language films in Southeast Asia in the 1950s indirectly fostered the collaboration between the left-wing and right-wing studios, as Shaw and MP&GI became regular distributors of left-wing productions through their theater networks in the region.[3]

The landmark event that completed the formal division of left and right in the film industry took place in 1953 when the Hong Kong and Kowloon Union of Free Workers in the Film Industry (the "Free Association") was established on 27 March.[4] Supported by the KMT, the Free Association was founded by a group of pro-Taiwan filmmakers. Zhang Shankun, co-founder of Yung Hwa and the former Great Wall, played a leading role in the activities of the Free Association.[5] Its mission was to scrutinize the political affiliations of all filmmakers and serve as the KMT's unofficial film censorship body in Hong Kong.[6] The Free Association had the full backing of the KMT government to directly identify and disclose names and titles blacklisted, organize group visits to Taiwan, and offer incentives to individuals associated with the left-wing film circle to "flee for freedom." (This was also why right-wing filmmakers were also called "freedom filmmakers," or *ziyou yingren*.) Over the years and until the early 1980s, the Free Association made its formidable power felt through overt and covert censorship and market access regulation. Since Taiwan was the largest Mandarin film market until the gradual resumption of commercial film imports to Mainland China in the 1980s, Shaw and MP&GI were the default co-opted supporters of the Free Association. The almost exclusive access to the Taiwan market by the two largest Mandarin studios of the time, and the decline of MP&GI after the death of its charismatic boss, Loke Wan Tho, in a plane crash in 1964 created a golden opportunity for Shaw to become the godfather in Mandarin cinema until Shaw's withdrawal from film production in the mid-1980s.[7]

It was a well-known fact that Free Association was an extension of both the KMT and the US's political interference in Hong Kong. In the same year, Asia Pictures was founded with financial backing from the US. Before its closure in 1958, Asia Pictures had produced a total of nine features carrying subtle propagandistic content.[8] Meanwhile, the colonial administration began to adopt a more rigorous approach to film censorship in view of the escalation of the left–right ideological battle in the early 1950s, in particular through the 1953 Film Censorship Regulations (under the *Places of Public Entertainment Ordinance*). While films displaying pro-CCP content was subject to "various forms of surveillance and control [from] spying, censorship, regulation of market access, deportation, media propaganda, and so forth,"[9] a principal duty of colonial censors was "to cleanse the movie screen of the spectacle and ideology of the nation state, that is, 'China.'" Under this principle, "all shots of Chinese leaders, political rallies, national flags and emblems, Communist or KMT, from films and documentaries" were prohibited."[10] Such surveillance remained in place for over two decades, during when numerous filmmakers had to denounce or deny their affiliations with the left-wing in "confession statements" to avoid being expelled from the Taiwan market. In the course of events, some iconic stars working for the left-wing studios made their dramatic "flight to freedom."[11] Another form of control came from the CCP. Through direct and indirect contact with filmmakers, senior party officials were keeping a close eye on the direction and management of the left-wing studios. At the local level, the left-wing film community felt the need of a united front to consolidate resources and keep up the morale of fellow filmmakers. In 1949, the progressive film community established the South China Film Industry Workers' Union (SCFU), whose initial membership and board of directors consisted of the key personnel of the "big four" left-wing studios that came into being between 1950 and 1952. Being the steam engine behind the Cantonese Cinema Clean-up Campaign, the SCFU's main strategies were to unify and engage left-wing filmmakers and like-minded supporters in fund-raising and organizing campaigns for the betterment of Cantonese cinema. In order to sustain a critical mass of film industry workers, the SCFU produced four fund-raising films between 1956 and 1962. All revenue and staff salaries were donated to support members' welfare and the Association's operation.[12]

The ideological battles between the KMT and the CCP had a direct impact on the filmmaking world. The KMT government's increasingly aggressive interference in the Hong Kong film industry was achieved through the control of market access. The rise to prominence of the two Mandarin film production giants, Shaw and MP&GI, were due in part to their right-wing credentials, which also worked to the advantage of their Southeast Asian theater operations. It can be said that, as far as

British Hong Kong was concerned, the Cold War was as much a war of the market as it was a war of ideas. The US trade embargo on China and Hong Kong after the outbreak of the Korean War in 1957 threw the film industry into further disarray, as shipment of film stocks from the Western Bloc countries were suspended. To stay in business, film studios regardless of political orientations had to abide by the law of the market. Whereas the cinematic left never lost sight of their loftier goals of social and cultural reform, the market remained the primary site of ideological and commercial rivalry. Decades later, the necessity to reclaim their position in the mainstream cinema in Hong Kong was a major catalyst for the reinvention of the left-wing film tradition into a more dynamic, Hong Kong–based conglomerate from where some of the city's best-known directors started their careers in the 1980s (Chapters 5 and 7).

The "left-wing business model": production, distribution, and exhibition

The duality of Cantonese cinema as a form of popular entertainment and a means for ideological persuasion somehow worked to alleviate the critical bias toward Cantonese films as inherently inferior to Mandarin films, especially since the political value of Cantonese cinema was endorsed by senior party officials overseeing the state's policy toward Hong Kong.[13] The most vocal supporter of a moderate left-wing approach among party leaders was Liao Chengzhi, who was then overseeing the cultural bureau's external affairs. (Liao would have a crucial role to play in the rehabilitation of left-wing film production in Hong Kong after the Cultural Revolution and the 1967 anti-British riots, discussed in Chapter 5.) In his 1964 summary report on the central government's policy on Hong Kong cinema, Liao reiterated his belief that "progressive thought," "national style," and "flexible approach" would best serve the course of a left-wing cinema in Hong Kong, while anti-imperialism and anti-feudalism would remain the guiding principles of patriotic filmmaking. In Liao's words, the localized left-wing cinema in Hong Kong should be producing "bourgeois revolutionary films" as a distinctive branch or "tributary" of the orthodox "socialist/proletarian revolutionary films" in Mainland China.[14] Under this rubric, left-wing filmmakers in Hong Kong were given greater creative freedom as long as they adhered to the principles of anti-imperialism, patriotism, and anti-feudalism. No doubt, Cantonese cinema's transnational popularity was a form of soft power much needed by the new regime to assert itself as the legitimate ruler of the new Chinese nation (Taiwan being a region or *diqu* in the PRC's official definition). The disjunction between Cantonese cinema's artistic quality and political value made the tasks set by the Third Cantonese Cinema Clean-up Campaign in 1949 all the more urgent and important. It was through a synthesis of Cantonese cinema's artistic, political, and market potentials that the localized left-wing cinema could most effectively answer the party's call to make "educational and morally uplifting" films to contribute to the society as well as the course of nation-building.[15] Obviously, given cinema's dual role as cultural capital and a designated branch of the CCP's "cultural united front" (*wen hua zhanxian*), at the core of this synthesis was the political agenda of the state. The pro-Taiwan Mandarin commercial studios affiliated with the Free Association were more co-opted agencies caught at the crossroads of interstate rivalry; hence their politics was also profit-driven despite the ideological inclinations of some of their leading figures.[16] Among the four major left-wing studios, three were under the direct supervision of senior party officials in Mainland China, who would advise on production directions and strategic planning in line with the central government's policy toward Hong Kong (discussed below).

The complex entanglement between Cold War politics and cultural production in Hong Kong at the time, and the CCP's proactive approach to grooming a cultural brigade on reserve for future political mobilization,[17] had shaped the general outlook of the left-wing studios and their positioning in the Hong Kong film industry. A third dimension of the left-wing cinema of equal importance was the self-perception and artistic-intellectual orientation of the filmmakers themselves, which amounted to an identity politics that helped define what it meant to be "on the left" at large. This question is raised from different perspectives in the following chapters. To gain a fuller understanding of what it means to be "on the left" of the filmmaking world, we must first consider the left-wing as a member of the local film industry subject to both the established rules and conditions of film production as well as the laws of the market, that is, demand and supply contingent upon the taste, interests, and viewing conventions of the target audience. As many filmmakers were committed to making spiritually and morally uplifting films to serve loftier goals than profit, hence the need to seek out alternative paradigms of film production to achieve the twin objectives of artistic excellence and commercial viability, the question of what it meant to be "on the left" is also about what should and could be done to develop a *popular* left-wing cinema that would challenge the hegemony of a commercial mainstream deemed to be perpetuating feudalistic and capitalistic values.

The extent to which the interstate power dynamics of the Cold War had penetrated the local film industry cannot be overstated; however, in the absence of an institutionalized "national cinema" (or a state-run "national film industry" as in Mainland China or the USSR) supported by public funding to balance an often lopsided commercial filmmaking environment, the cinematic left had to prove their worth against the harsher realities of the box office. It is therefore highly relevant to consider the idea of a *popular left-wing* as a self-positioning strategy even though the left-wing studios benefitted from the direct and indirect support from the CCP. After all, the aesthetics and politics of the left was to enlighten the "broad masses" in the Party's parlance; popularity measured by ticket sales was therefore both a commercial and ideological imperative. A closer look at the more mundane side of "being popular" in the filmmaking world, that is, the way studios adapted to a competitive market environment where the left, right, or middle were subject to the vicissitudes of the box office, yields a more vivid portrayal of the conditions under which the "popular left-wing" came into being. In this light, the inquiry below is guided by the following questions: what distinguished the corporate culture of the left-wing studios from their commercial counterparts in terms of production, distribution, and exhibition? How did the studios organize themselves, covertly or overtly, as a "cultural united front" pursuing collective, noncommercially driven goals? What kind of partnership existed between the studios? Did a similar or different pattern of competition/complementarity exist on the cinematic left? The discussion here proceeds in two directions: the financing and corporate models of the studios and their self-positioning as functional units of the CCP's cultural brigade in Hong Kong. As we shall see, Sun Luen is the studio that straddled two realms: it was among the three official left-wing studios directly under the auspice of the Communist Party leadership (commonly known as "Chang Feng Xin," designating Great Wall, Feng Huang, and Sun Luen by their Chinese character initials). On the other hand, it had a close connection to Union, a Cantonese film production collective founded by prominent filmmakers. Sun Luen and Union were in essence twin companies in terms of staff composition, resource sharing, and self-positioning in the Cantonese film market that differentiated it from the competitive mode of the right-wing studios. Sun Luen was also active in networking with non-left-wing investors to forge business alliances in the local and Southeast Asian markets.

The "big four" left-wing studios were set up between 1950 and 1952.[18] Great Wall Movie Enterprises Limited, founded by Zhang Shankun as Great Wall Pictures Corporation in 1949, went through a major restructuring in 1950. Zhang was a leading figure in the film industry in Shanghai. His initial success was short-circuited by financial miscalculation in a major project. Zhang's position was further weakened when his partner, Yuan Yang'an, had diverging views on production strategy. Yuan, a left-leaning entrepreneur who saw greater potential in the Mainland film market, took the helm when Zhang left the company in 1950. The studio was restructured with the support of shipping industry tycoon Lui Kin-hong.[19] The change of ownership and management signaled a "left turn" in the company's ideological and business outlook.[20] Modeled after Hollywood commercial studios in its initial set-up, Great Wall had been reputed for its lavish production budgets and strict quality control. The corporate reshuffle did not change the studio's commitment to producing high-quality films in Mandarin that were both socially engaging and accessible to the average filmgoer.[21] Feng Huang came into being as the successor of its two predecessors, Dragon-Horse and Fifties. Founded in 1948 by Fei Mu, the renowned director of Chinese cinema's all-time classic, *Spring in a Small Town* (1947), Dragon-Horse ran into financial difficulties shortly after Fei's death and ceased operation in 1951.[22] The same year also witnessed the deportation of left-wing filmmakers from Hong Kong, many of whom were founding members of Dragon-Horse and Fifties. As an initiative of the CCP to reorganize its filmmaking apparatus in Hong Kong, Feng Huang and Great Wall operated as complementary labels to capture the Mandarin film market. Similar to Union and Sun Luen, Feng Huang and Great Wall adopted a synergetic production model characterized by flexible resource sharing and crossover of acting and production talents, while the Cantonese and Mandarin studios would also collaborate on some occasions. It should not be a mere coincidence that Union and Sun Luen were set up in 1952, shortly after the deportation of eight left-wing filmmakers by the colonial government (see timeline). Between the two Mandarin studios, Great Wall's founding history marked the company's transition from self-initiated entrepreneurship to systematic consolidation through indirect state investment and institutionalization.[23] Feng Huang, on the other hand, is closer to the direct investment mode by the CCP with a predetermined ideological agenda. Whether through direct or indirect investment and ownership, Great Wall and Feng Huang marked a major advancement in the consolidation of left-wing film production base in Hong Kong. Throughout the 1950s and until more radical politics took over Mainland China on the eve of the Cultural Revolution, the two Mandarin studios were able to maintain a foothold in the local and overseas Chinese film markets while gaining access to Mainland China.[24]

Sun Luen functioned as a strategic node connecting the big three official studios and potential collaborators from outside the progressive camp. Lo Duen,[25] a veteran filmmaker and co-founder of Sun Luen, was a left-leaning intellectual whose experience in wartime China had shaped his anti-imperialist and anti-colonial worldview. Like many of his filmmaking peers (many of whom became leading figures in Sun Luen and Union), Lo Duen exemplified the patriotic Chinese intellectual whose artistic and social vision was attuned to the leftist course. As a senior member of the left-wing film community, Lo was recruited to set up Sun Luen with the support of Liu Yat-yuen, who was head of *Wenhui Bao*, a local newspaper known to be the CCP's official mouthpiece in Hong Kong. Before Liu left the news agency to work full-time in Sun Luen in 1956, the studio was operating on a co-op mode of production—or "brotherhood" (*xiongdi ban*) in Lo's words. Under Liu's charge, Sun Luen would venture into commercial genre films to increase its market presence.[26] With the addition of Sun Luen, the CCP by now had established its filmmaking apparatus in both the Mandarin and Cantonese cinema. Since Cantonese was a major regional dialect and a language of everyday life in the city, Sun Luen's strategic value to the Party was beyond doubt. As a left-wing studio, Sun Luen was actively engaging both left-leaning filmmakers and the moderate members of the right to maximize its business and ideological reach, for instance the co-production with Shaw of its 1953 film, *House of 72 Tenants* (1963, dir. Wong Wai-yat).

Union was founded in 1952 by twenty-one filmmakers acting in the capacity of co-directors of the managing board, many of whom were leading stars and directors of the time. Primarily a collective effort, Union offers an interesting example in contrast to the "big three" left-wing studios directly supported by the CCP. While direct support from the party might be a better guarantee of operational stability, the downside, as some critics have noted, was the inevitable constraints on creativity on productions under stricter party guidelines.[27] The leading figure of Union was Ng Cho-fan, an acclaimed actor with entrepreneurial charisma. As a "bottom-up" film studio, Union can be regarded as the "independent" arm of the cinematic left. Being senior members of the local film scene with similar wartime experiences, Ng and Lo's friendship was founded upon a shared belief in cinema's social and moral function and their commitment to raising the professional and artistic standard of Cantonese films. Commercial considerations aside, the two studios maintained close interactions and at times collaborated to resolve production and casting needs.[28] Similar to Sun Luen during its founding years, Union relied on a co-op business model and collective ownership.[29] In 1957, Cheung Ying, a leading actor who frequently starred in Sun Luen and Union productions, founded his own studio, Wah Kiu Film Company, with financial backing from Ho Yin, a tycoon and head of a powerful clan in Macau.[30] Wah Kiu specialized in *wenyi* films (lit. art and literary films with a melodramatic bent, hence often rendered as "melodrama" in English),[31] most of which were tailor-made for Cheung, who once took up the director's role. From 1957 to its closure in 1967, Wah Kiu was ranked among the four leading Cantonese film studios together with Sun Luen, Union, and Kong Ngee (a Singaporean-owned film company specializing in modern-style urban dramas, comedies, and popular genre films featuring younger icons).[32] According to Lo Duen, both Wah Kiu and Union were established with the support of Sun Luen as a continuation of the Cantonese Cinema Clean-up Campaign (Chapter 1). Apart from strengthening the left-wing Cantonese studios, Lo also facilitated the setting up of Kong Ngee's Hong Kong operation.[33]

With hindsight, Union's co-op business model enabled the company to go against the grain of mass production of formulaic genre films, raising the hope of an alternative film practice to become a player *within* the mainstream rather than a "counter culture." The left-wing's aspiration to becoming a *popular* cinema for the general public motivated its ambition to compete against and alongside commercial "exploitainment" films. Although Union was not an official filmmaking arm of the CCP in Hong Kong, its close relationship with Sun Luen—founded upon shared ideological, intellectual, and artistic convictions—fostered an unofficial alliance with the official left-wing studios, with Union serving as the independent arm of the left-wing film establishment.

The above topographical sketches of the left-wing studio's existential condition in post-World War II Hong Kong reveal an important characteristic of the left-wing cinema as a joint effort involving party officials in

Mainland China and cultural agents in Hong Kong. Against the backdrop of the macropolitics of the Cold War and the micropolitics of the struggle for legitimacy between two contending Chinese nations, the colonial city's filmmaking landscape was gradually transformed in terms of output variety, market stakeholders, sources of financing, business models, and division of labor. Nuanced silhouettes were layered on the preexisting linguistic divide between the Mandarin and Cantonese cinemas that resonated with the larger political and social climate of the time. Interestingly, while the original rivalry between two linguistic clusters was never free from internal strife within a single cluster (for instance, the competition between Shaw and MP&GI), the market success of left-wing productions magnified the distinction between different *types* of films and their covert political messages. While the commercial mainstream was mainly defined by market competition, the left-wing studios were employing a hybrid mode of collective corporate survival through product differentiation, label diversification, flexible crossovers, and openness toward new and potential allies, including collaborating with pro-Taiwan studios and overseas investors such as Kong Ngee.

A second observation has to do with the strategic importance of a "middle ground" actively cultivated by the major studios (left and right) as a backdoor to seek temporary relief from the stranglehold of Cold War politics. It must be noted here that, unlike the left and the right, the middle ground did not have readily identifiable contours and its boundaries were by necessity porous and unstable. One can say that the middle ground existed as an ad hoc and interstitial space that was called into being whenever the left–right politics was endangering individual and corporate survival. In this light, Sun Luen's strategic role as an incubator of new partnerships, the cross-fertilization of acting and production talents between studios, and the right-wing studios' readiness to open distribution avenues for left-wing films made visible the middle ground as a precarious "third space" in a bipolar world. Between Sun Luen and Union, Sun Luen was more active in playing the role of a strategic planner and facilitator of partnerships to consolidate the left-wing cinema's network in Hong Kong. As Lo Wai-luk observes, the subtle division of labor between the two companies made for a maximum flexibility in production capacity, industry engagement, and business strategies.[34] Back-tracking Ackbar Abbas's description of Hong Kong cinema to the Cold War era, if the left-wing cinema ought to "be popular in order to be,"[35] contemplating a *popular* left-wing must also take into account the final destination of film as a cultural product, that is, the projection screen where it meets the audience. On this note, we shall turn to the competition for screen space and the formation of alliances between studios and theater circuits in the making of a popular left-wing.

The making of a popular left-wing: film exhibition and theater circuits

From the 1950s to the mid-1960s, local theaters showing Cantonese films far outnumbered theaters specializing in Mandarin and foreign films.[36] As mentioned before, Cantonese films had a natural supremacy over other Mandarin and other Chinese-dialect films in Hong Kong. The popularity of Cantonese movies throughout the Chinese diaspora in Southeast Asia further boosted the confidence of filmmakers. Meanwhile, it was not uncommon for prominent stars to establish their own production companies to take advantage of the strong demand for Cantonese films in the region. As studios big and small were stepping up their productions, film companies were looking for ways to expand their screening facilities. The boom in Cantonese cinema came to a halt in the mid-1960s for two main reasons. At a time when overproduction led to a sharp decline in quality during the boom, identity politics in Southeast Asia began to turn inward, as newly independent nations adopted protective film policies that would effectively close the door for Chinese-language films.[37] Unable to access the Mandarin-speaking market in Taiwan, Cantonese films were the hardest hit when the overseas market conditions continued to deteriorate. In 1966, Mainland China entered into another prolonged period of political upheaval with the outbreak of the Cultural Revolution. The most direct impact on Hong Kong's left-wing studios, and the Hong Kong society as a whole, was the 1967 anti-British riots that brought the entire city into a standstill for eight months. The repercussions of this historic incident on the left-wing film network and its subsequent development is discussed in more detail in Chapter 5.

An interesting phenomenon during the postwar boom in the film industry was that the keenest competition seemed to come from theater operators, while the film studios themselves were flexibly navigating their courses in a thriving yet versatile market. The 1950s and 1960s saw a vibrant expansion in the film exhibition sector. Major studios were willing to acquire new venues, while numerous others underwent renovation to accommodate new exhibition technologies and rising venue standards.[38] Studios would also configure their theater circuits through direct ownership or forming alliances with independent, usually lower tier, operators, to maximize their market capture. In a nutshell, the theater boom during this time gave rise to a dynamic exhibition culture vesting on the softer edges of the ideological divide in the filmmaking world. Vertical integration of film production, distribution, and exhibition had been a stock in trade since the earliest days of Chinese cinema. Lai Man-wai, for example, started theater operation in Hong Kong in the 1920s with improved modern facilities for his studio's productions.[39] The Shaw family owned theater circuits in Southeast Asia before expanding their business into studio production in Hong Kong in the 1930s under the name of the Tianyi Film Company. With the establishment of the Shaw & Sons Co. Ltd. in 1950, and the Shaw Brothers (HK) Ltd. in 1958, Shaw became the official label of the family business that would continue to grow in scope and scale in the following decades. Cathay Organisation (MP&GI) sported a similar trajectory from a theater operator in Southeast Asia to one of the two largest film studios in Hong Kong in the 1950s and 1960s.[40] While the contest for screen space did not preclude flexible crossovers, studio-run theater circuits became a common industry practice across the left- and right-wing clusters, as both were aware of the need to better strategize their screening practices in an increasingly competitive environment. Vertical integration of film production, distribution, and exhibition by the leading studios and theater circuits continued to be a standard practice in the late 1960s and throughout the 1980s.[41]

A closer look at the intersections of politics and economics in film production, distribution, and exhibition as an organic whole illuminates the longer-term implications of this episode in the history of Hong Kong cinema during the Cold War. First of all, the linguistic divide between Mandarin and Cantonese films was complicated by the sources of financing, political affiliation, business strategies, and artistic preferences. The criss-crossing of commercial and political prerogatives, in turn, was reflected in the way in which theater circuits and studio-controlled screening facilities operated, which was also informed by the linguistic and cultural preferences of individual operators in addition to commercial considerations. The "political economy" of film screening, thus, was determined by an amalgam of sometimes incompatible motives and objectives that would upset the already delicate ideological equilibrium between the various interests at stake. In a predominantly Cantonese-speaking society, Cantonese films enjoyed a natural advantage even though they were deemed to be qualitatively inferior to Mandarin and imported films (mostly from Hollywood, followed by Britain, Italy, and France).[42] Since the film industry's postwar revival, film exhibition in Hong Kong had developed a pattern of linguistic specialization guided more by commercial logic than politics. The rise and fall in fortunes of the two major Chinese-language cinemas had a direct bearing on the profitability of showing a particular type of films, which was further complicated by differentiated market segmentation between Mandarin and Cantonese films. Apart from market versatility, a theater's screening program was also shaped by personal preferences. A senior staff in the Lee Theatre group (a leading partner in the foreign film circuit), Yuen Yiu-hung, was known to be a long-time fan of Cantonese opera and supporter of Cantonese films. Interestingly, Yuen was also appointed as the general manager of a left-wing theater (Astor; see below) by Ho Yin, the Macau-based tycoon and financial backer of Union star Cheung Ying's Wah Kiu Film Company. Due to Yuen's influence, the Lee Theatre would also program left-wing films from time to time.[43] These screening patterns, therefore, were often underscored by a combination of factors that were *not* necessarily political in nature. The screening preferences and interactions between theater operators and film studios point toward a dynamic lifeworld of film production and exhibition that traversed ideological and political boundaries. Instead of being dictated by political motivations, filmmakers and theater circuits were exercising their entrepreneurial skills to carve out a "middle ground" to negotiate the competing demands of their professional and political commitments. It was not uncommon to see popular left-wing stars issue public announcements to deny personal involvement in "political activities" (Figure 2.1).

While the biggest players in the field remained Shaw and MP&GI, left-wing studios were actively securing their own screen space through collaborating with theater operators and acquiring new exhibition venues. Beginning from the early 1950s, left-wing studios partnered with the Southern Film Corporation (official distributor of PRC productions in Hong Kong and overseas) to acquire screening facilities for their own films. Their joint effort resulted in two well-known left-wing theater circuits, the Ruby-Astor circuit and the South China–Nanyang circuit. The former consisted of two directly owned theaters, Ruby and Sil-Metropole, and two rented venues, Astor and Ko Sing; the latter was a conglomerate of South China, Nanyang, and Sunbeam Theatre, which came into service in 1972.[44] Another important link in the formation

Figure 2.1 Ng Cho-fan's announcement in *Wah Kiu Yat Po* (15 July 1952, p. 7).

of the left-wing theater circuits was the active support of Ho Yin.[45] Ho founded a holding company as the legal owner of Astor and consolidated the Ruby-Astor circuit. In 1963, Ho Yin once again played a pivotal role in acquiring the Ko Sing Theatre. Both Astor and Ko Sing were overseen by Xu Dunle, former general manager of the Southern Film Corporation and the chief architect of the two left-wing theater circuits.[46]

According to Xu, it was the market success of high-quality imported films (including imports from Soviet and Eastern Bloc, and feature and documentary films of a more propagandistic nature from Mainland China) that prompted left-wing filmmakers to further advance a "progressive film culture" in Hong Kong and expanded the scale of local productions.[47] The most unexpected box office hit during that time was a traditional opera film in the Yue dialect, *The Butterfly Lovers* (1953; released in Hong Kong in 1954),[48] which allegedly recorded over 500,000 ticket sales out of a population of 1.8 million.[49] As such, the left-wing theater circuits' screening programs projected an alternative interna-tionalism as a counter-discourse to the mainstream commercial cinema, while documentaries and feature films from Mainland China functioned as a window to the "New China" that was otherwise obscured or censored from public view in Hong Kong. If print technology and capitalism were the twin catalysts that brought the nation as an "imagined community" into being in nineteenth-century Europe,[50] the advance of the "moving image" since the early twentieth century had turned film into the most powerful medium for nations to deepen and popularize their collective imaginations. In a nuanced and somewhat ironic way, the left-wing studios in Hong Kong took advantage of the laissez-faire capitalist economy to operate an alternative apparatus of film production *within* the existing industrial system despite and against the constraints and setbacks in the localized Cold War context. Their historical trajectory was also a function of Party leadership during the founding years of the PRC before the outbreak of the Cultural Revolution in 1966. The left-wing cinema in Hong Kong would take an abrupt downturn when ripples of the political turmoil from Mainland China finally hit the shores of the British colonial enclave, a subject further examined in Chapter 5.

How left is the left? Notes on the middle ground

This chapter has set out to examine the filmmaking ecology in Hong Kong during the Cold War era through a topographical mapping of the major studios as primary stakeholders, and film exhibition practices that underwent constant adjustments and adaptations by both studio and theater operators to negotiate the economics and politics of the cultural Cold War in Hong Kong. Under the versatile conditions of film production and exhibition, the cinematic left's impetus to clean up the local film culture was inseparable from their effort to establish themselves as fellow industry players to be reckoned with in the commercial mainstream. The formation of theater circuits and alliances, and the increasingly active role played by film studios in theater operations, were evidence of the entrepreneurial flexibility of industry practitioners, when actual practice made it impossible to uphold the ideological divide as an overriding prerogative. Very often, when ideological doctrines were tested against the much less predictable lifeworld of human agents driven by contending motives, needs, and aspirations, new axes and patterns would come into play to realign vested interests or redraw old boundaries. Despite the overt attempts by the KMT government to exercise political censorship through market access control, the responses of cultural agents in the filmmaking world testified to the arbitrariness of an imposed political identity, whose perceived value was a coefficient of its market value. The 1950s and 1960s also witnessed some genuine effort by the cinematic left to claim a space in the film culture of the colonial city. Primarily an organized community of left-leaning filmmakers with organic and/or diplomatic ties with like-minded cultural agents and entrepreneurs, the cinematic left consisted of the studios' production, acting, and managerial talents, theater operators, and their business connections in Hong Kong, Macau, and Singapore. As far as their production and marketing strategies are concerned, the left-wing studios were functioning in much the same way as their rival commercial studios, with the exception of Union, which had upheld a communal, co-op mode of production throughout its fifteen-year lifespan.[51] As a progressive filmmaking community empowered by its social and ideological mission, the left-wing film studios were by and large producers of popular films with a view to claiming a place in the commercial cinema. (The way in which the left-wing studios engaged with the popular cinematic medium to advance their artistic and social ideals is discussed in Chapters 3 and 4.)

As a popular left-wing film network, Great Wall, Feng Huang, Sun Luen, and Union constituted a mini-united front in terms of corporate image building, product diversification, distribution and exhibition mechanism, and complementary modes of personnel deployment and resource sharing between and within the Mandarin and Cantonese film clusters. Such a corporate model distinguished the left-wing studios from other commercial studios. The above analysis also suggests that the left-wing studios were institutionalized to function as a progressive cultural force under the guidance of party leaders in Mainland China. Their ideological mission notwithstanding, the actual conditions of film production often compelled cultural agents, left or right, to steer a middling course. If one were to give a value to measure how far the cinematic left had gone in being "the left" as a political identity (*zuo pai*), a "middle ground cultural left" as a description would not be too far off the mark. This middle ground is characterized by constant adaptations and negotiations by the cultural agents to turn an unfavorable environment into an advantage. As we shall see in the following chapters, the strategic value of being a *popular left-wing* was crucial to their translation of the guiding principles of patriotism, anti-imperialism, and anti-feudalism into "spiritually and morally uplifting" films that carefully avoid political provocations. As such, the cinematic left in Hong Kong was self-consciously steering a middling course to carry out their progressive mission that would answer the party's call for "making full use of Hong Kong in the interest of long-term planning."[52] Without any aspiration to stir anti-British sentiments or overturn the status quo, the cinematic left perceived its mission as one of ideological persuasion and moral education. As a member of the CCP's cultural brigade in post-World War II Hong Kong, the left-wing studios entered their "battlefield" with a view to reforming—and *becoming*—the mainstream.

Notes

1. On the Seamen's Strike (1922) and the Guangzhou–Hong Kong Strike-Boycott (1925–26), see Loh, *Underground Front: The Chinese Communist Party in Hong Kong,* 44–52.
2. Zhou, "Glory Be with Cantonese Films," 32–33.
3. Mak, *Hong Kong Cinema and Singapore: A Cultural Ring between Two Cities,* 13; Lee, "The Best of Both Worlds: Hong Kong Film Industry during the Cold War Era," 86.
4. See Zuo, "The Free Association: Introduction and Chronology of Key Events," 271–289. The Union was renamed in the 1950s and 1990s to include theater workers.
5. Zhang was sabotaged twice by his left-wing colleagues at Yung Hwa and Great Wall. See Chapter 1 and timeline.
6. See Lu, "The Might of the People," 13–32.
7. On the history the two Mandarin studios, see Wong, *The Cathay Story*; and Wong, *The Shaw Screen: A Preliminary Study.*
8. See Lu, "The Might of the People," 13–32; and Leary, "The Most Careful Arrangements for a Careful Fiction," 548–558.
9. Yip, "Closely Watched Films: Surveillance and Postwar Hong Kong Leftist Cinema," 33.
10. Ng, "Inhibition vs. Exhibition: Political Censorship," 27.
11. Among whom were Linda Lin Dai and Li Lihua. Cf. Chapter 4.
12. Sil-Metropole Organisation, *Sixty Years of Sil-Metropole,* 122–123.
13. Ho, *Artistic Mission: An Exploration of Sun Luen Film Company,* 22–23.
14. Su, *Looking North from a Floating City,* 35.

15. Liao Chengzhi's widely quoted phrase "educational and morally uplifting" (dao ren xiang shang) was often reiterated by left-wing filmmakers as the guiding principle of artistic creation at all the major left-wing studios. Ibid., 35; Ho, *Artistic Mission: An Exploration of Sun Luen Film Company* 152.

16. MP&GI's founder, Loke Wan Tho, for example, was a champion of Western liberal values, which he tried to inculcate in the Chinese-speaking world through the cinema. See Fu, "Modernity, Cold War, and Hong Kong Mandarin Cinema," 24–33.

17. Historically, social and cultural organizations in Hong Kong directly or indirectly backed by the Communist Party would form a "united front" to exert influence on local affairs. The most evident example is the Worker's Union (工聯會), together with its affiliated smaller leftist unions, which has evolved from a social organization into a major political party over the last thirty years. Its strong presence in the Legislative Assembly (Hong Kong's law-making body) makes it the most important ally of the Democratic Alliance for the Betterment of Hong Kong (DAB), the largest political party in the city known to be Beijing's "shadow cabinet" in Hong Kong since 1997.

18. The dating of film companies varies in existing literature. The dates adopted in this study are based on the official company history published by Sil-Metropole and newspaper reports and announcements. Cf. timeline.

19. Chung, "A Film Industry In-between Two Political Powers," 176–179.

20. Ibid.

21. According to some sources, Yuan's managerial role was only "notional" due to the behind-the-scene control of the CCP. See ibid., 183–184.

22. Su, *Looking North from a Floating City,* 24–25.

23. Indeed, Great Wall had opened its doors to left-wing directors and script writers before the restructure. By the time Zhang stepped down, the company was already taking a "progressive" turn. See Chung, "A Film Industry In-between Two Political Powers," 179; and Su, *Looking North from a Floating City,* 56–57.

24. Wong, *An Age of Idealism: Great Wall and Feng Huang Days;* Zhang, "The Cultural Revolution's Impact and Damage," 216; Sil-Metropole Organisation, *Sixty Years of Sil-Metropole,* 37–38, 116–117.

25. Also spelled "Lo Dun" in other English-language sources. The current spelling is based on the Hong Kong Film Archive's Hong Kong filmography online catalogue.

26. See Ho, *Artistic Mission: An Exploration of Sun Luen Film Company,* 28, 45–46.

27. Ibid., 26–27.

28. The acting and production crews of the two studios were basically interchangeable, as shown in the production details and screening credits. The same can be observed in Feng Huang and Great Wall productions.

29. Chung, "The Story of Sun Luen," 42–44; Zhou, "Glory Be with Cantonese Films," 30–32.

30. Stokes, *Historical Dictionary of Hong Kong Cinema,* 184.

31. *Wenyi* film as a genre does not have a satisfactory English translation, and even in Chinese film studies its exact definition and generic properties can be slippery. In general, *wenyi* refers to drama films either adapted from literature or exhibit

"literary" characteristics. Compared to the social ethics drama, the *wenyi* film is a softer kind of drama films that appealed to the average filmgoer. For more detailed discussion on this concept in the Chinese cinema tradition, see Yeh, "A Small History of *Wenyi*," 225–249.

32. Kong Ngee was the only commercial studio specializing in Cantonese films that could rival the Mandarin film giants, Shaw and MP&GI, during the 1950s and 1960s. See, for example, HKFA's publications on the three studios, *The Glorious Modernity of Kong Ngee, The Cathay Story, The Shaw Screen: A Preliminary Study* (2003).

33. Yi, *Realism and Lyricism: Cantonese Cinema and the Hong Kong New Wave*, 86.

34. Lo, "Reflections on the Left-wing Cinema," 65.

35. Abbas, *Hong Kong: Culture and the Politics of Disappearance*, 21.

36. Chung, *100 Years of the Hong Kong Film Industry*, 140–141, 158–159.

37. Mak, "Hong Kong Cinema and Singapore: A Cultural Ring between Two Cities," 35.

38. Huang, *Rediscovering the History of Hong Kong Movie Theatres*, 41–58.

39. Chung, *100 Years of the Hong Kong Film Industry*, 56–64.

40. See Fu, "Modernity, Cold War, and Hong Kong Mandarin Cinema," 24–33, and Chung, "The Industrial Evolution of a Fraternal Enterprise," 1–18.

41. The three major commercial studios with the widest network of theaters were Shaw, Cathay (ceased operation in 1971), and Golden Harvest. This pattern continued in the 1980s with the inception of Cinema City (1980–1991) and D&B Films (1984–1992). The age of the big studios gradually gave way to newer, smaller scale production houses. Shaw ceased film production in 1987 to focus on television broadcasting (TVB), film distribution, and exhibition. Golden Harvest was the home studio of Bruce Lee, Jackie Chan, and Hong Kong's legendary comedian Michael Hui. The company was renamed Orange Sky Golden Harvest after its acquisition by a Mainland Chinese group, Orange Sky, in 2008.

42. Chung, *100 Years of the Hong Kong Film Industry*, 140–141, 158–159.

43. Huang, *Rediscovering the History of Hong Kong Movie Theatres*, 140–142.

44. Huang, *Rediscovering the History of Hong Kong Movie Theatres*, 144. According to the author, a Singaporean partner was involved in the running of South China Theater.

45. Widely known as one of the three most prominent clans in Macau, the Ho family has close ties with the Chinese government. Ho Yin's son, Ho Hau-wah, was the first chief executive of Macau after the former Portuguese colony's reunification with China.

46. Huang, *Rediscovering the History of Hong Kong Movie Theatres*, 140, 187–188. Born in Guangzhou, Xu came to Hong Kong in 1948 to take charge of Nanfang Film Company's propaganda unit and became its general manager in 1965. The chief architect of the left-wing theater circuit, Xu's credentials included the establishment of the Clear Water Bay film studio and major Mainland and Hong Kong–China co-productions during the 1980s. See Xu, "The Projection of Socialist vs. Capitalist Ideological Struggle," 270.

47. Xu, "The Projection of Socialist vs. Capitalist Ideological Struggle," 267–269.

48. Produced by the Shanghai Film Studio, this film has the same Chinese title, *Liang Shanbo yu Zhu Ying Tai*, as a later Shaw production in Mandarin, *Love Eterne* (1963).

49. Xu, "The Projection of Socialist vs. Capitalist Ideological Struggle," 268.
50. Anderson, *Imagined Communities: Reflections on the Origin and Spread of Nationalism*.
51. Union officially closed down in 1967, three years after its production was suspended due to the retirement and departures of its leading stars and a chronic shortage of younger talents.
52. Loh, *Underground Front: The Chinese Communist Party in Hong Kong*, 125.

Chapter 3

Remaking Cantonese film culture: Union and Sun Luen

Ranked among the "big four" Cantonese film studios in Hong Kong during the 1950s and the first half of the 1960s, the studio style of Sun Luen and Union can be defined by a creative adaptation of the aesthetic taste and preferences of the south-bound intellectuals from Mainland China, an émigré community who had maintained a strong emotional connection to their home country.[1] Unlike the elitist ethos of the south-bound community that saw the colony as a cultural desert, the filmmakers were guided by their vision of a healthy Cantonese film culture as an agent of more far-reaching social change, which explains their sense of urgency in using cinema as a collective wake-up call against a materialistic (capitalist) and decadent society that colonial Hong Kong presumably had become. Committed to elevating the Cantonese cinema to a serious form of art and agent of social transformation, leading figures of the left-wing film community took an active role in fostering a progressive filmmaking culture. Their work included the Third Cantonese Cinema Clean-up Movement and the founding of the South China Film Industry Workers' Union in 1949. Indeed, Cantonese cinema at the time was plagued by an overproduction of formulaic genre and opera films, many of which were shot on hasty schedules to maximize profitability. Union and Sun Luen became the labels of a number of Cantonese film classics that contributed to the distinctive "period look" of the black-and-white era. Without losing sight of their best-known classics, this chapter takes a closer look at the studios' genre films to shed light on the left-wing's effort to claim a space in the commercial mainstream. It is argued that alongside the more serious drama films, the lighter entertainment films also contributed to the "studio style" of the left-wing cinema. As we shall see, genre films were also an important constituent of the "popular left-wing" in Hong Kong cinema in the 1950s and 1960s.

A recurrent question pertaining to studio style is the way in which it interacts with the film culture of its time that gives rise to a set of stylistic signatures, hence a studio's public image or identity. The social dramas aside, Union and Sun Luen produced a wide range of popular genre films, from comedies and crime thrillers to traditional opera films, to capture a wider spectrum of audience. Seemingly sidetracking from the left-wing's original mission, these entertainment films also deliver moral lessons while displaying a readiness to embrace popular tastes and cultural trends. The diversification in studio productions bespeaks the existential condition of "being left-wing" in an unfavorable political environment. One can say that making entertainment films—otherwise condemned as being decadent if not a form of spiritual pollution (cf. Chapter 2)—reflected the reality and nature of the popular left-wing in Hong Kong, and more importantly the convictions of individual filmmakers that mark them off from the more doctrinal "revolutionary" left-wing across the borders. The cinematic left in Hong Kong, therefore, was sitting on a dynamic balance of ideological, commercial, and artistic imperatives. Existing writing on the left-wing cinema has emphasized the ethics of left-wing films, an argument that foregrounds the humanistic and egalitarian ideals of the filmmakers as a group of patriotic and progressive individuals. This chapter attempts to shift the spotlight away from an ethical perspective toward an understanding of the left-wing as both an advocate for the CCP's cultural mission in Hong Kong *and* a popular cinema that pitched itself as a rival to be reckoned with by the commercial mainstream. A selection of the left-wing's crime thriller and comic action films is discussed to make a case for the lighter side of the Hong Kong left-wing cinema by situating these entertainment films within the context of the commercial film market of the time. The weighted emphasis on the genre films of the left-wing is meant to supplement a less-noticed dimension of the left-wing to current discussion of left-wing films from the 1950s and 1960s. Diachronically, the more nuanced legacy of the left-wing is traced through their formal qualities that found their way into the work of two much later filmmakers, Wong Kar-wai and Johnnie To Kei-fung. The comparison with Wong and To is not intended to inspire a study of influence or direct lineage, but to draw attention to the dynamic, and mostly implicit, linkages in the transmission of artistic sensibilities as a constituent of local film history that might have been obscured by ideological and political critique.

Progressive protocol and film practices: localizing "south-bound" aesthetics

As mentioned in Chapter 1, the Third Cantonese Cinema Clean-up Campaign (1949) was a landmark event that any account of Hong Kong's left-wing film tradition cannot afford to miss. Shortly preceding the establishment of Union and Sun Luen, the campaign was a prelude to the organized effort of the cinematic left to claim their place in the local film industry in the coming two decades. Figure 3.1 is a newspaper report on the annual meeting of the South China Film Industry Workers' Union held in July 1952. In their address to members and the press, Lo Duen and Ng Cho-fan, two senior actors and leading figures at Union and Sun Luen, condemned the abhorring state of Cantonese cinema. Their pungent criticism of the malpractices and "chaos" in the industry was accompanied by a summary report on the problems faced by the local film industry, among which were the over-production of low-quality films, the impact of the US trade embargo, and growing concerns about unemployment and staff morale in the film industry. This lengthy statement reiterated the manifesto of the Cantonese Cinema Clean-up Campaign while drawing attention to the structural crisis faced by the local film industry at large. It is noteworthy that Sun Luen and Union were established in February and November 1952, respectively, followed by Kong Ngee (1955) and Wah Kiu (1956). With the addition of Kong Ngee as a commercial ally with a strong network of production and distribution in Singapore, the Cantonese arm of the cinematic left had secured a foothold in the Hong

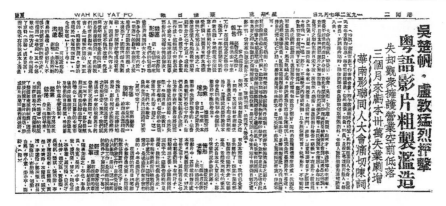

Figure 3.1 Newspaper report on the Annual Meeting of the South China Film Industry Workers' Union (*Wah Kiu Yat Po*, 9 July 1952, p. 8).

Kong film industry.[2] What these filmmakers set out to do marked them off as a critical mass of progressive cultural workers mediating between an inherited modern Chinese intellectual tradition[3] and the realities of filmmaking in a colonial city where their most dearly held values were found missing or indiscriminately ignored.

Embracing their ethical mission, the filmmakers' intellectual and aesthetic affiliation with the south-bound intellectual community was complicated by their roles as cultural agents and entrepreneurs, hence their aspiration to claiming a place in the image culture of colonial Hong Kong. In the spirit of "all for one, one for all" (a memorable movie quote that years later would become a shorthand for "Cantonese oldies" carrying serious social and moral messages), these filmmakers occupied a "middle ground" between their artistic and political vision. Bearing in mind the imperative of making films that would appeal to the broad masses, the challenge therefore was how the progressive vision could be translated into the popular medium of film to serve the greater good. The middling approach of Union and Sun Luen may explain the preference for melodrama and adaptations of well-known literary works that came to define their studio style. These iconic productions exemplified the visual politics of left-wing films of the time, while the lighter genres complemented the studios' effort in localizing the south-bound mentality in the creation of a popular left-wing cinema as a strong contender in the commercial mainstream.

The "Cantonese classics": the left-wing's studio style and influence

Among the Cantonese classics, the most talked-about films with original scripts included Chun Kim's *Neighbours All / Jia jia hu hu* (1954), *The Prodigal Son / Bai jia zai* (1956), Ng Wui's *Sworn Sisters / Jin lan zimei* (1954), and Lee Tit's *In the Face of Demolition / Wei lou chun xiao* (1953). Film adaptations of Chinese and Western literary works included *Family / Jia* (Ng Wui, 1953), *Spring / Chun* (Lee Sun-fung, 1954), and *Autumn / Qiu* (Chun Kim, 1954) (three novels constituting *The Torrents* trilogy by Ba Jin, one of the best-known writers of modern Chinese literature from the early twentieth century), *An Orphan's Tragedy / Gu xing xie lei* (Chu Kea, 1955; adapted from Charles Dickens' *Great Expectations*) and *Broken Spring Dreams / Chun can meng duan* (Lee Sun-fung, 1955;

adapted from Tolstoy's *Anna Karenina*). Equally worthy of mention among the left-wing productions during this period is the grooming of child actors who would become future superstars in Cantonese cinema, among whom were Bruce Lee, Josephine Siao Fong-fong (who won the Best Child Actress Award at the Second Southeast Asian Film Festival in 1955), Bobo Fung (aka Patrina Fung Po-po), and numerous popular stars who started their acting careers at an early age. Upholding the ethos of the Cantonese Cinema Clean-up Movement, the two studios' productions display an affinity in their representation of class and generational conflicts. The critique of traditional Chinese culture and Hong Kong's rootless capitalist society being a common trait, some of these films make room for charismatic female characters to outperform their male counterparts, a recurrent leitmotif in both the Cantonese and Mandarin productions (cf. Chapter 4). In *Neighbours All*, for example, the husband figure (played by Cheung Ying) fails in both judgment and action when the conflict between his mother and his wife escalates.

One of Lee Tit's best-known works, *In the Face of Demolition* (*Demolition*) is set primarily within the interiors of a subdivided apartment in a dilapidated vernacular building. The influx of immigrants from war-inflicted areas in Mainland China had created a chronic housing shortage since the end of World War II. The congested and hazardous living conditions of the working class was reaching an alarming state in the postwar decades. *Demolition* effectively exploits the psychosocial dynamics of an impoverished working-class community to deliver a convincing cross-section of everyday life. The film begins with a montage of squatter areas and alleyways of lower-class housing before the camera closes in on the main character, Luo Ming, entering a vernacular housing area (ironically named "Quick Fortune Lane") on a rickshaw. The next scene swiftly introduces the rest of the cast, all of whom are fellow inhabitants of the overcrowded apartment. This opening scene establishes the relationships and social dynamics within the working-class community and foreshadows the heavier-hearted crises to be unveiled. While working-class identity is venerated through a collective struggle against capitalist exploitation, the subdivided apartment community is threatened by evil and in-between characters from among its members, whose ambiguous values and split loyalty turn out to be both agents of destruction and self-redemption. In the film, the antagonists are a mercenary couple, Taipan Wong and

Mrs. Wong, who are bankrupt capitalists turned loan sharks. Wong's habit of bluffing in fragmented English expressions and half-boiled legalese is an all-too-transparent satire on those "native informants" who corroborated with the colonizer. An element of instability is found in the character of Luo Ming, an unemployed school teacher who aspires to becoming a fiction writer. As the newest member to join the community, Luo's educated background earns him respect and trust from fellow flat-mates. As the narrative unfolds, Luo ends up working for his landlord uncle as a rent collector when his overblown dream of wealth and fame falls apart. Luo's new position soon turns him into a class enemy in the eyes of his peers. The film climaxes at the moment of Luo's moral awakening, when he musters up enough courage in the last moment to defy his uncle's order to cover up the imminent collapse of the building.

Lee's film has been praised by critics as a masterpiece in Cantonese cinema. It is also the origin of one of the most memorable movie quotes from this period—"all for one, one for all"—that came to define Union's studio style, if not the left-wing cinema's founding principle as a whole. Critical reception of Lee's film tends to focus on the social significance of the film and Lee's directorial merit.[4] What is of interest here are some less noticed details that would find distant echoes in some of the best Hong Kong films half a century later. In *Demolition*, the gloomy lower-class world is occasionally animated by light-hearted episodes that help create a livelier picture of everyday life. To balance its otherwise heavy moral messages, the film builds in a romantic subplot between Luo and Bai Ying, a beautiful nightclub hostess. (In the film culture of the time, a nightclub hostess represents the victimization of lower-class women and occasionally is a co-culprit of capitalist corruption, the latter more prominently figured in crime and thriller films, discussed below.) The budding romance between Luo and Ying is structured around scenes of intimacy, where the couple enjoy quiet breaks from their stressful lives as they make coffee together. As a symbol of Western culture and a so-phisticated "taste" and lifestyle marker coterminous with the experience of modernity,[5] coffee symbolizes the mutual attraction and under-standing between Luo and Ying that is not readily shared by their less cultured neighbors. As a recurrent motif, coffee-making in *Demolition* underscores Luo's desire to break away from his working-class constraints and, to some extent, his unrealistic self-image as a literary-giant-to be. To Ying, coffee-making is a daily ritual for psychological comfort and a much-needed refuge from her shadowy profession. As a symbol of their emotional bonding, coffee-making creates an experiential space otherwise unaffordable in the young couple's compromised circumstances. In the film, coffee-making motivates the romantic subplot as the world outside begins to cave in.

Lee's penchant for teasing out the beauty and significance of the quotidian is also evident in another scene which finds interesting parallels in a much later movie, Wong Kar-wai's *In the Mood for Love* (2000), in which an unacknowledged romance between Chow Mo-wan (Tony Leung Chiu-wai) and So Lai-chun (Maggie Cheung) is also set against the background of a rooming apartment inside a vernacular building. In *Demolition*, Ying is filmed through street food stalls on her way home late at night. Her body movement is captured in a combination of medium, medium long and panning shots, accompanied by a musical sound track playing in the background. This scene also marks the developing romance between Ying and Luo, who, like Chow Mo-wan, is turning to fiction writing after losing his full-time job. Although Wong's film is neither left-wing-inspired nor social realist in style, interesting echoes are visible in his treatment of a signature scene where Maggie Cheung acts out a solo, MTV-like performance as she walks downstairs to buy a late-night snack. Carrying a container (which itself is an archaic object that serves as a period marker) and dressed immaculately in cheongsam (*qipao* in Mandarin), she walks elegantly through the narrow alleyways while the camera captures her body movement in slow motion with the film's theme song playing in the background. In *Mood*, this scene closes with Maggie Cheung walking up the stairs, paralleled by Chow Mo-wan coming downstairs on a split screen, suggesting a missed opportunity of a chance encounter. Employing a more elaborate visual palette with slow motion, close-up shots, camera movement, and sound track music, the setting and foregrounding of the solitary figure of a woman strolling through the back alleys of 1960s Hong Kong bear an uncanny resemblance to the much earlier film.[6]

Union and Sun Luen were the home studios of some of the best directors in Cantonese cinema of the time. Besides Lee Tit, Chun Kim and Ng Wui were the most prolific directors. In 1952, Ng Wui directed Sun Luen's first film, *The Prodigal Son*. The critical and popular success of this film set in motion the steam engine of left-wing film production that would transform the landscape of the Hong Kong film industry in the next fifteen years. As the title suggests, Ng's film tells the story of moral reform of a young man through a series of blunders and setbacks. As a social drama film, *The Prodigal Son* testifies to the cinematic left's protocol of making educational and socially uplifting films. Parent and child relationship became a favorite motif in subsequent left-wing films, such as Chun Kim's *Neighbours All* and *Parents' Hearts / Fumu xin*, Tso Kea's *Loving Father, Faithful Son / Fu ci zi xiao* (1954), and Ng Wui's *Father and Son / Fu yu zi* (1954). In addition to promoting filial love and the importance of the family as the foundation of society, the parent-child relationship is sometimes intended for social criticism. In *Father and Son*, a single father's misguided insistence on sending his son to an elite private school, which he believes will ensure upward social mobility, raises questions about the nature and purpose of education, and the detrimental effect of social stigmas on the underprivileged, especially when certain biases become internalized in the self-perception of the working class. The emphasis on the true meaning of education against the distorted values of a materialistic society might seem passé from today's perspective, but as a recurrent motif its influence would still be felt years after the left-wing studios went into decline toward the late 1960s, especially in the films of Lung Kong (Chapter 7).

While the left-wing cinema may have become a historical phenomenon bounded by its own spatial-temporal specificities, the legacy of the left-wing can still be traced in later filmmakers who may or may not share the ideological and moral vision of their predecessors. This line of inquiry informs my discussion of the genre films below. While serious social drama films helped raise the benchmark for the local film industry in the 1950s, the left-wing studios had also maintained a steady supply of genre films to broaden its popular appeal. Their self-conscious social mission aside, these films tend to be less confined by the ideological impetus of the social drama films in characterization and thematic design. Adapting their moral mission to the requirements of film genre, the left-wing filmmakers displayed an understanding of society and human nature that was more complex than the otherwise moralistic image of left-wing films that had shaped the public's perception of "Cantonese oldies." The following discussion looks at selected crime thriller and comic action films to examine more closely this less orthodox aspect of the left-wing cinema. As we shall see, there exists a less noticed lineage between these "oldies" and much later films that would redefine Hong Kong's genre cinema decades after the classical left-wing faded into oblivion.

The lighter side of the left-wing: genre films

While "film genre" can be a producer and critic's label,[7] the concept may not be directly applicable to the production context of the 1950s and 1960s, when "genre" was not yet a standardized market placement tool. A cursory glance at film advertisements during this period shows a very loose and intuitive approach to genre description. A film may be described as "martial arts-action-mystery-suspense-blockbuster," or "social realist family ethics tragedy classic." These overdrawn descriptions and phraseology were widely adopted by the film industry to promote all kinds of films. Very often, genre or sub-genre labels such as "thriller," "mystery," "detective" or "suspense" were usually accompanied by a cluster of thematic indexes that looks like a textual trailer or viewer's guide (Figures 3.2 and 3.3). Apart from serving the purpose of product promotion and managing audience expectations, a certain authorial intention is discernible behind these hybrid genre labels to educate the audience prior to viewing, as well as to emphasize

Figure 3.2 Genre description in film advertisement (*Wah Kiu Yat Po*, 13 September 1950, p. 10).

Figure 3.3 Genre description in film advertisement (*Wah Kiu Yat Po*, 27 October 1950, p. 7).

a film's social and moral meaning in the language of mass entertainment, a motto that gave the popular left-wing its distinctive quality since the time of its inception. It therefore comes as no surprise that the cinematic left had developed their own brand of genre films as a means of critical intervention without compromising their competitiveness in the film market. The following discussion takes a closer look at some recurrent themes in selected crime thriller and comic action films. Beginning with the critique of reckless capitalists in crime thrillers, the analysis moves on to explore the generic affinities between the left-wing's entertainment films with much later works in Hong Kong cinema. Without losing sight of generational difference, the purpose is to uncover the more nuanced legacy of the cinematic left, which so far is an under-researched area that deserves closer attention to obtain a more comprehensive understanding of the left-wing cinema, and no less of Hong Kong's film culture at large.

The reckless capitalist as usual suspect

The figure of the reckless capitalist is one of the most recognizable generic traits in left-wing films about moral failures under capitalism. Usually an unscrupulous businessman caught in a financial crisis, the reckless capitalist is a master of frauds and deception and, if need be, will go to any length to advance his self-interest and ambitions. In *The Cruel Husband / Du zhangfu* (1959), Jinming (Ng Cho-fan) turns into a cold-blooded murderer who attempts to kill his wife, Bijun (Tsi Lo-lin, aka Violet Wong), in order to marry a young woman from a rich family to save his failing business (Figure 3.4). This straightforward and commonplace

Figure 3.4 *The Evil Husband* (film advertisement, *Wah Kiu Yat Po*, 18 November 1959, p. 12).

anti-capitalist character symbolism, however, is more than compensated by its clever plot twists, supporting cast design, and stylish cinematography that deliver an impressive popular entertainment vehicle. The film wittily withholds crucial facts about the murder and subtly plants an unofficial detective subplot in the figure of a journalist who is a mutual friend of Jinming and Bijun. The journalist's covert investigation into the murder case develops alongside a series of suspense-driven episodes where Jinming and his mother are led to believe that their house is haunted by Bijun's spirit. Making effective use of lighting and optical illusion through skillful editing, the film stands out as an unsung masterpiece among its peers. The finale, in this regard, deserves special mention for its well-crafted mis-en-scène and cinematography, which captures the scene of action in a series of painterly shots, displaying a visual coherence apropos to the rhythm of the drama.

Ng's capitalist crime-monger persona is representative of the left-wing's social and implicitly political critique. The downfall of this figure is usually juxtaposed with the moral triumph of his working class or intellectual counterparts. In *A Home of a Million Gold / Qian wan renjia* (1953), *The Cruel Husband*, and *The Bloody Paper Man / Xue zhi ren* (1964), Ng's criminal character is the tragic anti-hero who brings the fatal curse upon himself. As Union's iconic leader and one of the most prominent film stars in Cantonese cinema of his time, Ng's performance in these films makes him the capitalist villain par excellence in left-wing films, a track record otherwise obscured by his best-known screen persona as a voice of conscience and working-class hero (*In the Face of Demolition, Typhoon Signal No. 10 / Shi hao feng bo* [1959], *The Orphan / Renhai guhong* [1960]). In playing diametrically opposed roles on screen, Ng's public standing as a spokesperson of the progressive film community and voice of social conscience worked to reinforce the proverbial undertone in his rendition of the "bad guy" character, whose negative charm is filtered through the light of its offscreen alter ego.

All about money

A symbol of the capitalist society, money is a favorite motif in the left-wing's crime thrillers and social comedy films. As a convenient plot device, money motivates the main action in *Money / Qian* (Ng Wui, 1959): a bag filled with banknotes takes a free ride on a private vehicle

Figure 3.5 *Money* (film advertisement, *Wah Kiu Yat Po*, 22 February 1959, p. 10).

after a failed bank robbery. A treasure hunt immediately follows as the bag falls into the hands of different parties by coincidence. Meanwhile, they are followed by one of the bank robbers who also wants to claim the booty. The adventure continues over a long trail of chance encounters until the passing-the-bomb game ends. Instead of drawing a line between the good and the bad, the film playfully brings in a random collection of characters, all of whom are common folks who cannot resist the temptation of unearned fortune. The bank robber ironically plays the role of the observer of the comic drama as he follows the trail of the treasure hunters (Figure 3.5). The same plot structure appears in *Blood and Gold / Xie ran huangjin* (Chu Kea, 1957), which tells the story of deception and betrayals as former allies conspire against one another in a deadly fight over a carton of gold bars robbed from some Japanese soldiers on the eve of the Japanese defeat in Mainland China. The film makes an effort to foreground Hong Kong as the main scene of action through one of the main characters, Scar-faced Li (Ng Cho-fan), who identifies himself as a Hong Kong native when his vessel was crossing the border. Casting Li, the archvillain character, as a Hong Kong native who worked for the Japanese invaders during the war reveals a geopolitics that seeks to localize the scene of action by explicitly naming Li's native township without losing sight of the problematic relationship between the colonial city and the Chinese motherland.

As a comic action-cum-social satire film, *Money* has a crisp, well-paced plot structured by a series of interrelated episodes, each containing a mini-cast of actors linked directly or indirectly from one scene to another. The treasure hunt continues through a chain of coincidences and culminates in a final encounter of all parties in a nightclub. While the ending resorts to the moral-of-the-tale style admonition, the best part of the film offers a cynical portrayal of society that traverses class and gender. As such, the politics of the film is steered away from the standard narrative of social(ist) realism, redirecting the viewer's attention to the absurdity of life and human intention. *Blood and Gold*, on the other hand, is a crime thriller (broadly and contextually defined) in which all the main characters are unscrupulous traitors ready to resort to the most hideous means in pursuit of their self-interest. Among them, a former school teacher, Dong, was the only one who survives the deadly intrigues between his peers, only because he is able to weigh between the odds and let go in the last moment. Similar to *Money*, *Blood and Gold* is cynical toward human nature and society, where evil seems to be ubiquitous. The juxtaposition between Japanese invaders and Chinese captives in the opening scene is complicated by the unscrupulous acts of betrayals among the ex-war victims: having outsmarted their Japanese enemies, they soon turn into fellows in crime and murderers.

To present-day audiences, these "oldies" may look dusty and uncouth compared to the more sophisticated gangster and crime films that have become a trademark of Hong Kong cinema today. Upon closer examination, it is not difficult to notice subtle resonances between these earlier films and much later ones at the level of plot and thematic design across a temporal spread of four decades. The episodic plot structure and use of coincidences as a linking device in *Money*, for instance, are skillfully executed in Johnnie To's *Life without Principle / Duo ming jin* (2011). To's film is structured by a series of coincidences involving a petty criminal, a banker, a cop, and his wife. Shot between 2009 and 2011, the film takes snapshots of individuals caught in the aftermath of the global financial crisis triggered by the 2008 financial tsunami in the US. Similar to *Money*, a treasure hunt begins when a bag carrying five million dollars (approx. USD 600,000) keeps changing hands. It is interesting to note that the Chinese title of the film—*duo ming jin*, meaning "gold that kills"—echoes its two predecessors discussed above, while the English title can be read as a thematic elaboration. To's modern-day rendition of "gold that kills" also features a good criminal character who happens to be the least consumed by greed due to his sense of loyalty to fellow gangsters. Compared to *Money*, To's film does not rely on caricatures and character types to reinforce its moral message; rather, the conflicting demands of "principle" and self-interest are played out in the individual dramas as they each face the temptation of an illicit fortune. The two films diverge in the finale: in *Money*, the treasure hunt has everybody's dream shattered when the scattered banknotes start drizzling from the rooftop. As the camera pulls away from the scene, we see startled passers-by gathering on the street, accompanied by the sound of police sirens in the background. At the peak of the fiasco, two witnesses, a musician and his singer wife, reflect on the moral lesson learned as they look out of the window of their apartment. In *Life without Principle*, the winner of the game is the banker, a young professional woman who leisurely walks away with the cash-filled bag in hand. Filmed in the aftermath of the 2008 global financial crisis, To's film offers a more concrete portrayal of a society caught up by an unprecedented economic downturn when many found their hard-earned assets evaporated overnight. It is quite obvious that while human folly is never out of sight despite the film's quick-paced action, the invisible culprit remains the global financial institution that seems to have gone out of control by any form of national or international governance. The film's Chinese title, "*duo ming jin*," is itself an indirect allusion to the financial world, which in Chinese is rendered "*cai jin*" (lit. money and gold), or "*jin yong*" (lit. gold exchange or circulation). In essence, both films are critical of the power of money to corrupt: *Money* begins with a bank robbery and the plot follows the itinerary of the spoils. It is therefore the *circulation* of the ill-gotten cash that unleashes the latent instinct of those who comes into contact with it like a contagious virus. The film's cynical view of human nature notwithstanding, the target of its critique remains the institution of money itself; yet it leaves room for individuals (the musician and his wife, the only intellectual figures in the film) to exercise their moral judgment to remain distanced and resist the temptation. *Life without Principle*, on the other hand, does not presume the existence of such a psychological space where one can be untouched by the power of "gold" in the age of global speculation. Instead, there are only victims and survivors in the uneven distribution of good and bad fortunes, a game of numbers in which all are co-opted players.

Compared to the light-hearted commentary on society and the human condition in capitalist society in *Money*, *Blood and Gold* stands out among left-wing productions in its unsparing cynicism toward the possibility of redemption. The film also utilizes a treasure hunt plot and a relay of intrigues and murders as buddies in crime try to uncover each other's darker motives. As the story unfolds, trust and loyalty are completely absent since the very beginning of the secret alliance. A growing sense of absurdity runs through the film's action, as each step taken to advance one's self-interest works only to quicken the demise of the schemer. The crisscrossing of malicious intentions inevitably disintegrates the group from within. In a more pessimistic and downbeat note from what we see in *Money*, the treasure hunt keeps spiraling down to an abysmal finale. Scar-faced Li met his fated ending when his murder plot backfires. With the exception of Dong, who turns himself in to the police, the same fate befalls the rest of the gang, including Li's wife, a *femme fatale* character who uses her charm to prey on her husband and his peers. More than coincidentally, *Blood and Gold* finds distant echoes in another Johnnie To film, *Exiled / Fang zu* (2006), in which a gangster group tries to outwit their boss to save the lives of a deserted member and his family. The great escape saga is complicated by the news of a truck gone missing, allegedly carrying a full load of gold that some Portuguese officials in Macau want to move out of the colony on the eve of the change of sovereignty in 1998. Unlike *Blood and Gold*, To's film makes a case for grassroots solidarity in defiance of a higher authority. Instead of celebrating the lone hero serving the course of justice, *Exiled* reinterprets heroism through male-bonding and group loyalty.[8]

Despite their different attitudes toward loyalty and solidarity, the two films can be read as a case of similarity in contrast. The end of the Japanese occupation in *Blood and Gold* and the end of colonial rule in Macau in *Exiled* are respectively the historical setting of a crime thriller in which different parties get entangled in a deadly fight over an illicit fortune seized from a colonizer/foreign invader in retreat. While *Blood and Gold* remains steadfast in its condemnation of the criminals, a notional possibility of moral reform is offered in the character of Dong, although his moral awakening comes not from within but at the exhortation of his wife. Loyalty and brotherhood are cast in a more positive light in *Exiled*, even though any attempt to subvert a ruthless and almighty boss by a dissenting few is next to impossible right from the start. In following the hit-and-run trajectory of the rebels over a wasteland-like Macau on the eve of the political handover, the film conjures up an alluring atmosphere of fin de siècle abandonment as the action-drama edges toward its fatalistic ending. The interest of juxtaposing these two films lies not so much in their difference in value judgment and assumptions about good and evil as in the way in which this difference is mitigated by a shared deconstructive impulse that drives the action-drama toward its logical conclusion. In both films, all parties at cross-purposes are conjoined in meeting their accursed fate. In *Exiled*, the only survivor is the widow of a deserted gangster whom the rebels vow to protect at all cost. As in *Life without Principle*, serendipity defeats human intent in the denouement: it is the widow, a "final girl" character, who picks up the booty when she walks away from the bloodbath. These two films by one of Hong Kong cinema's best-known action auteurs can be seen as contemporary reinterpretations of a time-honored critique of "money" in the left-wing cinematic tradition.

Entertainment through art: mainstreaming the popular left-wing

The endeavors of Union and Sun Luen to "clean up" Hong Kong's Cantonese cinema are met with enthusiasm by the local audience, and the two studios soon forged ties through partnerships and collaborations with the right-wing film companies, Shaw and MP&GI, to establish distribution channels in Southeast Asia. This chapter has taken a closer look at the thematic and formal qualities of the two studios' productions to shed light on the range and diversity of the "Cantonese classics" that distinguish the left-wing's studio style of this period. While the more serious social drama films have received frequent mention in critical writing on the left-wing cinema (which in turn has shaped public perception of left-wing films), the analysis above has paid attention to the left-wing's genre films as the lighter side of its critical intervention into the mainstream cinema. This aspect of the left-wing also gives credence to their founding principle of "art through entertainment," which was further materialized in the "big four" studios' effort to mainstream their productions in the making of a "popular left-wing" (cf. Chapters 1 and 2). In the films of Wong Kar-wai and Johnnie To, one discerns subtle resonances that point toward the nuanced legacy of the left-wing in Hong Kong's cinematic imagination decades later, a subject to be examined further in Chapters 6 and 7.

Notes

1. The work of south-bound writers very often expresses a sense of displacement and homesickness, which usually was accented by a self-perceived marginality living in a British colony cut off from the Chinese cultural tradition. Cf. Introduction.

2. Apart from Wah Kiu, numerous smaller and shorter-lived studios were founded by Union stars for strategic purposes. Cf. Chapters 2 and 7.

3. The ethos of the cinematic left has been compared to their predecessors in early twentieth century China associated with the May Fourth New Culture Movement (1919–1927), a cultural-reformist movement advocating anti-traditionalism and the embrace of Western culture, science, and technology to bring China up to par with the imperial powers of the West. Patriotism, anti-feudalism, and modernization were the basic tenets of the May Fourth intellectual tradition. See Zarrow, *China in War and Revolution*; Schwarcz, *The Chinese Enlightenment*; and Lin, *The Crisis of Chinese Consciousness: Radical Antitraditionalism in the May Fourth Era*.

4. See Ho and Chan, *The Cinema of Lee Tit*.

5. The café used to represent a new urban culture and a modern lifestyle in early twentieth-century China. See Lee, *Shanghai Modern: The Flowering of a New Urban Culture in China*.

6. On the symbolism of *qipao* and Wong's use inter-referencing of early Mandarin films and popular songs, see Teo, *Wong Kar-wai: Auteur of Time*, 118–119.

7. This refers to the Fordian Hollywood studios' use of genres as production models to standardize and differentiate products, and film reviews "as a sort of explicit statement of mediation among the distributors, exhibitors, and spectators." See Staiger, "Hybrid or Inbred? The Purity Hypothesis and Hollywood Genre History," 190–191.

8. This kind of "collective heroism" has appeared in many Johnnie To films since the 1990s. This aspect of To's new-style gangster films is discussed in Lee, *Hong Kong Cinema since 1997: The Post-Nostalgic Imagination*, 87–116.

Chapter 4

Class, gender, and modern womanhood: Feng Huang and Great Wall

The complex political landscape of Hong Kong during the Cold War era gave rise to distinctive forms of cultural politics. Against the versatile conditions of film production in the 1950s and 1960s, film studios, left or right, had to carefully steer their courses in the domestic and overseas markets where anti-Communist policies were stringently enforced (for instance in Taiwan and Singapore), while the left-wing studios still enjoyed limited circulation in parts of Mainland China. Feng Huang and Great Wall were major contenders from the left-wing cultural front for the Mandarin-language film market during the 1950s and 1960s. Competing against MP&GI and the Shaw Brothers,[1] the two industry giants with close ties to the US and Taiwan and extensive industry networks in Southeast Asia, the left-wing studios were operating at a natural disadvantage in Hong Kong. In the heat of the left-wing initiated Cantonese Film Clean-up Campaign,[2] the Mandarin studios were facing an existential challenge of a different sort: to contest against their formidable right-wing rivals who had distribution and exhibition chains in Hong Kong and Southeast Asia and an exclusive access to the Taiwan market.

This chapter revisits the left–right divide in Mandarin films through the lens of gender and class politics. It is concerned with the way in which a certain notion of modern womanhood is embedded in the cinematic imagination of modernity of both the progressive and "freedom" camps. No doubt, gender and class have enriched the critical discourse on modernity and its more ambivalent manifestations in the non-Western world. When it comes to the Cold War and its cultural implications in relation to the left–right ideological divide in Hong Kong cinema, the triangulated relation between gender, class, and the imagination of modernity under the whirlwind of intensifying interstate conflicts remains an under-researched area, despite the fact that the Mandarin cinema of this period had produced some of the most memorable and captivating female actresses and screen personae in the history of Chinese cinema. While critical literature in recent years has shown a keen interest in Chinese female film stars, Hong Kong actresses from the left-wing studios have received scanty mention in this growing body of literature on Chinese stardom. Indeed, research on film stars in Hong Kong cinema in general has tended to focus on the transnational appeal of names familiar to the contemporary audience, such as Jet Li, Maggie Cheung, Brigitte Lin (originally from Taiwan), Leslie Cheung, Jackie Chan, and Bruce Lee.[3] When it comes to the film culture of the 1950s and 1960s, high production value, star power, and a mature regional distribution network distinguished as much the studio style of Shaw and MP&GI as the "period look" of the Mandarin-language cinema itself. The predominance of the two industry giants is well reflected in the critical spotlight they attracted in film criticism.[4] Both Shaw and MP&GI were known for their blockbuster-style commercial genre films and the glamourous images of stars, especially iconic female stars, sporting a stylish and modern outlook. Modeling after the studio system of Hollywood, Shaw and MP&GI were two phenomenal transnational Chinese-language film enterprises during the 1950s and the 1960s.[5] Existing literature on Feng Huang and Great Wall, on the other hand, has shown a greater interest in the broader sweeps of ethical-ideological and national-political analysis, with fewer attempts to situate the studios' productions against the dominant cinematic practices that they self-consciously, and sometimes quite explicitly, critique through the film medium.[6] The following discussion therefore sheds light on the strategic positioning of the left-wing Mandarin studios to reinvent their own language of popular entertainment as a means to achieve their loftier goals of social and cultural transformation.

Sharing the left-wing Cantonese cinema's progressive ethos, Feng Huang and Great Wall films self-consciously, and discreetly, craft their counter-narratives of capitalist modernity through charismatic female characters in a variety of roles, from school teachers, nightclub hostesses, and single/unmarried mothers to "prodigal daughters" whose moral detours serve as cautionary tales to the young and uninitiated. The analysis below first looks at some exemplary models of modern womanhood in right-wing films, especially the screen persona of Grace Chang, the lead star in MP&GI's most successful musicals that defined Chang's transnational stardom. Featuring a refined contemporary lifestyle, MP&GI's lavishly embellished cinematic fantasies popularized an imagination of modern womanhood that finds its counter-image in left-wing films. As ideologically loaded image-texts, these female screen personae are constructs and embodiments of the cinematic discourse of modernity in which the politics of class and gender is personified in their charismatic female subjects.

Nightclub hostesses, prodigal daughters, and the fallen woman

Since the silent film period in Chinese cinema, the femme fatale and the fallen woman are among the most frequently invoked screen images to allude to the seductive allure and contradictions of modernity.[7] In the history of Chinese cinema, it was not uncommon to see female stars and their onscreen personae having a symbiotic relationship in the production of "star texts"[8] that sustained both the popular and critical reception of film stars and their posthumous stardom. Among female film stars from the 1950s and 1960s, Grace Chang, Linda Lin (Lin Dai), Ling Po, and Li Lihua are among the most written-about figures from the Mandarin cinema. With the exception of Ling Po, who is best remembered for her cross-dressing roles in traditional *huang mei diao* films,[9] Chang, Lin, and Li were known for their charismatic screen presence. Among the three, Li was the most senior. Her acting career began at an early age in Shanghai. After she came to Hong Kong, she was signed up by Great Wall, where she had earned critical acclaim for her iconic performances in dramatic roles that shaped her screen image as an unconventional woman of exceptional character. Li's career took a sharp turn when she deserted to the "freedom" camp in 1953. In the same year, Linda Lin also left Great Wall to join Yung Hwa,[10] and later became a star actress of Shaw. As Su (2014) observes, the departure of Li and Lin, among others, from Great Wall reflected an overriding mechanism of political scrutiny that accounted for the loss of acting and creative talents.[11]

Grace Chang was a legend on her own as the queen of Mandarin musicals at MP&GI, the studio best remembered for its urban romance films and Chinese musicals. Chang's musical talent well suited her in song and dance films that celebrate an active, modern, and at times decadent lifestyle. In *Wild, Wild Rose / Ye meigui zhi lian* (Wong Tin-lam, 1960), she plays a femme fatale–like nightclub songstress who falls in love with

Figure 4.1 *Wild Wild Rose* (film advertisement, *Wah Kiu Yat Po*, 4 June 1960, p. 24).

an impoverished musician (Figure 4.1). Her effort to salvage her lover's reputation and career takes the form of a cruel and sudden break-up, for which she is begrudged and strangled by the man she loves. Utilizing a conventional plot of star-crossed lovers trying in vain to defy their accursed fate, the film builds its artistic core around Chang's captivating performance, including a Chinese version of the *Habanera* from Bizet's classic opera *Carmen*, and a short segment from Puccini's *Madame Butterfly*. The same can be said of most, if not all, of Grace Chang films. *Mambo Girl / Manbo nülang* (Evan Yang, 1957), another celebrated Grace Chang vehicle, is a lackluster story about a young woman's reconciliation with her adopted parents after a short and unsuccessful attempt to find her biological mother, a secret she uncovered by accident on her twentieth birthday. Technically, not much happens between the initial song-and-dance sequence and the final birthday party sequence except more Grace Chang solos in flashbacks. The representation of parent-child relationship in *Mambo Girl*, however, deviates from the conventional emphasis on kinship: the protagonist's brief conversation with her biological mother (an ex-nightclub hostess) does not bring about a reunion of mother and daughter but a denial of kinship by the mother. Parent-child bonding and solidarity with the underclass, the left-wing's stock-in-trade, are evaded by the voluntary erasure of the mother's voice. *Mambo Girl* thus justifies the protagonist's return to an affluent middle-class life with her adopted parents. Clashes of values between social classes, which would have led to a very different conclusion, are ironed out to give way to a bourgeois dream of upward mobility and self-fulfillment. The young woman's short-lived rebellion, therefore, is

Figure 4.2 *Air Hostess* (film advertisement, *Wah Kiu Yat Po*, 5 June 1959, p. 27).

recontained and domesticated by the ideal middle-class family, presented in the ending as an image of eternal bliss.

Before we turn to the counter-images of the femme fatale and fallen woman in the left-wing cinema, a brief detour into issues of class in the cinematic imagination of modernity will illuminate the intricate "class consciousness" and its manifestations in both left- and right-wing films. *Air Hostess / Kong zhong xiaojie* (Evan Yang, 1959), an award-winning film at the Asian Film Festival, is a big-budget "event film" befitting the capitalist-modernist thrust of MP&GI productions (Figure 4.2). It features Chang as a beautiful air hostess trying to come to terms with the less pleasant realities of her profession, a demanding, sometimes demeaning, yet ultimately rewarding job. A romantic subplot involving a young pilot is developed along the flight paths that literally take the lovers to popular tourist destinations in Taiwan, Singapore, and Thailand, which also underscore Cathay's regional presence. In one scene, we see the couple walking past a building with the sign "Cathay" prominently displayed. As an entertainment film, *Air Hostess* delivers more than what it promises, not only in the sense of satisfying the curiosity and aspirations of its intended audience about modern air travel, but also in the sense of promoting a culture of leisure to a younger middle-class generation. Symbolically, the air hostesses and pilots represent this new social class, with whom the film's audience are encouraged to identify: "air hostess is a new profession, a most modern profession . . . They help shorten the distance between people and facilitate movement between nations."[12] Poshek Fu comments that *Air Hostess* is a projection of the

Mandarin-speaking "migrant community's changing lifestyle, attitudes, and gender relationship [in] an emerging culture of capitalist modernity in Asia."[13] Geopolitics certainly plays a role in this fairy tale of boundless freedom and romance: the mobile generation's trajectories frequently foreground Taipei as a metropolitan center of an emerging globe-trotting culture and a popular tourist destination, a politically loaded message that somehow does not sit well with what could have been a more discreet form of ideological persuasion.

Commenting on the personae of Grace Chang and Li Lihua, Stacilee Ford observes how Hong Kong female stars in the 1950s and 1960s "blended seemingly disparate cultural values and national ideologies, cherry-picking tradition and offering audiences a chance to 'try on' new ways of communicating, consuming, and being in the rapidly changing postwar world."[14] According to Ford, due to its US connections, MP&GI's films tend to be "escapist and elitist" in their engagement with issues on social class, which differ fundamentally from the "working class perspectives" in Cantonese cinema.[15] The assumption that Cantonese films were more working class-oriented presumes a linguistic division of labor, which upon closer examination may exhibit a more nuanced picture. The remainder of this section looks at how the politics of class and gender in left-wing Mandarin films self-consciously responded to the "escapist and elitist" discourse of the right-wing studios. If Grace Chang is the right-wing's cinematic incarnate of modern womanhood with all the trappings of an affluent, capitalistic world, her counterparts in left-wing films offer interesting parallels-in-contrast that reveal the inherent contradictions and uneasiness of this gendered modern subject. As we shall see, the bourgeois dream of happiness and self-fulfillment as projected through the image of modern womanhood receives a different inflection in the left-wing cinema, which self-consciously engages generic conventions to mount their ideological critique.

Of immediate interest here is the way in which female empowerment is materialized in certain character types, such as the nightclub hostess/ songstress and the fallen woman, who are neither the right-wing's ideal modern woman nor the "virtuous woman" bound by the patriarchal code of ethics in the Chinese cultural tradition. Indeed, Feng Huang and Great Wall's productions do not lack what can be called "woman-centered" films in which the dramatic presence of female protagonists outweighs their male counterparts. In these films, modern womanhood is defined less by their readiness to embrace the new opportunities and promises of the modern capitalist society than by their daringness to challenge the prescribed (screen) roles of women in such a society. A selection of left-wing films is examined below to see how a different imagination of modernity is articulated through "strong woman" characters. Spanning a broad range of social and professional positions, these strong women embody alternative expressions of modern womanhood that could well be more advanced and "experimental" than the normative culture of their time.

In *Sunrise / Ri chu* (Hu Siaofung and Su Chengshou, 1956), *Green Swan Nightclub / Lü tian'e yezhonghui* (Li Pingqian, 1958), and *Rendezvous / Jiaren you yue* (Li Pingqian, 1960), the celebratory discourse of capitalist modernity is turned inside out to reveal a more ambivalent, if not ominous, side that undercuts the glossy picture exemplified in *Mambo Girl* and *Air Hostess*. *Sunrise*, *Green Swan Nightclub*, and *Rendezvous* present a palette of nightclub songstress characters that can be seen as parallels-in-contrast to the modern woman prototype discussed above. All three films feature the most representative female star of Feng Huang and Great Wall, Hsia Moon, whose charismatic screen presence earned her the title of "Great Wall's Crown Princess,"[16] for which she is still fondly remembered by filmmakers and audience today. Arguably, Hsia Moon was the left-wing's answer to Grace Chang, MP&GI's queen of Chinese musical, although Hsia's screen persona is not as closely associated with a particular genre or character type. The stories of *Sunrise*, *Green Swan Nightclub*, and *Rendezvous* revolve around a femme fatale–like character (Hsia) whose personal charm and intelligence are of equal importance to survival in a clandestine world dominated by predatory men. *Green Swan Nightclub* utilizes elements of the crime thriller to tell a tale of redemption and retribution. A young woman (Zhenyi) gets involved in a series of intrigues and sabotages after being persuaded by her father's business acquaintance, Mr. Ou, to avenge her father's death by infiltrating a syndicate. Posing herself as a high-flying socialite from Australia, Zhenyi begins her detective work as a songstress at the Green Swan Nightclub, only to realize that Mr. Ou is the mastermind behind the murder of her father, who himself was Ou's partner. Suspense is built around Zhenyi's search for a document allegedly bearing crucial evidence of the syndicate's illegal dealings. Zhenyi's artistic talent and charismatic charm are foregrounded in a solo performance at the nightclub, culminating in an aerial shot of a ballroom dance sequence in which Zhenyi, elegantly dressed, is at the center of a concentric circle of dancers. The layered plotline makes room for the protagonist to play out her double-agent role through a series of intrigues and decoys. The denouement is motivated by a romantic subplot between Zhenyi and Xu (a former syndicate member looking for a clean start), when the young lovers join hands to sabotage their god fathers.

Compared to *Wild, Wild Rose, Green Swan Nightclub* puts much greater emphasis on female agency in the figure of Zhenyi. While Grace Chang's femme fatale persona gradually settles into a more conventional tragic heroine character and a victim of misogynistic violence, Zhenyi in *Green Swan Nightclub* decisively tracks down on the real enemy after Xu discloses the truth about her father's murder. Adopting the conventions of a crime thriller to reinvent the femme fatale as an agent of change and subversion, *Green Swan Nightclub* is a progressive version of the songstress character type and an experiment in female empowerment in genre cinema. The film's portrayal of the nightclub as an inferno-like extension of a society dictated by greed and violence remains in line with the left-wing's ethos, an ideological subtext that is more suggestive than intrusive at the storytelling level. The characterization of Fei in *Rendezvous* strikes a similar chord with Zhenyi in *Green Swan Nightclub*. The film begins with a close-up on a caged bird, accompanied by a woman (Fei) singing a song about the unhappiness of being a pet bird. Soon we learn that Fei is groomed by her uncle (Fang) to bewitch rich suitors. On one such mission, Fei meets Ding, a former crook who has made good. Like Zhenyi and Xu in *Green Swan Nightclub*, Fei and Ding become fellow allies in their revolt against Fang, who happens to be blackmailing Ding at the same time. As an agent of change and liberation, the *femme fatale* figure in both films does not bring about the demise of her male counterpart. Instead, her subversive femininity is a self-transforming and emancipating energy that short-circuits the authority of an evil and controlling father figure (Figure 4.3).

A less benevolent fate befalls the fallen woman in *Sunrise*. A seasoned socialite active in the circle of the wealthiest men in town, Bai Lu finds herself at a crossroads when she tries to save "Tiny" (*xiaodongxi* in Mandarin pinyin), an orphaned country girl—in whom she sees her long-gone younger self—from the hands of a gangster boss. Surrounded by the obscenely rich and their lavish presents, Bai's alienation is dramatized through a juxtaposition of this decadent world of sex and money with the tranquil simplicity of her home village, where Bai reunions with her teenage lover, Dasheng, after years of separation. The story revolves around Bai's

Figure 4.3 *Rendezvous* (film advertisement, *Wah Kiu Yat Po*, 24 November, 1960, p. 11).

effort to protect Tiny, her young protégé, at great personal risk. The film ends with Bai's suicide as the heroine's final resolution. This tragic closure may sound counterintuitive to the film's title word, "sunrise." One wonders whether Bai's suicide is necessitated by the plot to drive in a message about hope: the suicide scene fades into the ending shot where Dasheng and Tiny, hand in hand, embark on a new journey at daybreak. If, in *Wild, Wild Rose*, the heroine's murder brings about the moral downfall of her lover, in *Sunrise* Bai Lu's death is a moral protest that precedes the symbolic "sunrise." More than a footnote to mitigate the demoralizing effect of Bai's suicide, this brief moment of hope alters the course of events to underscore the ethical-ideological significance of her tragic end (Figure 4.4).

Gender and class politics take the center stage in *Joyce and Deli / Zimei qu* (Zhu Shilin, 1954) and *Girl on the Front Page / Xinwen renwu* (Li Pingqian, 1960), in which the fallen woman finds expression in "prodigal daughter" characters. In both films, young women from humble origins fall victim to the flattery and deceit of unscrupulous acquaintances posing themselves as decent members of the social elite. Deli (Hsia Moon), the younger sister of Joyce (Wei Wei), quits high school to work in a trading company, only to find that the boss has been using her as a pawn to woo his rich and powerful clients. Ignoring her family's

Figure 4.4 *Sunrise* (film advertisement, *Wah Kiu Yat Po*, 12 September 1956, p. 12).

opposition, Deli turns a blind eye to the dubious conduct of her acquaintances in the business circle, and soon transforms herself into a social
butterfly supported by wealthy patrons. Deli's world of endless parties
and banquets is juxtaposed with the working-class lifeworld where Joyce,
a school teacher, sets up a free school for the poor with her like-minded

colleagues. As in most left-wing films, criticism of capitalist exploitation and moral degradation is channeled through character symbolism. The clash between the capitalist and socialist worldviews is dramatized through the frequent transition between Deli and Joyce in their diametrically opposed worlds. A failed plastic surgery marks a dramatic turning point in Deli's fortunes. Deserted by her patrons and friends, Deli ends up in a hospital in great agony and distress. The final message of hope is delivered by a female doctor, who confidently reassures her family that Deli will be cured, body and mind. The interest of this film lies not so much in the ethical-ideological message but in its gendered character symbolism and the incremental rhythm of the narrative along which Deli's moral downfall is plotted. Deli comes across not so much as an unthinking, passive victim but a talented teenager gone astray. A prodigal daughter character, she pays a dear price for the lesson learned. Deli's nuanced and complex characterization is accompanied by a line-up of "strong woman" characters, from her elder sister Joyce to the female doctor in the final scene. The "good doctor" is subtly juxtaposed with the male plastic surgeon, a charlatan who runs away at the first sight of Deli's deformed face. The film's gendered character symbolism is also evident in the absence of father figures: Joyce and Deli's father is diseased, and hard-working mothers are predominant in the poor neighborhood that the charity school serves. The "bad capitalist" role, not surprisingly, is reserved for men as symbols of power and corruption. These malicious male figures are in sharp contrast to Joyce's male colleagues as models of the "good proletariat." This streamlined gender-class accounting suggests that women are considered to be playing a more central and active role in the working-class world, as professionals, single/working mothers, and leaders of social change. This observation can be applied to the femme fatales and fallen women in the films analyzed above, whose self-empowerment is seen through their ability to sabotage a clandestine, male-dominated regime and act on their moral choice.

One can say that the intertwinement of gender and class is a hallmark of the left-wing's counter-discourse of modernity. In *Girl on the Front Page*, a missing person notice motivates the detective plot of the film. A female journalist is tasked to investigate the case of a missing person named Xiao Qin, a former student nurse who has disappeared under unknown circumstances. It is soon revealed that Xiao Qin has resigned from the hospital shortly before her disappearance. The plot is made up of two parts: the journalist's investigation in the first part is followed by a flashback sequence in which Xiao Qin, hospitalized after an attempted suicide, recalls how she has been misguided by Mr. Pei, a senior hospital administrator and career opportunist, in fabricating her academic qualification in the hope of getting a promotion. As in *Joyce and Deli*, the film juxtaposes two systems of values through character symbolism. Attracted by the sophisticated, westernized outlook of Pei and the promise of a professional career, Xiao Qin shuns her working-class boyfriend, Xia Ling, and falls prey to Pei's sexual advances. Like Deli, Xiao Qin is a "prodigal daughter" whose moral awakening comes through a symbolic ritual of death and rebirth. Both *Joyce and Deli* and *Girl on the Front Page* are cautionary tales for young women who are vulnerable to the lies and intrigues of "bad capitalists," the perpetrators of evil in the modern society. The two women's suffering in body and mind, the films suggests, is a necessary step toward self-redemption. In *Girl on the Front Page*, class conflict is also articulated through diametrically opposed characters. In one scene, the clash of values is pitched at a metatextual level in an argument between working-class Ling and bourgeois Pei over good and bad movies. Expectedly, Ling's distaste for sentimental and self-indulgent films is dismissed by Pei, who seeks only pleasure and entertainment—in movies as well as in his relationships with women. Ling and Pei's debate on the ethics of cinema amounts to a dramatic restaging of the central message of the Cantonese Film Clean-up Campaign in a potentially comical love triangle scene, where two suitors are going out with the same girl on a three-party date.

The selective analysis of woman-centered films above shows how the politics of class and gender shaped the imagination of modern womanhood in the Mandarin films of Feng Huang and Great Wall. The femme fatale and the fallen woman are the two primary (sometimes overlapped) tropes employed in these films to critique the modern capitalist society. The character symbolism in these films further extends to the supporting cast in the clash of values and worldviews between the progressive working class and the unscrupulous capitalists. In this ideological tug of war, women's suffering is a catalyst for the struggle against a misogynistic and oppressive regime. The alignment between female agency and the anti-capitalistic ethos in these fallen women films is echoed in a different type of woman-centered films that turn the conventions of female virtue upside down. Instead of utilizing the troupe of the "fallen woman," these films offer alternative interpretations of the more conventional roles of women, as housewife, mother, and widow.

Marriage, widowhood, and motherhood

Another category of woman-centered films presents a different cast of strong woman characters who upset the status quo of the ethical regimes of family and marriage. *Mama Sings a Song / Fu chang fu sui* (Zhu Shilin, Chan Ching-po, and Ren Yizhi, 1957), *A Widow's Tears / Xin gua* (Zhu Shilin, Chan Ching-po, and Long Ling, 1956), *Suspicion / Zhuo gui ji* (Huang Yu, 1957), *An Unmarried Mother / Wei chu jia de mama* (Zhu Shilin and Wen Yimin, 1958), and *The Wedding Night* (Zhu Shilin, Jiang Ming & Wen Yimin, 1956) span a spectrum of comedy, family drama, and crime thriller films in which the central protagonist(s) actively resist or reinvent the normative roles of women as housewife, mother, and widow. As we shall see, the foregrounding of female agency in these films is achieved through the undoing of taboos and patriarchal authority. Instead of positing class solidarity as a pathway to women's liberation, female subjectivity is reasserted through shaking up the hierarchy of power from within the social institutions of marriage, family, and motherhood.

A first example in this category is *Mama Sings a Song*, a comedy that puts into question the micropolitics of gender in the ordinary household. The film begins with a singing performance in which a young songwriter, Zhongming, debates with his wife, Ruiqing, over the subservient status of women in the family. It soon reveals that Zhongming has been snubbed by a record company manager for his old-fashioned taste in music. As husband and wife decide to switch roles in the family, Zhongming's underappreciated song-writing talent is overcompensated by Ruiqing, who by accident is signed up by his boss, a self-professed star-maker in the show business. The main action revolves around the contrast between the husband's comic mishandling of domestic chores and the wife's preoccupation with her new career. Jealousy and suspicion lead to brief moments of tension and distrust before a happy ending ensures that all's well that ends well. This light-hearted treatment of gender stereotypes inside and outside the family does not lose sight of the malpractices of the entertainment industry: Zhongming's songs are rejected by the company because they are "too serious" and lacking in sensational appeal. Ironically, when Ruiqing plays her husband's latest composition in an ad hoc audition at home, she is immediately signed up by the manager mainly because she is a woman. Ruiqing's serendipitous good fortune reveals a deeply held assumption about women's position in the music industry: they are performers who entertain, not artists who create. As a woman composer,

Ruiqing commands an exceptionality that makes her conservative style acceptable. This indirect criticism of the ingrained attitude toward women in the music industry foreshadows a more direct comment on the state of popular entertainment in a later scene, when Ruiqing starts her first song recording session. The song carries the familiar beat and rhythm of Grace Chang–style Chinese musicals, but the lyrics repeatedly question the purpose of such endless mirth-making and the superficiality of the hyperactive body movement that defines the genre's form and style. The mis-en-scène, too, self-consciously distances itself from its generic reference: formally dressed in a lady's suit (in contrast to the teenage fashion in *Mambo Girl*), Ruiqing remains standing behind the microphone in a self-composed manner throughout the entire session. Staging a dance song without a dance with lyrics that satirizes the Cathay-style musicals, the scene draws attention to itself as a mockery of what it calls "crazy dancing" in the lyrics.

More outspoken statements about women's virtue and sexuality are found in *The Unmarried Mother* and *The Wedding Night*. As its title implies, *The Unmarried Mother* challenges a widely held bias against premarital pregnancy, one of the biggest taboos in Chinese society. The film begins with a woman's consultation with her family doctor (Qiao) about undergoing an abortion. Qiao, in flashback, recalls his upbringing as an illegitimate child and how he was nearly killed at birth by his own grandfather (Dong), who would not allow this shameful incident to tarnish the family's reputation. An earlier attempt to force his daughter to abort the child has been intercepted by his wife and her maid servant, who takes the infant away and brings him up as mother and son. The scene of reunion some twenty years later dramatically plays off the gender and generation gap: the grandfather stands alone as the defender of tradition against the rebellious Qiao, Aizhen (Qiao's biological mother), and "mama," his adopted mother. Like the elder sister Joyce in *Joyce and Deli*, Aizhen lives an independent and unmarried life as a school teacher. *The Unmarried Mother*'s head-on confrontation with the tabooed subjects of premarital pregnancy and single-motherhood was atypical of its times even among the ranks of progressive films, especially in the conspicuous absence of a positive male character in the older generation.[17] Qiao, the child of two remarkable women, is the only male voice that resonates with the strong women who protect, nurture, and inspire him.

The disparity between strong women and weak men is no less visible in *The Wedding Night*, which speaks for rape victims who are stigmatized as "unclean" and "immoral." Lin Fen, a young woman happily in love with her cousin, Shaozong, is horrified to witness how her uncle cold-bloodedly disowns his daughter, a rape victim whom he blames for having brought shame to the family. Shaozong, son of the head of the clan, tries to interfere to no avail. At a gathering with his fellow college-mates, he vocally speaks up against the social taboo on rape victims and the misogynistic obsession with women's virginity on their wedding night. Shaozong's liberal thinking is put to test on his wedding night, when he realizes that the same fate has befallen Fen, his young bride. Outraged and confused, he steps back and lets Fen fight a lone battle with her father-in-law, who threatens to revoke the vows because Fen is now regarded as an unclean woman. In a surprise counter-move, Fen walks up to the patriarch and tears the marriage certificate into pieces. In rejecting an unjust and humiliating verdict of the father-in-law, the young woman's exceptional strength and character stands in sharp contrast to Shaozong, who proves himself a weaker character unable to live up to his ideal self-image.

Similar to *The Unmarried Mother*, *The Wedding Night* makes a daunting statement about women's subjugation under a misogynistic regime that seeks to control and regulate women's sexuality through a relentless system of shaming and punishment. Seen against their historical and cultural context, the direct confrontation with controversial issues about premarital pregnancy, illegitimate birth, single motherhood, rape, virginity, and female virtue puts the two films at the forefront of the left-wing cinema's progressive agenda. What distinguishes these two women-centered films, as well as the others discussed in this chapter, is the conscious effort to *exclude* men from an organic network of women that can be called upon to resist or mitigate the consequences of misogynistic practices. Instead of being victims awaiting delivery, women in these films are subjects in control of their destiny. On this note, we turn to the final pair of strong woman characters who break out of the confinement of widowhood.

In *A Widow's Tears*, widowhood subjects a young woman to public scrutiny and constant surveillance. The film starts off with the standard devices of a family drama in which Fang Mei's seemingly happy universe collapses after her husband's death in a car accident. Previously latent tensions with her mother-in-law (Mrs. Shen) surface as the older woman's grief for the loss of her beloved son turns into suspicion and hostility toward the young widow, who happens to be the only beneficiary of her husband's estate. Mei's isolation is paralleled by a developing, and unduly scandalized, friendship between Mei and Jun, her husband's friend and ex-colleague. At the center of this family drama is Mei's struggle to come to terms with her widowed life and compromised circumstances in the family before the final moment of self-reckoning. The plot follows a classic formula that runs through all the films discussed so far: the clash of values between two diametrically opposed worlds distinguished by age, class, and gender difference. In *A Widow's Tears*, widowhood brings into sharper focus the psychological distortion of women's domestic confinement across generations. The conflict between Mrs. Shen and Mei points toward a generational shift in women's self-perception as it reexamines the relationship between female subjectivity, women's virtue, and the conventional role and status of women in the family. In her decision to move out of the Shen household, Mei leaves behind the psychological encumbrances of a *domesticated* widowhood and walks into a new, though uncertain, life. As in *The Wedding Night*, the world outside the family is only an allusive presence vaguely depicted. This limitation of the script might also be the reflection of a subconscious anxiety about what might be in stock for the young rebels after their jump into the brave new world, and no less a reality check on the triumphalism otherwise implied in the ending. The presence of a male companion to complete the tales of women's self-awakening reveals a conservative edge to this pragmatic caution.

Two strong woman characters present themselves in the final example in this category, *Suspicion*, in which a school teacher's investigation into a murder mystery draws her into another woman's traumatic life (Figure 4.5). A young man, Gao, is wanted by the police on a murder charge. In an act of chivalry, Xiao Ping vows to find out the true culprit to clear her friend's name. An opportunity presents itself when the widow of the victim, Mrs. Shen, decides to rent out a room in her spacious mansion. Xiaoping's friendship with Mrs. Shen and her loyal housemaid leads her into the darker secrets of the Shen couple and their shady dealings with dubious acquaintances. As her detective work continues in what looks increasingly like a haunted house, atmospheric suspense is sustained by the skillful manipulation of lighting and sound effects. While Xiaoping's discoveries in her new abode fail to yield a solution to the mystery, the truth reveals itself when Mrs. Shen, after confronting a gangster with what appears to be evidence of the murder, breaks out of her silence in a confession in flashback: she killed her husband to avenge her father's death. This plot detail told through Mrs. Shen's recollection

Figure 4.5 *Suspicion* (film advertisement, *Wah Kiu Yat Po*, 22 March 1957, p. 12).

establishes her as both a victim of male sexual violence and an avenging angel who takes justice into her own hands, though in the moral universe of the film the murderer must surrender herself to the course of justice. At this point it would not be too far-fetched to place Xiaoping and Mrs. Shen side-by-side as a female dual whose pursuit of justice bifurcates into a course of chivalry and a course of revenge. With the main action driven by two leading female characters and the supporting male cast relegated to subsidiary roles, the film has turned the gender balance in commercial crime thrillers upside down. The narrative has even disposed of the chance of a romantic subplot between Xiaoping and Gao, who could have played a less dependent role. Instead, as the prime suspect-in-hiding at the center of an unsolved murder, Gao is at best a passive and well-intentioned blunderer who pales in the presence of his much more charismatic female counterparts. As a murder mystery, the film's "whodunit" plot is turned into an occasion for recentering female agency in the figures of two strong women in antagonistic roles.

Conclusion

While the ideological tug-of-war between left-wing and right-wing cinema in Cold War Hong Kong has attracted a lot of critical spotlight, more work needs to be done on how this left–right divide is translated and crafted in the cinematic medium. It was the films themselves, as both propaganda and as art, that ultimately reached their audience to deliver their supposed ideological mission. This chapter therefore has adopted a microscopic approach to revisit the imprint of Cold War politics on Hong Kong screens through the lens of gender and class in Mandarin film productions. Focusing on how women are cast into both traditional and nontraditional roles in both left-wing and right-wing films, it has argued that the cinematic imagination of modernity of both the progressive and "freedom" camps tends to utilize certain prototypes of the strong woman in articulating their respective visions of what it means to be modern, or more specifically what it means to be a modern woman. The right-wing's construction of modern womanhood in *Mambo Girl*, *Wild, Wild Rose*, and *Air Hostess* is juxtaposed with the left-wing's counter-symbolic fallen woman and prodigal daughter characters. While the modern girl/woman in these right-wing films displays a stylish, charismatic allure that speaks for a gendered vision of capitalist modernity, such a vision is debunked in the left-wing's critical appropriation of these prototypes. The final section has shown how this counter-symbolism is employed in a range of strong woman prototypes in drama, comedy, and crime thriller films to recenter female agency and female subjectivity within the social institutions of marriage, widowhood, and the family. As mentioned earlier, political affiliations did not preclude collaborations and flexible realignment among film companies in response to market versatilities. It is hoped that this preliminary survey offers points of departure for future inquiries into how the politics of gender and class has informed the cinematic imagination(s) of modernity in both the left- and right-wing cinema at a time when filmmakers were navigating the stormy waters of national, colonial, and international politics.

Notes

1. The Motion Pictures & General Investment (MP&GI) was the Hong Kong arm of the Cathay Organisation in Singapore. See Fu, "Modernity, Cold war, and Hong Kong Mandarin Cinema," 26–28. Shaw Brothers, also based in Singapore, set up its Hong Kong headquarters in 1958. See Wong, *The Shaw Screen: A Preliminary Study*, 7. Cf. timeline.
2. The third of its kind since the 1930s, the Clean-up Campaign published its manifesto on 8 April 1949 in major Chinese newspapers, including *Ta Kung Pao*, China's official mouthpiece in Hong Kong, as well as two other non-left-wing newspapers, namely the *Wah Kiu Yat Po* and the Kung Sheung Daily. Cf. Chapter 2.

3. See Farquhar and Zhang, *Chinese Film Stars*; Leung, *Multimedia Stardom in Hong Kong*; Chan, *Butterfly of Forbidden Colours*.

4. Two edited volumes dedicated respectively to Shaw and MP&GI were published by the Hong Kong Film Archive. See Wong, *The Shaw Screen: A Preliminary Study*; and Wong, *The Cathay Story*.

5. The untimely death of MP&GI's founder, Loke Wan Tho, in a plane crash in 1963 led to the gradual decline of the industry giant, clearing the path for Shaw's regional dominance.

6. *An Age of Idealism: Great Wall and Feng Huang Days* is an oral history collection published by the Hong Kong Film Archive in 2001. Among Chinese-language sources, more detailed treatment of films and directors from the two studios can be found in Zhang, *Studies on Hong Kong Leftist Films*; and Su, *Looking North from a Floating City*. Lo Wai Luk has also written on the depiction of female desire and sexuality in the films of Great Wall director, Li Pingqian, for the catalogue of the Hong Kong Film Archive's special screening program "Writer/Director Series" in 2018.

7. See, for example, Ma, *Sounding the Modern Woman: The Songstress in Chinese Cinema*; Mazilli, "Desiring the Bodies of Ruan Lingyu and Linda Lin Dai," 69–94; Harris, "The Goddess: Fallen Woman of Shanghai," 111–119.

8. On stardom and star texts, see Dyer, *Stars*; Farquhar and Zhang, *Chinese Film Stars*.

9. The *Huang Mei Diao* film has its roots in traditional stage art combining song and dance, modern cinematic techniques, and period costumes. It was a very popular local film genre with transnational appeal during the Cold War era. Chen, "Musical China, Classical Impressions: A Preliminary Study of Shaw's Huangmei Diao Film," 51.

10. Yonghwa was eventually taken over by Loke Wan Tho's International Film Distribution Agency in 1955 and restructured into MP&GI in 1956. Cf. timeline.

11. Su, *Looking North from a Floating City*, 33. Cf. Chapter 5.

12. From Cathay's official magazine, *International Screen*, quoted in Fu, "Modernity, Cold war, and Hong Kong Mandarin Cinema," 29.

13. Fu, "Modernity, Cold War, and Hong Kong Mandarin Cinema," 29–30.

14. Ford, "'Reels Sisters' and Other Diplomacy," 186.

15. Ibid., 186.

16. Hsia and two fellow Great Wall actresses, Shek Hwei and Chen Sisi, were known as the studio's "three princesses."

17. Another representative example in this category is a much earlier film from the silent film period, *The Goddess* (1934). The story of a prostitute in Shanghai struggling to bring up her son in dignity became a star-vehicle for the actress Ruan Lingyu, whose rendition of the "fallen woman" character remains one of the classic moments in the history of Chinese cinema. See Harris, "The Goddess: Fallen Woman of Shanghai."

Chapter 5

Corporate repositioning, transnational cultural brokerage, and soft power: Sil-Metropole

In the heat of the political upheaval in Mainland China during the Cultural Revolution, Hong Kong left-wing films were condemned as "lacking class consciousness" and "poisonous." Many filmmakers were forced to attend "thought reform" training sessions in Guangzhou, where they were also dispatched to "join the workers" in factories. The interruptions caused periodic shutdowns and a total suspension of production at Sun Luen between 1970 and 1971.[1] The most direct impact of the Cultural Revolution on the left-wing studios was two-fold. As the party's liberal film policy was replaced by extremist doctrinal imperatives and direct political interference, left-wing films suffered from a dramatic decline in productivity and creative freedom, which inevitably led to setbacks in output quality and popular appeal. The dwindling prospect of left-wing films was intensified by a widespread disillusionment among studio personnel, resulting in the dispersal of stars and production talents. Where productions were still possible, strict party guidelines would be imposed at each stage of the production process. As one filmmaker recalled, much time was wasted on work meetings that were counter-productive to creative work, while some simply found the political climate debilitating.[2] This said, changing market trends and audience preferences may also explain the decline of the left-wing cinema in Hong Kong. Union, the unofficial arm of the left-wing film network, suffered from a talent drain as its leading stars began to retire by the mid-1960s. The studio ceased production in 1964 and officially closed down in 1967. Union's fading out from the film scene coincided with the expansion of the Kong Ngee group studios (Kong Ngee and Sun Ngee) founded by former Union director Chun Kim between 1955 and 1962 (cf. Chapter 6). Under Chun's leadership, the studios' urban romance and youth films grew in popularity, and its young screen icons eventually replaced their predecessors as the new face of Cantonese cinema.

From 1967 to 1976, the left-wing screen space was dominated by revolutionary films or imports from nearby Communist countries. Between 1971 to 1976, more than half of the combined output of the three studios were documentaries showcasing scenic landscapes or the nation's achievements in sports and infrastructural projects.[3] As studio staff were under pressure to "stay close to the latest political course,"[4] a majority of the left-wing's feature films during this period were propagandistic films that glorified class struggle, many of which had little appeal and relevance to the local audience. Meanwhile, Shaw and MP&GI continued to roll out star-studded blockbusters sold through their local and regional distribution networks. The second half of the 1960s, therefore, was a watershed period in the history of left-wing and right-wing studios.[5] It was also a time when the commercial Mandarin studios reached the apex of their glory, before Cantonese cinema's revival in the 1970s.

Another turning point in the haphazard fortunes of the left-wing studios was the outbreak of anti-British riots in 1967. Also known as the Hong Kong Riots, the territory-wide public disturbance lasted for eight months, during which leftist organizations and labor unions were joined by intellectuals and cultural workers, as well as college and high school students, in mass protests and armed conflicts with the police. At the peak of the chaos, the city was shaken by escalating violence, street bombings, and mounting tension between the leftist groups and the colonial administration, as both sides of the conflict were agitated by the casualty among their numbers. The details of the events are not yet fully disclosed to this day, and eyewitness accounts from both sides suggest that the trauma has left a lasting wound in those who were involved, and no less in their family members.[6] The most direct impact on the left-wing film apparatus was the arrest and detention of filmmakers, stars, and those who were suspected to have left-wing sympathies. Among them were screen icons Fu Chi and Shek Hwei, who took part in a mass protest outside the Governor's House, and Liu Yat-yuen, the head of Sun Luen and also the unofficial leader of the left-wing film establishment in Hong Kong. A member of the standing committee of the All-Circle Struggle Committee (believed to be the control center behind the riots),[7] Liao was arrested on 16 November 1967.

A ten-year hiatus was more than a temporary interruption in film production. To reverse the downward spiral caused by the structural damage, a comprehensive corporate restructure and reorientation was in order. After a few attempts to resume regular production in the late

1970s, Feng Huang, Sun Luen, and Great Wall launched their first joint production, *Shaolin Temple,* the debut film that introduced Jet Li (Li Lianjie) to the Hong Kong audience.[8] *Shaolin Temple's* significance lies not only in its being a precursor to subsequent Jet Li films that propelled the new martial arts screen hero into international stardom, but also in its being a catalyst for the consolidation of the three studios into a new conglomerate, Sil-Metropole (Hong Kong). The merger was an important turning point in the history of left-wing studios in Hong Kong. As the CCP began to retreat from political radicalism and refocus its energy on economic rehabilitation and restoring public morale, China and Hong Kong were on their ways to developing a new economic order that would transform the social and cultural landscapes of the two societies. Under the new reformist environment, the left-wing film establishment in Hong Kong was in need of a strategic retooling or risk facing oblivion. By the mid-1980s, "progressive film" had become an obsolete label with little relevance to the film industry and the general audience.

Sil-Metropole's story offers an insightful case study of the historical transformation of the left-wing cinema in Hong Kong. Beginning as an organized collective effort guided by an explicit ethical-ideological mission, the left-wing film apparatus in Hong Kong was eventually reconfigured into a more diversified cultural enterprise seeking to redefine itself in the local film industry and the Hong Kong society at large, at a time when the repercussions of the Cultural Revolution began to have an alienating effect on the locals, and as the colonial government was tactfully stepping up its modernization projects in a series of social and economic reforms. More importantly, Sil-Metropole was born at the dawn of China's Reform and Opening-Up Era under the leadership of Deng Xiaoping, which set in motion an ambitious project of nationwide economic reform that would transform China into a new global power— and Chinese cinema into a global(ized) cultural phenomenon—in the next three decades. Indeed, the quickening pace of market reform in China during the 1990s had deep repercussions in the film industries of Taiwan and Hong Kong, where more and more filmmakers seek investment and collaboration opportunities with their Mainland counterparts to gain greater access to the lucrative China market. The reconfiguration of the left-wing studios in Hong Kong was also the outcome of a paradigm shift in the PRC's cultural and economic policy, from propagating class struggle and political doctrines as the foundation of socialist nation-building to selective adaptation of the market economy as the steam engine of social and economic development. "Socialism with Chinese characteristics," which essentially means the fusion of socialist politics and capitalist economics, would soon become the motto of the next generations of CCP leaders. The Chinese film industry was not immune from this deep-rooted and far-reaching economic reform. Structural and institutional reforms carried out since the 1980s included the integration of major state-run studios into a gigantic conglomerate, The China Film Group Corporation (CFGC), in 1999; the emergence of privately owned production companies (such as the Huayi Brothers Media Corp in 1994);[9] the easing of institutional constraints on foreign investment in film production and exhibition; and the gradual relaxation of import quotas upon China's accession to the WTO in 2001. These are among the state's proactive measures to strategically relaunch Chinese cinema in the global film market.[10]

Film, after all, remains an effective instrument and embodiment of a nation's soft power that necessitates continuous self-reinvention to stay at the top of the game. What follows is an account of how Sil-Metropole, a product of the cinematic left's self-reinvention in the context of the institutional reform in China, maintains its presence in the changing social and cultural environment in Hong Kong, an undertaking that coincided with both Chinese cinema's rise to global prominence and Hong Kong cinema's passage through its "golden era" to a more sober stage of national-regional repositioning in the post-handover era.

The discussion below is informed by these questions: the way in which Sil-Metropole, as a state-owned "patriotic cultural organization" and a Hong Kong-based cultural enterprise, has been steering its corporate wheel to negotiate the duality of its mission; how the company has acted as a cultural broker between Hong Kong filmmakers and the Mainland film industry since the political handover in 1997; and the extent to which it serves as a strategic node in the state's policy to strengthen China's soft power by leveraging its economic, political, and cultural capital. The indirect legacy of the classical left-wing is traced through the development of social realist films and the working relationship between Sil-Metropole and emerging talents who would later become prominent figures in Hong Kong's arthouse cinema. As we shall see, Sil-Metropole's effort in grooming local film talents belonged to a larger project of the company's identity construction and localization, which is not limited to investing in art films but also encompasses its commercial projects that soon became an important vehicle for further regionalization and internationalization. These undertakings reveal the strategic role played by Sil-Metropole in aligning creative and production personnel in Hong Kong to forge a closer partnership between the local and the Mainland film industries. Sil-Metropole's most recent project of producing "Hong Kong-themed" blockbusters for the China market offers further insight into the latest phase of the company's self-reinvention under a dual mission to "lure (Mainland) audience back to Chinese cinema" and to "keep Hong Kong cinema alive."[11]

Indirect Legacy: social realist films and arthouse cinema

As a state-owned enterprise, Sil-Metropole has maintained its status as a "patriotic cultural organization," a common reference used by the Chinese authorities to refer to pro-China cultural agencies in Hong Kong; on the other hand, its commitment to increasing its local relevance by producing high-quality films was behind its active support of Hong Kong's best-known auteurs in the early phase of their careers. Indeed, Sil-Metropole's structural reform and strategic reorientation have retained traits of the left-wing tradition's commitment to cinema's social function, which is evident in its filmography of social realist films over the years. Alongside its regular theater circuits, the company operated a successful arthouse theater, Cineart (1988–2006), which used to be an important conduit of international art films in Hong Kong. Since its inception in 1983, the company has been increasing its production capacity in Hong Kong and China, maintaining a steady output of arthouse and popular genre films to reach out to broad bases of film audiences in the Greater China and international markets. Sil-Metropole's comprehensive program of commercialization to cultivate a mainstream studio label suggests that the left-wing's strategy of using the popular cinema as a platform for mass education and social action has become passé. This said, an indirect legacy of the classical left-wing is still discernible in the effort to sustain an alternative stream of socially committed films that may not be immediate crowd-pleasers, yet many of which were important landmarks in Hong Kong cinema in the 1980s and 1990s (discussed below). One can say that the most tangible and immediate reward brought by a successful corporate self-transformation is the rising prestige and influence of Sil-Metropole as a cultural broker between the Hong Kong and Chinese film industries, hence a facilitator of the state's policy of further integration of city and nation.

In the post-handover era, Sil-Metropole's public profile is enhanced through its closer relations with the Hong Kong SAR Government. As the state's official film and media enterprise in Hong Kong, Sil-Metropole amounts to a de facto partner in Hong Kong–China co-productions because of its special status as a Mainland state-owned studio. This is especially true when local filmmakers are generally less conversant with the bureaucratic mechanism of film censorship and licensing in Mainland China. Sil-Metropole's comprehensive corporate structure was completed with the integration of the Southern Film Corporation, the PRC's sole distribution agency in Hong Kong that also operated two local theater circuits. From the late 1970s to 1990s, Sil-Metropole worked with a number of younger directors who would soon become iconic figures of Hong Kong cinema, from future action film auteurs such as Tsui Hark, Johnnie To, and Benny Chan, to New Wave and "second wave" directors including Ann Hui, Allen Fong, Jacob Cheung, Mabel Cheung, and Clara Law (cf. Chapter 7). Understandably, China's model of the "market economy with socialist characteristics" necessitated a reorientation of its filmmaking apparatus in Hong Kong. In terms of output ratio, Sil-Metropole's commercial productions outnumbered its low-key social dramas. Spanning a wide range of genres, styles, and subject matter, the company's production strategy is both a continuation of and departure from the classical left-wing. Its close working relationship with younger directors known for their "local content" films is further evidence of the company's shift from the left-wing's emphasis on patriotism and anti-imperialism to reposition itself more firmly in the Hong Kong society since the 1980s. Despite its reorientation toward market-driven projects, its production history shows a commitment to cinema's social function and a willingness to take up projects that did not promise immediate profits. These experimental projects signaled the beginning of a new phase of socially committed cinema that distinguished itself from the classical left-wing.

From Allen Fong's *Father and Son* (1981) and Lawrence Ah Mon's *Gangs* (1988) to Jacob Cheung's *Cageman* (1992, discussed in more detail in Chapter 7), the new social realist films speak to the Hong Kong society with a distinctively local voice stripped of didactic messages and ideological subtexts that distinguish the left-wing films of the previous decades. More nuanced in their social vision and critique, the new social realist cinema differs from the previous generation's progressive rhetoric, capturing a budding urban sensibility that reflects not only the coming of age of the local cinema, but also the city's growing awareness of its historical becoming. Throughout the 1980s and 1990s, films that focalize on local subject matters continued to garner awards in Hong Kong and overseas. More recent examples in this category include Samson Chiu's *Mr. Cinema* (2007), a melodrama about the life story of a veteran leftist worker who finds his beliefs out of sync with reality; Ann Hui's *A Simple Life* (2012), a quietly evocative film about the a film producer and his aging caretaker in her final years of life; and new director Wong Chun's *Mad World* (2016), a debut film that zooms in on mental illness with poignant criticism of the healthcare system and social stigma on mental patients and their families.[12]

Sil-Metropole's identity construction can be seen as a self-conscious attempt of localization that would prove to be instrumental to the company's strategic repositioning as a regional cultural broker. This task is complicated by the company's official ties with the Chinese government and the necessity to reinvent its left-wing pedigree in the new corporate package. Allen Fong Yuk Ping's working relationship with Sil-Metropole serves as a good early example of the company's self-re-invention. A leading figure of the Hong Kong New Wave, Fong directed four features and two documentaries during his tenure at Feng Huang/ Sil-Metropole, which happened to be the director's most productive period. His first film, *Father and Son* (1981), was winner of the Best Film Award at the First Hong Kong Film Awards. Two years later, Fong won the Best Director at the Third Hong Kong Film Awards with his second feature, *Ah Ying* (1983). Fong's third film, *Just Like Weather* (1986), won the Best Director award at the Hong Kong Film Awards and the Jury Grand Prize at the Turin International Film Festival. Mixing reality and fiction in an experimental style of storytelling, the director's onscreen persona interviews characters in front of the camera in the documentary segments. Frequently used in Ann Hui's docudrama films, this technique was further exploited in Stanley Kwan's *Centre Stage* (1990), a critically acclaimed biopic of the legendary silent film era actress Ruan Lingyu (1910–1935), in which the director mounted a fictional interview with Ruan through her present-day screen incarnation, Maggie Cheung. Focusing on a Hong Kong couple's struggles over emigrating to the United States, *Just Like Weathers* deserves credit as a forerunner of a new category of "migrant films" that allude to the 1997-triggered existential impasse. Migration, displacement, gender, and diasporic identity soon became popular leitmotifs in Hong Kong cinema as the city began its countdown to the end of colonial rule.[13]

Insisting on making non-mainstream films with experimental elements, Fong is far from being prolific, but his track record of winning three Best Director awards out of four feature films in less than ten years testifies to his status in Hong Kong's arthouse cinema. From the late 1970s on, social realist films became a vital part of Hong Kong cinema alongside the burgeoning commercial cinema that saw the rise of new-style action and martial arts films. Fong clearly identifies himself as an experimental filmmaker who puts the art and substance of a film before its entertainment value: "I . . . let audiences know that the film is fake. Once I have lured them into the [theater], they will discover the fun stuff underneath the fictional veneer."[14] Seen against Fong's oeuvre, "fun stuff" probably refers to delivering the pleasure of artistic decoding as a form of entertainment in itself. This apparently light-hearted comment encapsulates a similar artistic temperament discernible in fellow arthouse directors, such as Fruit Chan, Stanley Kwan, and Wong Kar-wai. Apart from cultivating its arthouse label, Sil-Metropole's corporate reinvention of the left-wing film establishment has also reinterpreted its "middling role" to better serve its dual mission at a time when Hong Kong and China were gearing up for a new phase of economic and political integration, a subject discussed in more detail below.

Entertainment through art: Sil-Metropole's middling role

Sil-Metropole maintains a head office and a studio in Hong Kong, and a solely owned subsidiary in Guangzhou with studio and production facilities. Incorporated in 1983, the company's official history begins in 1950, the same year when the "new Great Wall" came into being. In 2010, the company celebrated its sixtieth anniversary with a series of activities, including exhibitions and a retrospective on the left-wing cinema's history and filmography. In addition to a 500-page commemorative volume, a leading film journal in Mainland China, *Contemporary Film*, published a special issue to tie in with the anniversary. Both publications stress the company's contributions to the Hong Kong film industry, downplaying any possible political overtones that might arise from its association with the Chinese government. Over the years, Sil-Metropole has been making a conscientious effort to cultivate a more polished corporate image to harness its cultural and economic missions without completely disavowing its political origins:

> Political labels such as "progressive films," "united front," "ideology" and even "red capital" are routinely used whenever [the left-wing studios] and Sil-Metropole are mentioned. As such, Sil-Metropole has been criticized, if not purposely attacked, for being a political tool. Even though Sil-Metropole cannot be completely severed from politics, it must be stressed that politics alone cannot account for the scale of its operations and influence on Hong Kong cinema. Over the past sixty years, the organization has produced approximately 500 films and distributed nearly 1,000 titles from Mainland China. A conglomerate of over twenty subsidiaries, Sil-Metropole's total asset value is reaching 30 billion HKD. Sil-Metropole should be recognized, first and foremost, as an established film production company with a track record of industry and artistic success. Its contribution should not be obscured by political discourse.[15]

Acknowledging its left-wing origins, Sil-Metropole's self-positioning and business strategy remain in tune with the new mission given to progressive filmmakers in the post-Cultural Revolution era:

> We have to speed up the recovery of [left-wing] film production in Hong Kong . . . Any projects that can contribute to the course of national unity will be supported . . . We won't impose restrictions on subject matter as long as a film is not against the interest of the country and stays away from decadent and pornographic content. We encourage you to develop your own style to suit the taste of the Hong Kong audience. You should have the ambition to surpass the achievement of the Shaw Brothers in a couple of years. We have very good conditions now. We hope to see more films that are both healthy and attractive to the general audience.[16]

Restructured under a new corporate label, Hong Kong's left-wing film establishment entered a new phase of commercialization and product diversification. The new corporate mission has obliged the company to move away from Mandarin film production in Hong Kong, which was suffering a dramatic downturn in the 1970s. With Run Run Shaw turning away from film production to television broadcasting, Cantonese popular culture went into an unprecedented boom and was fast making its way to becoming a regional dominant in the Chinese-speaking world. Sil-Metropole's production strategy since the mid-1980s reflects this irreversible trend. Apart from commercial considerations, the refocusing on Cantonese films was also in line with the party's call to "stay close to everyday life" and make films that can appeal to the "overseas Chinese and regional audience."[17] The company's portfolio today spans from film production, co-production, and distribution to concurrently expanding digital media production and supporting services. Positioning itself as an industry player, the company's website highlights several core activities: talent grooming, market expansion, and active cultivation of Hong Kong–China co-production through facilities sharing, cross-border projects, and joint ventures with state- and privately owned film companies in Mainland China.[18]

Like all left-wing cultural organizations in Hong Kong, Sil-Metropole enjoys privileged treatment in its activities in Mainland China. This privileged status was particularly significant during the early stages of the Reform and Opening Up era under Deng Xiaoping, the grand architect of China's massive modernization project in the late twentieth century that jet-lifted the nation from a struggling socialist state to one of the world's leading powers at the start of the twenty-first century. While other Hong Kong-based production companies had to get through protracted bureaucratic hurdles, Sil-Metropole could directly approach central government authorities for permits with additional logistical support for location shooting. Special screening quotas for Sil-Metropole films further strengthened its position as a bridge between the Hong Kong and Mainland film industries.[19] During the 1980s and 1990s, these privileges worked to the advantage of both Sil-Metropole and younger filmmakers who were making headstarts in their career. Johnnie To's debut film, *The Enigmatic Case* (1980), a martial arts film shot on location in Northern Guangdong, was among the earlier projects that benefited from the new policy. Stripped of conventional studio sets and props, the film's action is driven by atmospheric suspense and visual contrast. To's distinctive visual language was later developed into his stylistic signature, a Hong Kong version of neo-noir, or what Stephen Teo calls "Kowloon noir,"[20] that characterizes To's action aesthetic. Stylistic borrowing from the Japanese samurai film in *The Enigmatic Case* prefigured a popular trend of intertextual referencing in martial arts films, where Japanese and Hollywood genre conventions were adapted in the reinterpretation of traditional Chinese folklore and martial arts fiction, for example, Ching Siu-tung's *A Chinese Ghost Story* I, II, III (1987, 1990, 1991) and Tsui Hark's *Seven Swords* (2005). In 1996, Johnnie To founded his own production house, Milkyway, which is famous for its "To-style" action drama. As one of Hong Kong's most internationalized action auteurs, To stands together with John Woo as stylistic masters of the "Hong Kong action film," a mark of distinction that helped To and fellow filmmakers gain inroads into regional and international markets. Over the years, Milkyway has developed a close working relationship with Sil-Metropole as a gateway to the China market. To's 2008 feature, *Linger*, was the director's first Mandarin-language film produced and distributed by Sil-Metropole in Mainland China.[21]

Leveraging the strengths of Hong Kong's creative talent pool to diversify its output, Sil-Metropole's China connection gave it a unique edge in the production of films that emphasized authenticity; for instance, social dramas and historical films set in China could take advantage of the greater accessibility to scenic sites and shooting locations on the Mainland. This was especially important before China's economic reform and modernization further increased the openness of the country to international collaborations. In addition to *Shaolin Temple* and two follow-up Jet Li vehicles, Sil Metropole collaborated with Li Hanxiang and two other Mainland production companies on a historical epic, *The Burning of the Imperial Palace* (1983). A best-selling film in Hong Kong and winner of a special award from the Ministry of Culture (reconstituted into Ministry of Culture and Tourism in 2018), it was celebrated as the first Hong Kong–China co-production film in the Reform and Opening Up era. As a leading martial arts film director of his time and a close affiliate of the right-wing studios, Li's "political" choice reflected the pragmatism and a general condition of the filmmaking world. As we have seen in the previous chapters, Li's attitude toward politics is typical of many during and after his time. One of the biggest ironies revealed by the personal stories of filmmakers caught in the left–right divide seems to be Hong Kong filmmakers' general aversion to politics, in the sense of expressing political views that might expose them to the sensitive radars of various state agents, while at the same time having to succumb to political pressure to declare their loyalty to the power that be. Perhaps this depoliticized politics has been an essential quality that keeps the film industry going, and that which accounts for its versatility, adaptability, and vulnerability when politics, or political complacency, became a precondition to survive in their trade. This middling attitude has run through generations of filmmakers, if not the film industry at large.

Similar to its left-wing predecessors, Sil-Metropole was under pressure to redefine itself in the presence of formidable rivals. While the Mandarin cinema was gradually fading out in Hong Kong, the return of Cantonese film as a market dominant was accompanied by the rise of new studios at the dawn of Hong Kong cinema's golden age. As far as the commercial mainstream was concerned, new studios such as Golden Harvest, D&B, and Cinema City were churning out blockbuster films. It was during this period that Hong Kong's big-budget kung-fu, comedy, martial arts, and action films outperformed Hollywood imports in the domestic box office. The landscape of film exhibition paralleled this paradigm shift in film production: Golden Harvest, founded by former Shaw CEO Raymond Chow and the launchpad of Jackie Chan's international kung fu stardom, operated an extensive network at prime locations, while D&B and Cinema City were actively expanding their theater circuits. A concomitant development was the phasing out of the traditional single-screen theater by multiplexes in Hong Kong, a material challenge to the well-being of the left-wing's exhibition channels. Facing these challenges from new and old rivals, the traditional left-wing theaters soon found their commercial viability in jeopardy. By 2009, all the six major theaters and subsidiary venues were either sold for redevelopment or ceased operation upon the expiry of their rental contracts.[22] As one senior member of Sil-Metropole recalls, both Sil-Metropole and Shaw failed to get on the express train of Hong Kong cinema's golden age.[23] As a reconstituted left-wing film and media producer, Sil-Metropole's market presence hinges upon its middling role, which in turn is necessitated by its dual identity as part of the national film industry and a Hong Kong-based cultural enterprise subject to the ebbs and flows of the local and regional markets. This middling position harks back to the time of the classical left-wing studio era, revealing a consistency in the Chinese government's cultural policy toward Hong Kong, albeit subject to constant fine-tuning and adjustment as well as periodic disruptions in Hong Kong–China relations over time.

Transnational cultural brokerage: pan-Chinese cinema as soft power

If the Cultural Revolution and the Reform and Opening Up policy in Mainland China were two crucial turning points in the history of left-wing studios in Hong Kong, the local film industry, if not the city as a whole, was shaken to its foundations by a series of unfortunate events not long after the political handover in 1997. Probably more dramatic than the Asian financial crisis and the avian flu in 1997, 2003 was a year of unprecedented turbulence: SARS, a global epidemic allegedly originated in China, hit Hong Kong in February 2003. The highly contagious and largely unknown virus soon sent the city into frantic chaos. Apocalyptic apprehensions escalated on every news update on the death toll, and stock and property prices continue to plunge in the face of massive fallouts. Mounting public discontent over the Hong Kong government's below par performance in managing the avalanching public health and economic crises culminated in the 500,000-strong mass protest on 1 July, the day when the former Chinese premier Wen Jiabao officiated the reunification ceremony in the heart of the city. An epidemic out of control thus snowballed into a political crisis that called into question the fitness to rule of the new SAR administration. What the premier and his party colleagues witnessed on 1 July was a catalyst to the next phase of Hong Kong's economic integration with China. Shortly after the premier returned to Beijing, the Closer Economic Partnership Arrangement (CEPA) was announced. To be implemented in successive stages, CEPA would benefit a broad spectrum of Hong Kong businesses and professional services seeking opportunities in Mainland China. Under its provisions, Hong Kong-made films would be exempted from foreign import quota restrictions upon satisfying a prescribed percentage of Mainland capital investment and personnel involvement.[24]

Since 2004, CEPA has activated an industry-wide reorientation toward the China market with an increasing number of filmmakers and companies relocating to and/or establishing production bases in the Mainland. Meanwhile, the special provisions for Hong Kong–China co-produced films have been reshaping the Hong Kong cinemascape in form as well as in substance, as Hong Kong filmmakers have to accommodate the viewing preferences and taste of the Mainland audience, and no less the censorship practices and regulations of the Chinese authorities. The relative merit of CEPA has been a matter of debate for some time in Hong Kong. Arising from the critical discourse are concerns over self-censorship, the constraints on creative freedom, and most of all the systemic marginalization of local content films, which are deemed to be unappealing to the Mainland audience due to their unfamiliarity with Hong Kong's history and culture. The tendency of co-produced films to stay within the comfort zone of ideologically safe and Mainland market-friendly content is another source of complaint. Despite this critical apprehension, co-production has become the default path in the local industry today, while a mini-current of "local films"—that is, local in content, cast, capital, and production crew—is recently showing signs of a moderate revival, as the local audience are also seeking alternatives to formulaic co-production films.[25]

Against this background, Sil-Metropole's role as a cultural broker deserves closer attention, not only because it has been a key player in the integration of the Hong Kong and Mainland film industries, but also because it has been a strategic node in Chinese cinema's expanding transnational network. The implications of the latter are more far-reaching. In China, cultural power is understood as "an important component of comprehensive national power,"[26] hence a means to augment China's cultural deficit vis-à-vis foreign (developed) countries. The emphasis on soft power was formally embedded in the state's latest drive to develop the cultural industries in 2007:

> We . . . must enhance culture as part of the soft power of our country in order to better guarantee the people's basic cultural rights and interests, enrich the cultural life in Chinese society and inspire the enthusiasm of the people for progress . . . The great rejuvenation of the Chinese nation will definitely be accompanied by the thriving of Chinese culture.[27]

Since then, increasing China's soft power to "give a good narrative" of the country to the world has been a state policy priority.[28] While the eventual outcome of this "soft power" incentive remains to be seen,[29] it is beyond doubt that China's cultural capital has been substantially globalized, considering the willingness of Hollywood producers to accommodate to "China friendly" content, setting, and casting in the last ten years or so (for instance, *Mulan* and *Kung Fu Panda*). Chinese cinema has also become a popular subject in film scholarship since the early 1980s, beginning with the growing reputation of China's Fifth Generation directors to today's more commercialized blockbusters and a smaller cluster of documentaries and independent films. These developments illuminate the broader context of Sil-Metropole's strategic positioning in the process of Chinese cinema's globalization. The company's increasingly active role in fostering Hong Kong–Mainland collaborations in the CEPA era can be dated back to an earlier "event film," Zhang Yimou's *Hero* (2002). Zhang's film is regarded as an important landmark that signaled the arrival of Hollywood-style blockbusters in

Chinese cinema, and a new mode of filmmaking combining top stars and creative talents from Taiwan, Hong Kong, and the Mainland.[30] As a "benchmark film," *Hero* set a new standard for the transnational Chinese martial arts genre.[31] It also proved the viability of the pan-Chinese film production formula in the global market. This narrative, however, should not overlook the ultimate "model" film that preceded Zhang's project, Ang Lee's *Crouching Tiger, Hidden Dragon* (2000), a Taiwan-US joint venture, and their Hong Kong connection: film producer Kong Chi-keung, who acted as a bridge between the Taiwan-US production team and the Chinese authorities to facilitate the filming of Li's transnational martial arts blockbuster.

The success of *Hero* consolidated Sil-Metropole's new role as not only the state's film production arm in Hong Kong, but also a transnational cultural broker contributing to the nation's soft power. This new objective is materialized in two broad types of products: transnational arthouse films and commercial genre films targeting a regional, pan-Chinese audience. The first category includes Ang Lee's *Lust Caution* (2007), Ann Hui's *A Simple Life* (2011), and Wong Kar-wai's *The Grandmaster* (2013). Affiliated to this category is Johnnie To's edgier action thrillers and his Milkyway catalogue, which has become an international label on its own. The second category spans a wider spectrum of detective, action, and horror films, including box office hits by veteran action directors Andrew Lau, Dante Lam, Benny Chan, and the Pang Brothers, who have established a reputation in the pan-Asian horror cinema after the critical success of *The Eye* (2002) and *The Eye 2* (2004).[32] The first category consists of art and popular art films or, in Cindy Wong's words, "festival films,"[33] aimed for an international niche audience. The second category reflects the importance placed on popular genre films in the pan-Chinese market. The films in this category significantly outnumber those in the first, a reflection of the filmmaking ecology in Hong Kong, and no less the company's weighted business and cultural objectives.

While "soft power" is generally understood as a nation's use of culture as a means of co-option, that is, a product and a means of interstate rivalry in cultural economics,[34] the status of Hong Kong as an ex-colony perceived to be lacking a sense of belonging to the Motherland (and therefore in need of reinforced patriotic education) means that national soft power in the ex-colony is also a form of domestic rivalry for cultural supremacy. Sil-Metropole certainly is not the sole agent on this mission.

Compared to its left-wing predecessors who acted as a cultural brigade in the struggle for political and cultural legitimacy, Sil Metropole participates in the construction of a pan-Chinese sphere of cultural imagination, utilizing its locational advantage to engage filmmakers and investors in the Greater China region in the production of a new "China imaginary." While success can be measured by numbers, there is also a qualitative nuance in the game of statistics. Fifteen years after its first implementation, it seems the CEPA effect on Hong Kong–China co-productions since 2004 has reached another turning point. If China-oriented co-produced blockbusters have dominated Hong Kong screens as a result of the hegemony of the Mainland film market, this trend seems to be partially reversed by a growing interest, in both Hong Kong and China, in Hong Kong-themed films, which may be a signal of a maturing popular film culture in Mainland China, and no less the result of a long process of adjustment and fine-tuning by local filmmakers to negotiate the disjunctions in audience preferences, working culture, and censorship practices in the two places. In early 2017, Sil-Metropole announced a rigorous program of Hong Kong-themed productions to "bring mainland Chinese audiences back to the cinema": "We observed that a lot of well-received films in mainland China had strong Hong Kong flavors, or were directed by Hong Kong film makers who brought their unique storytelling to the mainland. We feel that we must keep Hong Kong cinema alive."[35] After one and a half decades of experimentation, the co-production regime has proved to be less inflexible than it used to be and audience fatigue has become a cause of concern. The refocusing on Hong Kong-themed productions by Sil-Metropole suggests that the soft power of the China market is actively, though selectively, engaging and utilizing the cultural capital of Hong Kong as part of a greater effort to bring the two markets—and the two societies—into a closer partnership. This could be a positive turn for the local film industry to reinvent itself as not just a beneficiary (which connotes dependency) of the state's well-intentioned policy, but a shareholder of mutual interest in the cultural market. This said, the centrality of Sil-Metropole as both the state's official film and media production base in the territory and an industry heavyweight in Hong Kong bespeaks the uneven scales of cultural currency exchange between Hong Kong and China, a condition that likely will remain in the foreseeable future. After all, Sil-Metropole's statement above captures the essence of the company's dual mission: the Hong Kong-themed project is both a commercial decision to lure

Mainland audiences back to Chinese cinema and an ethical-political initiative to "keep Hong Kong cinema alive" in the post-handover, post-SARS era.

Notes

1. Zhou, "Only Cantonese Films Can Take Roots in Hong Kong," 65.
2. Zhang, "The Cultural Revolution's Impact and Damage," 216–217.
3. Despite their propagandistic mission, the quality of documentary films produced by the three studios were generally less hampered by the stringent political censorship during the Cultural Revolution. The best of these films outperformed the left-wing feature films during this period. Ibid., 222.
4. Ibid.
5. The premature death of Loke Wan Tho in a plane crash cast a fatal blow to MP&GI, which did not survive the business downturn thereafter. The company's film production unit was closed down in 1971.
6. There are bifurcating views on the 1967 Riots. One holds that the riots originated from domestic social crises and labor disputes; the other suggests that the organized manner of the major protests and the violence that erupted were an extension of the Cultural Revolution in China. See Ching, *The Origins of the Hong Kong Riots*; and Cheung, *Hong Kong's Watershed: The 1967 Riots*. A recent documentary, *The Vanished Archives*, presents interviews with former leftist leaders, students, unionists, and other eyewitnesses of the 1967 riots together with archival documents and news footages to reconstruct the historical events. The documentary was met with hostile reactions from unknown parties during public screenings in Hong Kong and was rejected by the Hong Kong International Film Festival in 2017.
7. Also known by its full name, The Committee of Hongkong–Kowloon Chinese Compatriots of All Circles for Struggle Against Persecution by the British Authorities in Hongkong.
8. Li's screen image as an "authentic" martial arts genius from Mainland China and his innocent, country-boy character led to two subsequent Jet Li films produced under the label of Sil-Metropole. It was Tsui Hark's *Once Upon a Time in China* series, where he plays Huang Feihong, a real-life kungfu legend back in the late Qing and early Republican period, that formally launched Li's international career in the late 1980s and 1990s.
9. Huayi is by far the most successful case of private film companies with an impressive record of domestic and international blockbuster films. Its creative core is director Feng Xiaogang, whose initial success with two "Chinese New Year Films," *A World Without Thieves* (2004) and *Cell Phone* 2005, was followed by a series of box office hits that consolidated Huayi's market leadership. Feng's recent films showed the director's ambition in translating his characteristic black humor into subtle social and political criticism, for instance *Assembly* (2007) and *Back to 1942* (2012).
10. See Yau, "Watchful Partners, Hidden Currents," 17–48.

11. Chow, "Filmart: Sil-Metropole Sets Hong Kong Slate as Chinese Cinema's Saviour."

12. Both Chiu and Hui's films are Sil-Metropole productions. Wong's film was produced by Golden Scene, another production and distribution company known for its investment in new and innovative projects from serious drama to genre films.

13. See Marchetti, *From Tian'anmen to Times Square*, Chapters 6 and 7.

14. Fong, "Half a Glass, Half a Director." See also director's profile on the Hong Kong Directors' Guild website, available at http://www.hkfilmdirectors.com/en/director/fong-allen (last accessed 18 January 2018).

15. Sil-Metropole Organisation, *Sixty Years of Sil-Metropole*, 318–319.

16. Ibid.

17. See Liao, "On the Work on Hong Kong Cinema," 452; Liao, "Developing a Patriotic Cinema in Hong Kong," 553–556.

18. Information extracted from Sil-Metropole's official website, available at www.sil-metropole.com/m/infopages.aspx?mid=1000001 (last accessed 18 January 2018).

19. Sil-Metropole Organisation, *Sixty Years of Sil-Metropole*, 430–432.

20. A term coined by Stephen Teo, *Director in Action: Johnnie To and the Hong Kong Action Film*, in his study of Johnnie To.

21. Boasting a pan-Chinese cast of Taiwan, Mainland, and Hong Kong stars, To's hand at the romance film failed to impress. Apart from a weak plot and undistinguished acting of the lead characters, the film falls victim to the ban on the supernatural in Mainland China. While borderline cases do exist, *Linger* dispenses with the central enigma (the ghost of a young man lingering around his beloved) by way of an ambivalent explanation: drug-induced hallucination. This is the dilemma faced by filmmakers who try to get around the ban on supernatural contents by "scientific" rationalization.

22. Sil-Metropole Organisation, *Sixty Years of Sil-Metropole*, 520.

23. Ibid.

24. See Yau, "Watchful Partners, Hidden Currents."

25. This recent trend in Hong Kong cinema is discussed in Lee, "Relocalising Hong Kong Cinema."

26. Zheng Bijian, political advisor of Jiang Zemin, quoted in Keane, *Creative Industries in China*, 29, emphasis added.

27. Former President Hu Jintao's address to the 17th National Congress. See Hu, "Report at the 17th National Congress of the Communist Party of China."

28. "We should increase China's soft power, give a good Chinese narrative, and better communicate China's message to the world," said Xi Jinping in his address to the 18th National Congress, 2014, quoted in Biswas and Tortajada, "China's Soft Power is on the Rise."

29. As one scholar remarks, "China's problem is more complex than whether or not its national image is 'good' or 'bad,' but hinges on a more difficult puzzle: China's image of herself and other nations' views of her are out of alignment." Ramo, *Brand China*, 12.

30. The year 2002 also marked the implementation of a nationwide reform to deepen the marketization of the film industry. Li and Si, "Taking Off Again after 1997," 431.

31. According to Davis and Yeh, a "benchmark film" is a blockbuster-style production and a trendsetter that will serve as a template for future imitation. Davis and Yeh, *East Asian Screen Industries*, 9–13.

32. The sequel was produced by Applause Pictures, a pan-Asian film company founded by Hong Kong director Peter Chan and two partners in 2000. It is worth noting that the Pang Brothers' later films for the China market cautiously worked around the supernatural element (which remains a censored subject in Mainland China) by way of rationalizing the uncanny in the language of medicine, so that the "ghost" is either a hallucination or the effect of schizophrenia.

33. See Wong, *Film Festivals: Culture, People, and Power on the Global Screen*, Chapter 2.

34. See Nye, "Soft Power," 153–171.

35. This ambitious scheme aims to produce ten films per year, most of which will be commercial genre films. Chow, "Filmart: Sil-Metropole Sets Hong Kong Slate as Chinese Cinema's Saviour."

Chapter 6

Critical transitions on the non-left: Patrick Lung and Cecile Tang

The decline of left-wing studios during the Cultural Revolution and their subsequent consolidation into a market-oriented conglomerate, Sil-Metropole Ltd., marked the end of what can be called the "classical period" of Hong Kong's left-wing cinema. As mentioned in Chapter 5, the left-wing's progressive ethos was adapted into the corporate mission of Sil-Metropole as both Hong Kong and China entered a new phase of political and economic transformation. While the reconfiguration of the classical left-wing into a multimedia conglomerate marked an important transition in China's cultural policy, which sees culture as both soft power and an instrument of economic modernization, the local cinema was seeking new orientations that would eventually render the left–right divide obsolete. While politics and society continued to inspire local filmmakers, the decline of the left-wing studios signaled a gradual shift from the classical left-wing's commitment to cinema as a form of social action and mass education to more individualistic visions of society and culture. These new voices were harbingers of a home-grown art cinema, a critical transition that anticipated the arrival of what came to be known as the "New Hong Kong cinema" in the 1980s.[1]

This chapter takes a detour into the critical transition made by Patrick Lung Kong (1934–2014) and Cecile Tang Shu-shuen (b. 1941). Different in background and artistic orientation, both Lung and Tang stirred up controversies and debates over their filmic interventions into politics and society. Lung's 1970 feature, *Yesterday, Today, Tomorrow*, came under fire by pro-China groups for its barely disguised condemnation of the violence and chaos instigated by left-wing activists in Hong Kong during the 1967 riots. Didactic and prescriptive at times, Lung's films display a greater confidence in the city's modern institutions and the liberal values they represent, which inevitably alienated him from the anti-capitalist and anti-colonial politics of the left-wing. Born in Yunan and educated in the US, Tang made her debut, *The Arch*, in 1969, an award-winning film showcased at film festivals in Taiwan and Europe. Tang's most overtly political film, *China Behind* (1974), tells the story of college students trying to illegally cross the border to escape the turmoil of the Cultural Revolution. Critical of both the Communist regime in Mainland China and the capitalist society of Hong Kong, Tang's film was banned from public screening until the 1980s. Tang has also been regarded as a pioneer in women's cinema. Her small corpus and short-lived directorial career notwithstanding (see below), her work exhibits an avant-garde quality in foregrounding female subjectivity and gender identity. Tang's Western film school training and cosmopolitan sensibility gave her a critical edge in the treatment of subject matters closer to home. Her work foreshadowed the arrival of the Hong Kong New Wave in the early 1980s, when a new generation of directors, most of whom had overseas film school training, began to transform the local film scene.[2] Looking back to these notable non-left-wing (if not counter-left-wing) directors sheds light on the split character of the left-wing's legacy, as both Lung and Tang daringly tackled the political taboos that suffocated the once dedicated left-wing artists, many of whom quitted filmmaking or defected to Taiwan at the peak of the Cultural Revolution.[3] More importantly, the trajectories of Lung and Tang revealed the complex entanglement between film and politics, or more generally the conditions of political representation, even when law and order together with the capitalist lifestyle had remained intact under colonial rule well after the Cultural Revolution and the 1967 riots. Lung and Tang's stories testify to the precarious nature of the "middle ground," and why it has remained a shifting yet indispensable domain, if not refuge, for Hong Kong filmmakers to continue their work regardless of the presence or absence of (unstated) political messages.

Patrick Lung: a new ethic of socially committed cinema

The decline and corporate restructure of the cinematic left not only cleared the path for the Shaw Brothers to become a regional filmmaking giant, but also opened up a space for a different approach to making "educational and morally uplifting films" that put greater emphasis on individual volition, humanistic values, and collective responsibility under the institutions of a modern society. Lung's films are critical of the utilitarianism and inequality perpetuated by the capitalist system while embracing Western egalitarian values as the foundation of social progress. Using film as a medium to challenge social taboos, Lung's subjects range from call girls, young rebels, juvenile delinquents, ex-convicts, and nuclear bomb survivors. In the context of 1960s and 1970s Hong Kong, Lung's films are both departures from the progressive film culture of the classical left-wing and a continuity of their humanistic ethos and commitment to film's social and educational function. Born in Shanghai and relocated to Hong Kong as a teenager, Lung saw filmmaking as both an artistic and social mission. Instead of using cinema to instill anti-capitalist and patriotic thinking, Lung's films express a strong sense of belonging to the local society and a desire to make it a better home for the younger generations. Signed up as an actor by Shaw, Lung developed a keen interest in script writing and production under the mentorship of Luk Chow, the most senior director at Shaw. Lung later was recruited by Chun Kim, former Union director and founding partner of Kong Ngee and Sun Ngee.[4] It was under Chun's mentorship that Lung made his debut, *Prince of Broadcasters* (1966), and subsequently *Story of a Discharged Prisoner* (1967), *Teddy Girls* (1968), and *The Window* (1969). Looking back, Lung played a significant role as a successor and pathfinder of the social realist tradition in Hong Kong cinema at a time when the film industry was gearing up on Hollywood-style genre films and blockbusters.

Considering the mostly positive portrayal of Hong Kong's modern (colonial) institutions in Lung's films, his criticism of the leftist-instigated 1967 riots in *Yesterday, Today, Tomorrow* (1970) would not be surprising. The film soon came under fire by pro-China groups, and the film's final cut was a substantially shortened version as a result of the controversy. A word of caution is in order before a case of the left-wing's hybrid legacy can be made. It would also help to contextualize and clarify the meaning of "hybrid legacy" in relation to non-left-wing films. As suggested in previous chapters, the left-wing in Hong Kong cinema is a porous entity despite the collective and institutionalized character of the leading studios, whereas a germane and pragmatic collaborative relationship was maintained between the left, right, and middle of the film industry against the ebbs and flows of colonial, national, and international politics. Meanwhile, the decline of the classical left-wing studios and their consolidation under Sil-Metropole coincided with a new phase in the PRC's film and cultural policy toward Hong Kong under the quickening pace of economic modernization within the country. This "economic turn" bespeaks the dynamic and versatile positioning of left-wing film production in the British colony. The legacy of the left-wing in Hong Kong cinema therefore may not be limited to a direct lineage of progressive film or the corporate history of left-wing studios that culminated in the founding of Sil Metropole as the PRC's official film and media enterprise in Hong Kong. Rather, it is in the actual practice of filmmaking, in terms of social and artistic attributes, that one begins to discover traces of the left-wing film tradition, which by necessity had to shake off the ideological convictions and political ties that gave the cinematic left its distinctive character in the 1950s and 1960s. Despite his nonchalance toward the socialist-nationalistic undertones that defined the classical left-wing, Lung's commitment to a *critical* cinema of social conscience with a reformist bent makes him an apt example of the left-wing's hybrid, and in a way contradictory, legacy, understood here as an indirect and *deviant* continuity unhinged from the spell of party politics and entrenched ideological alignment.

As an actor, scriptwriter, and director, Lung is famous for his urban youth films starring popular young idols of the time. Maintaining an average output of one film per year, Lung wrote and directed fourteen films from 1966 to 1979. From *Story of a Discharged Prisoner* (1967), *The Window* (1968), *Teddy Girls* (1969), *Yesterday, Today, Tomorrow* (1970), and *Hiroshima 28* (1974) to *The Call Girls* (1972) and *Nina* (1976), Lung's films bespeak a critical urgency to unpack latent social tensions, teasing out the entangled origins of embittered relationships between individuals, social classes, and generations. Despite his preoccupation with the "moral of the tale," Lung departed from the progressive tradition in choice of subject matter, character symbolism, and thematic focus. Probably Lung's most celebrated films, *Teddy Girls*, *Discharged Prisoner*, and *Window* probe the effect of social stigma on ex-convicts, the efficacy of the penal system, and the possibility of genuine reconciliation and rectification through institutional means and individual effort. Lung liked to emphasize his dislike for the "happy ending" plot, which he thought would weaken the social impact of the film. Compared to the left-wing's unequivocal criticism of colonialism, capitalist decadence, feudalism, and class exploitation, Lung's subject matters reflect a budding civic consciousness and a cautious optimism in the efficacy of a modern (Western-style) system of government in bringing about social and human progress. This is especially obvious in the opening scene of *Yesterday, Today, Tomorrow*, where tourists are given a panoramic introduction to Hong Kong's modern cityscape and metropolitan lifestyle through a uniformed female tour guide. The coach tour turns out to be a crash course on the city's impressive social development, substantiated by the latest employment and housing statistics. While such a detailed and informative orientation was (and still is) out of proportion for packaged guided tours, this rosy picture of the metropolitan city shown at the beginning of the film is intended to magnify the destruction and chaos brought on by a "plague" that soon follows. Adapted and originally named after Albert Camus's novel *The Plague*, the epidemic in the film is widely interpreted as an indirect reference to the 1967 riots, and the ubiquitous presence of rats as primary carriers of the deadly virus tellingly alludes to the instigators of the riots and their CCP affiliation. Political allegory aside, the apocalyptic crisis in Lung's film turns out to be a litmus test of human nature, and the director was undeterred when he inserted explicit political references to the riots, including the murder of a television broadcaster, Paul, whose Chinese name alludes to Ben Lam, a popular radio commentator and vocal critic of the riots killed in a car bombing in 1967. Succumbing to the mounting pressure from the left-wing media (which called for the burning of the film), the film company agreed to a substantial "editing" that effectively cut out more than half of the original film.[5]

Lung's individualistic approach to exposing the darker side of society and human nature is also evident in *Teddy Girls* and *The Window*, in which teenage rebels and social outcasts struggle to shake off their social labels. Their desperate attempts to make good are cast against the bigger failures in the adult world, which repeatedly dampens the hope of the young delinquents. Lung's sympathy for young people is anchored in the perspective of a figure of authority representing the benign and liberal side of the mainstream society. Acting as a voice of conscience, this character is usually an educator or social worker. As an enlightened member of society, he or she is an advocate of social equality and justice who firmly believes in the importance of education, rather than penalty, as the ultimate solution to social problems. While the left-wing film hero(ine) who champions similar values is often a member of the working class and the underprivileged, the voice of conscience in Lung's films embodies the professionalism of the educated elite. Sometimes this privileged position would become a hurdle when he or she tries to reach out to those in dire straits. This dilemma is most apparent when these characters are compromised by their in-between roles as the guardian of the public good on the one hand, and a lucid critic of unexamined assumptions and biases held by the mainstream society against their less fortunate members on the other.

Compared to the classical left-wing, Lung's films are more firmly grounded in the local society, where the quickening pace of modernization results in both blessings and setbacks. While the majority of his films carry strong social and moral messages, what distinguishes Lung's films from the left-wing's progressive ethos is his affirmative view of the modern (colonial) institutions, thereby obscuring the less desirable consequences of colonial rule while remaining highly critical of the injustice perpetuated by the ignorance and moral failures of individuals. In *Teddy Girls*, the rebellious inmates of a reformatory facility for girls are sympathetically pitched against a society oblivious to the root causes of youth crimes. Lung's portrayal of the facility as a supportive and benign institution under the enlightened guardianship of its principal, Rector Do (Kenneth Tsang Kong), for instance, borders on the idyllic when we see teenage female delinquents receive a disciplined education that resembles middle-class boarding school life. The world outside, however, is a bleak and unaccommodating environment where pimps, petty criminals, and drug traffickers rip off the innocent and the poor. Despite Lung's general confidence in the city's modern institutions, in *Teddy Girls* (and also in *Discharged Prisoner*) the police are very much an indifferent law-enforcing agency with little sympathy toward the plights of the young delinquents. The simpler, minimalist world of the reformatory and the "adult world" outside are juxtaposed throughout the film to create an ironic contrast to call for collective self-reflection by the mainstream society at large. The voice of conscience here is Do, who is torn between protecting his students, that is, the aggrieved youths under his care, and upholding the mandate of law and order. As an educator well versed in social psychology, he is a figure of authority who constantly cautions against entrenched assumptions and discrimination against young offenders. An intellectual committed to public service, Do speaks for a new generation of educated elites in whom Lung places his hope for a better society. *The Window* continues to explore the relationship between the individual and society through the love story of a criminal and a blind girl. The story revolves around a petty criminal's moral education through repentance and self-sacrifice. A good-for-nothing youngster, Yeh Hsia (Patrick Tse Yin) accidentally kills the father of a blind woman, Lu-ming (Josephine Siao), during a street robbery. His attempt to destroy the evidence of his crime brought him to the home of Lu-ming. Remorseful for his crime,

Hsia determines to change course and begins a new life. In the film, the love story between Hsia and Lu-ming is rendered in scenes of their "sight-seeing" tours. Repeatedly we see Hsia describing the colors, shapes, and textures of the scenery in meticulous detail as the couple travel to different parts of the city. Scenes of the metropolitan urban center and the natural beauty of the countryside are juxtaposed in a measured, rhythmic pace that yields an alluring image of the city far more inviting than the capitalist haven in left-wing films. Parallel to the police investigation plot, the more benign side of the institution is represented by the Catholic Church, which operates a school for blind girls. The romance of the young couple was curtailed as Hsia is fatally wounded in a fight with his ex-crime buddy, who raped Lu-ming out of jealousy. Hsia's self-redemption is completed when he makes his final will to donate his corneas to Lu-ming. The finale takes us back to the girls' school, where Lu-ming is now a nun and teacher (Figure 6.1).

In these films, the plight of the underclass is an occasion for self-reflection from within the institution, rather than a challenge to its legitimacy. *Discharged Prisoner* is an influential "social problem" film that inspired John Woo's action film classic, *A Better Tomorrow* (1987), a remake that would define the genre's period style and consolidate Woo's status as an action film auteur in Hong Kong cinema thereafter.

Figure 6.1 *The Window* (film advertisement, *Wah Kiu Yat Po*, 10 May 1968, p. 20).

In *Discharged Prisoner*, two polarized views on the treatment of ex-convicts are personified by a social worker, Mak Siyan (Patsy Kar Ling), and a police officer (played by Lung himself). In the film, Mak is an immaculately dressed professional woman in charge of a rehabilitation service facility. Her active lobbying for equal opportunities and greater social integration of ex-convicts is pitched against the police officer's skepticism and hostility toward her clients. This contrast is further magnified by gender difference: as a social worker, Mak is a champion of enlightened values, while Lung's detective is close to a conservative patriarch who holds onto his moralistic bias against all the "bad elements" of society.

While the youth films offer vignettes of a modern society troubled by its own restless impulses and contradictions, *Hiroshima 28* is a more ambitious attempt to tackle one of the world's most contentious issues since the end of World War II: the aftermath of the US atomic bombing and the global nuclear crisis.[6] Lung plays the journalist who visits Hiroshima on the twenty-eighth anniversary of the bombing. His tour guide, Yoshiko (Josephine Siao), recounts her family history and how she has been hiding her father's identity as a nuclear bomb survivor. Fears of radiation double up as social stigma fractures marriages and human relationships. Shot mostly on location in Hiroshima, the film was neither a critical nor a commercial success. A sentimental family drama cast against a larger-than-life apocalyptic scenario, the film was plagued by technical flaws and an untimely reception context back home, as the local audience was not yet ready for a Hong Kong film adopting a Japanese perspective on the Second World War.[7] It took another two decades before this "Japanese connection" was revitalized in Hong Kong cinema, when bitter memories yielded to the allure of Japanese popular culture, from television, comics, and pop music to cosmetics, fashion, and electronic products.

As a transitional figure, Lung's social critique is articulated through a paternalistic voice that calls for compassion, tolerance, and empathy toward the young and the underprivileged. The didactic undertone of Lung's films is therefore a reflection of his confidence in the efficacy of modern institutions to bring about social progress. As such, the challenges posed by social reformist characters in Lung's films are often recontained within the patriarchal system of values rather than questioning, much less unsettling, the status quo.[8] On this note, it is tempting to suggest that Lung's conservative leanings, in terms of his paternalistic admonitions for social equality and progress, make for an interesting parallel in contrast to the classical left-wing's humanistic ethos and egalitarian aspirations despite their very different ideological orientations. Lung's conservatism also departs from the classical left-wing in the sense that, even at his most moralistic moment, he did not adhere to a rigorous set of protocols that used to define and confine the classical left-wing's social vision. To Lung, instead of serving preexisting ideological and political purposes, making morally and socially meaningful films is an artistic pursuit in its own right. As we have seen in *Teddy Girls* and *The Window*, Lung's treatment of social injustice, generational schism, class conflict, or the human condition at large—perennial themes of the left-wing cinema—exhibits an interest in the human psyche and the individual as the fundamental unit of society. As such, characters are less specimens of a social class or spokespersons of a larger collective than human beings struggling through everyday traumas. This is not to say that these qualities are missing in the classical left-wing cinema, but that the cinematic left's collective self-identity and their communal, (semi-)institutionalized mode of filmmaking had preempted certain potentialities from blossoming in the creative process, an inherent inhibition that became more pronounced when the political situation deteriorated in Mainland China. From 1966 to 1979, Lung's directorial career roughly coincided with the Cultural Revolution and its immediate aftermath, a period that also marked the decline and reconfiguration of the left-wing studios. The 1970s also saw the revival of Cantonese cinema after a dramatic downturn.[9] In their attempt to give voices to the dispossessed caught within the shadowy substrata of society, Lung's films marked a critical transition toward a new social engagé cinema that stays in tune with the restless impulse of the city on its own terms. More than coincidentally, the first films that signaled the arrival of the Hong Kong New Wave were released between 1978 and 1979,[10] when Lung completed his last film. Lung's career can be fruitfully compared with that of Cecile Tang, an independent woman director whose artistic merit gained recognition only belatedly despite the provocations her small corpus managed to stir up among her contemporaries.

(Un)timely intervention: Cecile Tang

In the context of late 1960s and 1970s Hong Kong cinema, Cecile Tang was a pioneer without peers. Not only did her work stir up controversies and critical debates, but her public image was also the unprecedented outcome of a self-conscious identity statement vis-à-vis the patriarchal institution of filmmaking and film criticism.[11] Another marker of Tang's lone-wolf status was her transnational reach as a filmmaker capable of mobilizing her cultural capital to carve out a space of filmmaking that is both intimately personal and intensely political. Here it must be added that "politics" in Tang's work is a far cry from the politics of left and right that dominated the film scene in the previous two decades. Tang's politics as a filmmaker is registered in her daringness to speak in a different tongue to and against the prevailing discourse and practice of filmmaking of the time.

Of the critical writing on Tang published so far, Yau Ching's book-length study offers the most comprehensive study of her work from the perspective of a feminist scholar, filmmaker, and critic, revealing how both Tang's films and her identity as a "woman director" had been used to effectively *marginalize* her as a critical voice that challenged the status quo of filmmaking and no less the masculinist regime of film criticism both in Hong Kong and overseas. Yau's close reading of Tang's corpus and the critical discourse and press materials on her work and life in Chinese and English pays attention to how the director's public image stood out as a subversive gesture against the inquisitive gaze of her (male) critics, who insisted on a gendered (as a "woman director") and racialized (as a "Chinese director") decoding. Tang was the founder of a film magazine, *Close Up*, which was the first to announce the arrival of "a new wave . . . which will sooner or later replace the current so-called big directors who only occupy a seat but produce nothing."[12]

Here I would like to revisit Tang's career in terms of her interstitiality and multiple in-betweenness comparable to, and constitutive of, the "middle ground" that used to inform the actual practice of filmmaking during the Cold War era. The purpose is to shed light on the mobile and mutating character of the middle ground as an in-between space in which dissonances are negotiated and conflicting interests realigned. In the case of Tang, this space was complicated by her nonconformism as an "outsider" to the institution of filmmaking. Unlike Lung, Tang did not have personal or professional connections with filmmakers or studios. Coming back from the US with little experience in the filmmaking world, she had to rely on her own resources to reinvent a film production mechanism that would enable her to articulate her artistic and intellectual vision. According to Yau, Tang's incessant effort resulted in an alternative transnationalism that asserted its independence from the industrialized studio system exemplified by Shaw in the 1960s and early 1970s.[13]

Critical writings on Tang tend to focus on *The Arch* (1969) and *China Behind* (1974) to establish, if not rehabilitate, her status as an "iconoclast" and art film director.[14] *China Behind* is a controversial work about four individuals who fled to Hong Kong during the Cultural Revolution. The very first Hong Kong feature film to reflect on the turmoil of the Cultural Revolution and the issue of illegal immigrants in Hong Kong, *China Behind* was banned by the colonial government until 1980. Different from most other much later films about the Cultural Revolution, Tang's film was shot at a time when Mao's mass mobilization campaign was reaching a peak. Shot in Taiwan and Hong Kong, *China Behind* eschews the standard narrative of collective victimhood and suffering to focus on an elaborate escape plan of four individuals (a doctor and three senior university students) who decide to flee the country as their future and personal safety are at risk. Much of the story is about the hardships and hazards on their journey to Hong Kong, where they find entry-level jobs with little satisfaction or hope of upward mobility. Consistent with Tang's storytelling, the film's ending does not offer comfort or closure to either the characters or the audience. As we shall see, this kind of ambivalent ending is also found in *The Hong Kong Tycoon* (1979) and *Sap Sam Bup Dup* (1975),[15] Tang's apparently more commercial films.

Set in seventeenth-century China during the Ming Dynasty, *The Arch* tells the story of repressed female desire in the figure of Madame Dong, a widow who falls in love with a military officer temporarily stationed in her village. A lyrical atmosphere is sustained throughout the film as the emotional drama between Dong, the military officer, Dong's daughter (who is also in love with the same man), and the mother-in-law unfolds. The quiet suffering of Madame Dong slowly builds up to the final scene of emotional outburst: a series of flashbacks is followed by a close-up shot on Dong. In distraught, she suddenly dashes out into the backyard, knife in hand, and slashes open the neck of a hen. After a quick succession of shots to dramatize Dong's emotional uproar, Tang cuts to the ending shot, when Dong, looking indifferent and detached, attends a village ceremony where the "chastity arch" was erected.[16] Described by a US film critic as an "experimental melodrama" that was "sadly forgotten after its successful release [in 1969],"[17] *The Arch*'s belated rediscovery by critics and film festival curators is not an isolated phenomenon. The Hong Kong Film Archive, for instance, hosted a retrospective on Tang's films with post-screening forums in 2014. Apart from *The Arch* and *China Behind*, generally deemed to be her representative arthouse films, the program also showcased the restored versions of *The Hong Kong Tycoon* and *Sup Sam Bup Dup*. At first glance, the latter two films seem to have come out of completely different hands than Tang, and film critics regard these films as Tang's compromise to the mainstream cinema. A closer analysis of *The Hong Kong Tycoon* and

Sup Sam Bup Dup, however, yields a very different understanding of Tang's intention and interest behind these commercial projects.

In her analysis of *Sup Sam Bup Dup*, Yau discovers how Tang uses a popular everyday hobby, mahjong (a Chinese tile game), to explore the absurdities of life and the psychological distortions whose origins go far deeper than mahjong playing. As a feminist scholar and filmmaker, Yau's reading of Tang's film draws attention to female subjectivity and the politics of gender, ethnic, and class identity. *Sup Sam Bup Dup* portrays a world where individuals regardless of gender, race, and class backgrounds are obsessed with playing mahjong, and the pervasiveness of this obsession is panoramically captured in thirteen unrelated episodes. The film's title, *Sup Sam Bup Dup*, literally means thirteen pieces of unconnectable mahjong tiles, the worst combination that a player can get in any single round where the chance of winning is next to nil. The episodic structure enables Tang to condense and compress her observations of everyday life across a wide spectrum of social clusters, from affluent middle-class couples and business tycoons to new immigrants, unemployed workers, and imposters. Tang's first "mainstream" film was neither a critical nor commercial success. Not only does the film's fragmented plot and disconnected episodes frustrate expectations of an entertainment film, but it also refuses to offer dramatic closure to the conflict, mystery, intrigue, or scandal that sustains viewer's interest in each episode, leaving the viewer in a state of hanging disbelief at the end of each story. The film's play with anti-climax and anti-closure in the disguise of a mainstream comedy certainly raises its stake as a postmodernist experiment ahead of its times.

The Hong Kong Tycoon has a more conventional linear plot in telling the success story of a working-class man, Kim (which puns with "gold" or "money" in Cantonese), who manages to transform himself into a property tycoon within a relatively short time. A happy-go-lucky young man with no real ambition to begin with, Kim's only talent is his quick-mindedness and exceptional arithmetic skills. Kim's humble beginnings make him the ideal representative of the "Hong Kong man," the embodiment of the "rags to riches" narrative of Hong Kong's historical transformation from a humble village to an international financial center. If Kim is a metaphor of the capitalist society in which money is the only measure of self-worth, the supporting cast consists of a diversity of voices that subtly undercut the rhetoric of money. In the film, Kim's sexual advances on women are met with different forms of resistance. In one episode, a woman next door confronts him with her naked body in rebuke of his peeping into her shower. This unexpected move of an anonymous character early in the film not only foreshadows Kim's predatory behavior toward women but also the resistance he would face in his later adventures. By deconstructing the subject/object power structure, this scene turns the "male gaze" inside out in a swift and matter-of-fact manner, something that was rarely seen in Hong Kong films at the time. The film's foregrounding of female agency to unsettle a male-centered hierarchy of power in a capitalist society resonates with the left-wing's woman-centered films discussed in Chapter 4. This could be a reason why the film was released through the left-wing's theater circuits (Figure 6.2) despite the political controversy over Tang's earlier film, *China Behind*.

Figure 6.2 *The Hong Kong Tycoon* (film advertisement, *Wah Kiu Yat Po*, 5 July 1979, p. 21).

Tang's turn toward making commercial films also necessitated a linguistic code-switching from Mandarin to Cantonese. By the time Tang finished her debut film, *The Arch*, in 1969, the Mandarin-language cinema in Hong Kong was beginning to lose its market dominance with the re-orientation of the Shaw Brothers toward television broadcasting and the decline of MP&GI after the death of Loke Wan Tho. By the early 1970s, Cantonese films were regaining strength with the rise to global popularity of Bruce Lee's kung fu cinema, which coincided with the phenomenal success of the Hui Brothers' urban comedies in the domestic film market. At the same time, Sam Hui, the younger brother of Michael Hui, came to redefine Cantonese pop music (which soon took on a new label, Cantopop) with original compositions and lyrics that echoed the sentiments and aspirations of the working class. One can say that a distinctively local culture began to take shape in the 1970s,[18] and Cantonese became the unofficial lingua franca of popular culture. It is therefore no coincidence that Tang switched to Cantonese when she decided to test the waters of the commercial cinema. It is tempting to dismiss the film as Tang's failed exercise in an unfamiliar genre, if not a disappointing compromise to the realities of the film industry. However, when seen against the director's corpus and her non-conformist public persona, Tang's commercial projects can be seen as the director's dialogue with the local cinema and a critical inquiry into the possibility of social critique using the commercial film medium. *Sup Sam Bup Dup*'s structural incoherence and anti-closure endings reveals that the film's technical flaws and rough edges might well be a deliberate gesture to problematize the prevailing practices of commercial film production. For one thing, the thirteen episodes do not add up to any coherent storyline, but in different ways they are composed of easily recognizable genre elements that effectively turn the film into a generic remix of overused clichés in Hong Kong cinema. In addition to foregrounding female subjectivity as a basis for questioning and destabilizing class, gender, and ethic identities, Tang's tactic of self-conscious citation, appropriation, and recycling of cinematic clichés amounts to a postmodernist subversion of the very logic of making a commercial film in the context of 1970s Hong Kong. In *Hong Kong Tycoon*, the critique of the "money cult" is subtly intertwined with the critique of a sexualized hierarchy of power in the commercial world in the figure of Kim. Tang was probably the first director who had a precocious awareness of the disastrous consequences of the property boom that started in the early 1970s in her plot and character design. Precisely because the real damage to society and individuals of the government's lopsided land policy would not materialize until much later, Tang's critical intervention into the looming crises of the capitalist city deserves to be reevaluated.

Rethinking the left-wing's "afterlife"

This chapter seeks to go beyond studio history to examine the critical transition made by two "middle ground" directors, Patrick Lung and Cecile Tang. If the classical left-wing's critique of imperialism, feudalism, and colonial capitalism had been guided by their political idealism and patriotic sentiment, Lung and Tang's films display a more individual-istic vision of society, culture, and local/national identity that would become important points of departure for later filmmakers. Tang, in particular, has been widely regarded as a precursor of the Hong Kong New Wave who came of age in the early 1980s. Despite his confidence in the modern institutions under colonial rule, Lung's artistic orientation is closer to the social realist cinema of Chun Kim, in whom he found echoes of his own belief in the educational and moral function of the cinema. Like Chun Kim and other left-wing directors, Lung's camera stays close to the experience of the dispossessed and underprivileged, especially marginalized youths. Lung's criticism of the radical politics of the 1967 anti-British riots in *Yesterday, Today, Tomorrow*, however, was no longer confined by the left–right politics of the time; instead, Lung's politics is grounded in an optimistic view of social change and the rationality of modern government. Instead of left and right, it is more appropriate to situate Lung as an individualist wary of the dire consequences of radical politics.

Compared to Lung, Cecile Tang occupied a more marginalized position as a "Chinese woman director" who tried to make a difference in an unwelcoming environment. Tang's small corpus reveals her effort to accommodate her artistic vision to the systemic constraints of the film culture of her time. Whereas Lung's *Yesterday, Today, Tomorrow* was substantially shortened before it was approved for theatrical release, Tang's most political film, *China Behind*, suffered a fifteen-year ban. As illustrated in the discussion above, *Sup Sam Bup Dup* and *The Hong Kong Tycoon* were less the director's compromise to the mainstream than self-conscious interventions into the practices of commercial filmmaking by reinventing a critical film language out of clichés. In different ways, the careers of Lung and Tang are indicative of the instability and changing nature of the "middle ground" in Hong Kong's filmmaking world. Both Lung and Tang have succeeded the classical left-wing in their respective attempts to reinvigorate a critical cinema within and alongside the mainstream. Lung had a stronger sense of belonging to the colonial city where he spent most of his adolescent and adult years. The way in which he relates to and reflects on the "colonial city"—more as a hometown than a transitory refuge or place of exile—is simultaneously marked by a critical intellectual distance, often mixed with appreciation of its modern capitalist trappings that have ensured long-term social and political stability, which was unavailable in either Mainland China or Taiwan for the better part of the twentieth century. Tang, on the other hand, maintains a detached critical distance from both China and Hong Kong due to her diasporic upbringing. The "middle ground" that the two directors occupied, therefore, is by no means homogenous. The examples of Lung and Tang perhaps can shed light on the flip-side of the left-wing's legacy: the shock waves of the Cultural Revolution not only shattered the hopes of many left-wing filmmakers in advancing the socialist ideals in the British colony, but also brought into being a more diffused and de-centered form of socially engaged cinema that began to zoom in on Hong Kong's cultural and identity politics through the cracks and holes of local history, understood not only as textbook versions of British colonialism but also as an amalgam of unarticulated or suppressed voices that inform the mundane everyday experience of the here and now. Bringing two generations of socially engaged filmmakers in Hong Kong's film history into a dialogue, this chapter has attempted to discover the hidden linkages of two disjoint clusters of filmmakers to shed light on their nuanced (dis)continuities. After all, the historical legacy of the cinematic left can be more fruitfully gauged through the prism of their contemporary resonance, which is further explored in the next chapter.

Notes

1. Abbas, *Hong Kong: Culture and the Politics of Disappearance*, 16–47.
2. See ibid.; Teo, *Hong Kong Cinema: The Extra Dimensions*, 137–206; Cheuk, *Hong Kong New Wave Cinema*; and Lee, "The Hong Kong New Wave: A Critical Reappraisal" for more detailed discussion on the Hong Kong New Wave.
3. During this time, a large number of movie stars, left-wing or not, turned to the television to continue their acting career.

4. Kong Ngee (est. 1955) and Sun Ngee (est. 1962) were subsidiaries of Kong Ngee (Singapore). Chun was himself a shareholder of both the Hong Kong branches. Shing and Lau, *Oral History Series 6: Director Lung*, 46–47; Cf. timeline.

5. Lung had been labeled a "British spy" and traitor back in 1967, when a photo in which he was sitting next to a senior government official at the charity premiere of *Prince of Broadcasters* was released. The current seventy-two-minute version of *Yesterday, Today, Tomorrow* is dubbed in Mandarin. The film's original version is believed to be permanently lost. See Shing and Lau, *Oral History Series 6: Director Lung*, 59–61, 107–109.

6. *Hiroshima 28* was selected for Udine Far East Asian Film Festival (20–28 April 2018). It is also listed under "Archival Gems," a compilation of representative works in Hong Kong cinema by the Hong Kong Film Archive.

7. The "Japanese perspective" on World War II has been a contentious issue in Chinese cinema. A more recent example to negotiate patriotic expectations and nonpartisan artistic expression is the wartime drama *City of Life and Death* (Lu Chuan, 2009). The film drew criticism from official media, and its theatrical screening was curtailed due to its use of a Japanese soldier's perspective in recalling the tragedy of the Nanjing massacre in 1937.

8. Yau, *Filming Margins: Tang Shu Shuen*, 143; Fu, "The 1960s: Modernity, Youth Culture, and Cantonese Cinema," 83.

9. After a dramatic downturn in the early 1970s, signs of revival appeared with the box-office success of a Shaw-TVB production, *House of 72 Tenants*, an all-TV-star cast, working-class comedy, followed by the Hui Brothers' slapstick comedies and Bruce Lee's kung fu cinema.

10. These included Yim Ho's *Extra*, Ann Hui's *The Secret*, and Tsui Hark's *Butterfly Murders* (1979).

11. In *Filming Margins: Tang Shu Shuen*, Yau Ching offers a detailed analysis of how critical reception of Tang's work during the late 1960s and 1970s was founded upon masculinist assumptions and biases toward Tang as a "woman director," if not a "Chinese woman director." See discussion below.

12. Cheuk, *Hong Kong New Wave Cinema*, 10.

13. Yau, *Filming Margins: Tang Shu Shuen*, 11.

14. Teo, *Hong Kong Cinema: The Extra Dimensions*, 140.

15. The English titles are based on the information provided on the website of the Hong Kong Directors' Guild. Other alternative titles of the films include *The Boss*, *The Tycoon* (for *The Hong Kong Tycoon*), and *Shi San Bu Da* (for *Sup Sam Bup Dup*).

16. The chastity arch or chastity *paifang* is a monument in the form of an arch in traditional Chinese architecture, given as an honor to virtuous women who remained unmarried after the death of their husbands.

17. According to one report, Henry Miller, Fritz Lang, and Anais Nin are among the literary and cinematic heavyweights who praised the film upon its international release. Berkeley Art Museum and Pacific Film Archive, "The Arch, Cecile Tang Shu Shuen."

18. See, for example, Lui, *The Story of Hong Kong in the 1970s Retold*.

Chapter 7

From political alibis to creative incubators: the left-wing film network since the 1980s

In Chapters 5 and 6, the nuanced legacies of the classical left-wing cinema are delineated through the corporate history of Sil-Metropole as a cultural broker between Hong Kong and Mainland China, and the careers of Patrick Lung and Cecile Tang as critical transitions in the late 1960s and 1970s. Seen as cultural agents seeking to renegotiate a space to advance their interests in response to the changing parameters of local and national politics, their middling roles are defined against a combination of institutional, industrial, and volitional factors. The rapid expansion and internationalization of Hong Kong cinema in the 1980s and the emergence of new rivals that challenged the preeminence of Shaw and Golden Harvest brought in the so-called "golden age" of Hong Kong cinema. As a film enterprise mediating between institutional objectives and commercial interests, Sil-Metropole did not reap immediate harvest in the industry boom.[1] As suggested in Chapter 5, its influence on the Hong Kong film industry goes well beyond box office takings at a particular cross-section of time. This chapter turns to another arena where the reconfigured left-wing film network mobilized its economic and institutional resources in cultivating a niche cinema that would have a lasting impact on Hong Kong's arthouse cinema, which came of age with the arrival of the Hong Kong New Wave in the late 1970s.[2] In an attempt to further diversify its output and discover new talents, the realigned left-wing film network extended horizontally through smaller satellite studios. From production strategies to partnership cultivation, one discerns a consistent effort in engaging younger filmmakers to incubate less commercially oriented projects inspired by local experience and perspectives.

Presented below are some underarticulated subcurrents in the development of left-wing film production in the post-Cold War, post-Cultural Revolution era. A brief overview of satellite studios during the 1950s and 1960s serves as the immediate background to the developments since the late 1970s, when the left-wing film network entered a more experimental stage in terms of talent-grooming and creative incubation. An overlooked case in this phase of the left-wing's self-reinvention is the Bluebird Film Company founded by former Great Wall superstar, Hsia Moon (1933–2016). The discussion examines Hsia's behind-the-scene diplomatic labor as the left-wing's "star producer." While current scholarship has rightly noted the symbiotic relationship between the local television and the Hong Kong New Wave, greater emphasis has been placed on the auteurist character of what came to be known as the "New Hong Kong Cinema."[3] A less noticed subcurrent within this coming-of-age story is the incubator's role played by the left-wing film network. No doubt, Sil-Metropole's rise to a heavyweight player in Hong Kong cinema in the post-handover era has increased its social visibility and recognition, but its duality as both a cultural enterprise and state-level cultural agency bespeaks not only its special status in the film industry in the postcolonial era, but also its sometimes atypical business strategy and corporate ambition whose implications are not limited to box office success and industry prestige. In this scenario, the left-wing film network is seen through a plurality of agents who were directly or indirectly related to the core studio establishment, that is, Sil-Metropole or its former incarnations. Its collaboration with a new generation of homegrown filmmakers deserves closer attention because, first of all, smaller studios became the launchpads of future high-flyers in the field. In most cases, the collaboration between the left-wing film network and individual filmmakers reveals an eagerness to forge apolitical strategic partnerships through the active cultivation of a middle ground, a congenial trait discernible in successive generations of Hong Kong filmmakers. The extended production arm spinning out of the core establishment can be seen as a mini-left-wing film network, whose role and function changed from being political alibis for their parent companies to creative incubators since the 1980s. The middle-ground politics revealed through the historical trajectory of the left-wing film network is both constitutive and symptomatic of Hong Kong's film production environment, in which "politics" is often seen as an undesirable and inconvenient label from which one should keep a safe distance.[4] The biggest irony in this culture of political disavowal is perhaps the compulsion to declare one's political position or "desert" to the opposing camp. What happened to Ng Cho-fan and his left-wing colleagues, and likewise to the "freedom filmmakers," in the 1950s and 1960s was only a prelude to latecomers such as Patrick Lung and Cecile Tang. Like the strategic in-betweenness of Hong Kong in the Cold War ideological warfare, the middle ground in the local cinema exists as both a discursive and existential space that has enabled generations of filmmakers to navigate the erratic terrain of colonial, national, and international politics at critical historical junctures.

From political alibis to creative incubators: the left-wing film network

According to published filmographies and oral history accounts,[5] the major left-wing studios used to establish satellite studios as a stop-gap measure in times of political and economic adversities. Since the late 1970s, these smaller studios were the training ground for younger directors who used their cameras to capture emotions and sentiments that resonate with the experience of the local people. Small in number and mostly short-lived, these satellite studios were a flexible and contingent entity born under the specific conditions of the filmmaking environment of their times. Of immediate interest here is that strategic adjustment and realignment across political clusters was not only a common resort among filmmakers but also a distinguishing quality of their middle-ground politics (cf. Chapter 2), which is also a kind of apolitical politics that would remain an unofficial protocol of the film and entertainment industry in years to come.[6] The satellite studios were notionally set up by individual filmmakers with financial and infrastructural support from their parent companies and/or institutional backing from the Chinese government. As discreet sub-labels of the left-wing film apparatus, these smaller studios reflect the changing role of the left-wing in Hong Kong cinema, and more generally the reorientation and fine-tuning of China's cultural policy toward Hong Kong in the late colonial era.

The precursors

Prior to the 1980s, the left-wing's satellite studios were a contingent measure—a "disguise" according to Lo Duen—to mitigate the adverse consequences of an over-politicized filmmaking environment.[7] Lo did not elaborate on how and to what specific ends such "disguise" was set up, but if Sun Luen, Great Wall, and Phoenix were the official face of progressive film studios in Hong Kong, using new and lesser known sub-labels as alternative channels made perfect business sense.[8] Satellite studios were also a useful diversification tool to assemble resources, maintain output level, and ensure a steady cash flow to keep staff on the payroll. Union, the unofficial member of the left-wing film establishment, had seven subsidiaries serving as the studio's sub-units. These satellite studios were set up at various times. According to one account, these diverse sub-units collectively produced twenty-nine films between 1953 and 1964.[9]

By the mid-1960s, the political climate in China continued to deteriorate as the CCP was under the sway of ultra-leftist thought after a series of witch hunt-style purges within the Party.[10] While the left-wing studios were busy tackling the stringent requirements for ideological compliance in the film production, stars and production crews had to find ways to stay afloat in the industry. Allegedly, Flying Dragon Pictures Corporation was established as an alibi to facilitate overseas distribution.[11] Sixteen film titles were accredited to the studio between 1963 to 1970.[12] As a subsidiary of Sun Luen, Flying Dragon films were distributed through its mother company's network in Hong Kong, Southeast Asia, and North America.[13] Another shorter-lived subsidiary, Modern Film Company, was set up by actor Chow Chong to serve as a shelter for his colleagues to get around the ban on left-wing films in Southeast Asian countries.[14] Founded in 1969, the company only managed to produce three feature films before it closed down in 1972. The closing of these studios happened at a time when their mother company, Sun Luen, was itself in dire straits to stay afloat during the peak of the Cultural Revolution.[15]

As an extension of the core studio establishment, the satellite studios were a survival tool in turbulent times. By the mid-1950s, the left-wing cinema in Hong Kong had already developed two main nexuses: Mandarin film production was led by Feng Huang and Great Wall, while Cantonese film production exhibited a more diverse structure, with Sun Luen being the official left-wing studio, and Union and Wah Kiu serving as the independent arm of the progressive cinema.[16] Since the satellite studios were focused on Cantonese film production, the division of labor between Mandarin and Cantonese films on the progressive front was tilted toward the latter. While this corresponded to the demographics of the local market, the effort put in expanding the left-wing's presence in the Cantonese film market was consistent with the goals of the Clean-up Campaign laid out by the founders of Union and Sun Luen. The dynamic balance between politics and economics would continue to inform the left-wing film network's later transformations.

Bluebird Movie Enterprises: a pathfinder in the new era

As far as China's literary and cultural scene is concerned, the "New Era" refers to the time when the country began to take stock of the damages of the Cultural Revolution, and party leaders shifted toward a more pragmatic style of social reengineering and economic rehabilitation. The consolidation of the left-wing film apparatus in Hong Kong was a reflection of the pragmatic shift in China's cultural and economic policy, which was increasingly geared toward marketization and international-ization of cultural enterprises. As far as the film industry was concerned, party leaders reacted quickly to the plight of the left-wing film community shortly after the torrents of the Cultural Revolution subsided. At a meeting with progressive filmmakers in Beijing in January 1978, Liao Chengzhi called for a concerted effort to revive the Hong Kong film industry (that is, left-wing film production in Hong Kong). Beginning with a diatribe against the extremism of the Cultural Revolution and its damage to progressive filmmaking in Hong Kong, the CCP's top Hong Kong affairs expert also outlined a general direction to revitalize a "patriotic cinema" (which he also called a "new democratic revolutionary cinema") in Hong Kong. Apart from the standard admonitions about patriotism, anti-imperialism, and anti-feudalism, Liao's speech was intended to dismiss the taboos imposed on left-wing filmmakers during the Cultural Revolution. As one of the CCP's most experienced officials in Hong Kong affairs, Liao was indirectly delivering the latest party guidelines for the rehabilitation of left-wing film production in Hong Kong.[17]

It was under this open and collegiate atmosphere that Liao invited Hsia Moon, who decided to quit acting during the 1967 riots, to return to filmmaking.[18] Already in her forties, the former Great Wall superstar preferred to retire from acting to work behind the screen as a film producer. Hsia's film company, Bluebird Movie Enterprises Ltd., was founded in 1979. According to Hsia, "bluebird" is an allusion to a classical Chinese poem in which it means "delegate" and "pathfinder."[19] As we shall see, the company fulfilled its pathfinding mission during its active period (1979–1984), which also coincided with the beginning of the latest phase of the left-wing film establishment's corporatization and interna-tionalization. As a production company, Bluebird has maintained a low profile and an extremely small output of just three feature films released between 1982 and 1984, all produced by Hsia. Nonetheless, the studio made its lasting impact on Hong Kong cinema with the local and international success of two ground-breaking films, *Boat People* (Ann Hui, 1982) and *Homecoming* (Yim Ho, 1984).[20] *Boat People* was the winner of Best Director, Best Film, Best Screenplay, and Best Art Direction at the 1982 Hong Kong Film Awards. In 1984, it was outperformed by *Homecoming* in the Best Actress category. Both films were also Hong Kong's Best Foreign Film nominee for the Academy Awards, and are listed among the "100 Must-See Hong Kong movies" recommended by the Hong Kong Film Archive. Enthusiastically received by critics locally and internationally, critical literature has focused on the two films' aesthetic merit and sociopolitical significance.[21] While the "author-text" approach is indispensable to the interpretation of a film's (or any artwork's) meaning, for the purposes of this chapter the analysis below adopts a producer-context approach to shed light on the role of the producer in the creative process. Using *Boat People* as a case study, the discussion focuses on the strategic importance of Bluebird as a pathfinder to the subsequent development of the left-wing film apparatus in Hong Kong.

The first Hong Kong feature film about post-liberation Vietnam under the Communist regime, *Boat People* was shot on Hainan Island in southern China with the official support of the local government in Hainan. At the time of production, China was still engrossed in armed conflicts at the Sino-Vietnam border despite its announcement of withdrawal in 1979.[22] According to Hsia, Bluebird was established after she had come across the script of *Boat People* and lined up Ann Hui as the film's director.[23] While a direct cause-and-effect relationship cannot be taken for granted, the circumstances under which an "anti-Communist" film such as *Boat People* came into being were more than a mere coincidence. Nonetheless, the "filmed in China" label turned out to be a mixed blessing in the film's reception, which happened at a time when former political foes were just beginning to renegotiate new terms of diplomatic engagement in the post-Cold War era. In many ways, *Boat People* was a product of the changing dynamics of the Hong Kong–China relationship and the haunting presence of Cold War politics in Asia.

While it is generally true that the job of the producer is "probably the least recognized and, at the same time, the most difficult to define,"[24] in the case of *Boat People* the cultural and political capital of Hsia Moon as a film producer proved to be crucial to the creative process. Other than script selection and editing, Hsia's stature as the most important female star of the left-wing cinema was beyond doubt when a special screening program dedicated to her films was launched at about the same time as the Third Plenary Session of the Eleventh Central Committee of the CCP in December 1978. Hsia was among the guests at a reception of Hong Kong filmmakers in Beijing in January 1979, where she was invited to return to filmmaking by Liao Chengzhi.[25] Years later, Hsia fondly recalled her conversation with Liao as a "turning point" in her life, revealing both her reverence for the party elder and also her own aspirations as a filmmaker.[26] At the helm of her new production company, Hsia earned her reputation as a producer of high principles. Disenchanted by the violent and sexually explicit content in popular movies, Hsia kept a conscious distance from the commercial cinema when selecting scripts and crew.[27] While Hsia's vision as a producer was consistent with the left-wing's practice in the past, the decisions she made were also the outcome of a risk-taking personality and independent judgment that sometimes yielded unexpected results. Unpredictability, too, could also be a motivation to enlist less experienced directors and stars instead of established names. The third film in Ann Hui's "Vietnam Trilogy," *Boat People* certainly bears the entrepreneurial imprint of its charismatic star producer.

Hui's interest in Vietnamese refugees in Hong Kong originated in a television drama, *The Boy from Vietnam* (1978), commissioned by the RTHK (Hong Kong's public broadcaster). Hui went on to make her second Vietnam-themed feature film, *The Story of Woo Viet* (1981), starring Hong Kong's top male star, Chow Yun-fat, as a Vietnamese Chinese in Hong Kong. *Boat People* went further to take on the political situation in Vietnam from the perspective of a Japanese journalist, Akutagawa (George Lam), who returns to Vietnam three years after the liberation to witness the disturbing truths of life under the new regime. Hui's portrayal of postwar Vietnam is so unflattering that it irritated some sensitive political nerves elsewhere. Due to the sensitivity of its subject matter, the film was banned in China and was moved from the Competition program to a last minute "film surprise" at the 1983 Cannes Film Festival with virtually no publicity.[28] Interestingly, this "anti-Communist" film was also censored in Taiwan, on the ground that it was filmed in China with the support of the Chinese authorities. The reaction of the Taiwan government was not unforeseen, as Chow Yun-fat, the leading actor in *Woo Viet*, had declined to act in *Boat People* at the last moment for fear of losing the Taiwan market. Ironically, the controversies over the film's politics became a rallying call to the audience in Hong Kong, whose enthusiasm instantly transformed an off-beat drama film into a box office winner. *Boat People* broke the local box office record with a total revenue of over 15 million HKD, which was considered phenomenal for a non-mainstream drama film.[29] Indeed, 1982 was a year of significance for Hong Kong: Margaret Thatcher, the former British prime minister, visited Beijing in September and reached a tentative agreement with the Chinese government to draw up a blueprint for the return of sovereignty of Hong Kong to China. The agreement materialized in the *Sino-British Joint Declaration* in 1984. To the local people, it was tempting to make metaphorical connections between the world of *Boat People* (released in October 1982) and the as yet unknown world of Hong Kong under Chinese rule, despite Hui's repeated statements of disinterest and ignorance in "politics."[30]

As Bluebird's debut production, the film brought many surprises to both Hsia and Hui. Hsia's reputation and personal connections were crucial for securing filming locations and work permits in China. The local authorities went so far as to order a citywide curfew to facilitate the shooting. Thousands of troops and a few tankers were mobilized as props, and a local military detachment was called in to advise on the use of explosives.[31] This level of institutional mobilization to support the production of a Hong Kong film would be unimaginable without the political capital and diplomatic finesse that Hsia pulled together during the three-month shooting in Hainan. In a media interview in 2014, Hsia only gave an off-hand mention of her role behind the scene: "Before moving to a new shooting location, I would go there ahead of the team and host a dinner gathering [with the relevant parties] before we brought in [the actors] and other crew members."[32] Hsia did not go into the details of her communication with the various work units and officials, but it is not too far-fetched to read this casual remark as a condensed version of the protracted diplomatic labor Hsia had undertaken in her capacity as film producer.

Bluebird virtually went into perpetual hibernation after the release of *Homecoming* in 1984, the same year when the *Joint Declaration* was signed between Britain and China. The reason why Hsia did not continue film production despite the critical success of *Boat People* and *Homecoming* has puzzled many observers. A frequently cited explanation, offered by Hsia herself, borders on the fatalistic: Hsia had been waiting for "good scripts" to come her way. Judging from the company's track record and the vitality of the Hong Kong film scene in the 1980s, the scarcity of "good scripts" falls far short of being a convincing reason behind Bluebird's fading out right after *Homecoming* won five major prizes at the Hong Kong Film Awards.[33] Hsia was reported to have dropped another hint on a later occasion, saying that "one should know when to stop winning" (*jian hao jiu shou*), a colloquial expression about the need of self-restraint after making a fortune.[34] What lies behind Hsia's tongue-in-cheek statement about her withdrawal from filmmaking remains an unanswered question. One possible reason is the reservation of party officials in charge of Hong Kong affairs toward the "anti-Communist" content of *Boat People*.[35] Looking back at the brief history of Bluebird, the company's active period coincided with the arrival of the Hong Kong New Wave and the local cinema's increasing diversification and internationalization. More importantly, the years 1979–1984 saw the completion of the left-wing cinema's restructure into its present incarnation. Sil-Metropole as a production label first appeared in the left-wing studios' integrated filmography in 1982 (Zhang Jianyan's Jet Li vehicle, *Shaolin Temple*, and ex-TVB producer Stephen Shin's urban comedy, *Eclipse*) when the studios' combined annual output sank to a record low of five titles. From then on, the studio labels of Great Wall, Feng Huang, and Sun Luen were gradually phasing out. By 1985, Sil-Metropole became the exclusive studio label of Hong Kong's left-wing film production.[36]

Hsia Moon had kept a low profile after her brief yet impactful career as film producer at Bluebird. Her self-evasiveness has obscured the strategic importance of Bluebird to the later development of Hong Kong's left-wing cinema. As a pathfinder and "delegate" on a cultural mission, Bluebird's historical mission can be regarded as completed. Having successfully launched two important New Wave films, it had tested the local and international reception of non-mainstream films by new directors. Its small yet influential output signaled an emerging production partnership between Hong Kong and China at the dawn of the New Era, and anticipated the collaboration between Sil-Metropole and other New Wave and arthouse directors in making some of the finest works in Hong Kong cinema. As a bridge between two phases in the historical development of the left-wing cinema in Hong Kong, Bluebird's middling role displayed a more complex and nuanced "politics" than its predecessors. It can be seen as a forerunner of the left-wing cinema's self-reinvention in the post-Cold War, post-Cultural Revolution era.

Sil-Metropole's independent labels and arthouse projects

Localization and internationalization were two complementary trends in Hong Kong cinema in the 1980s. No doubt, Hong Kong cinema was responding to a society-wide sense of identity crisis as the clock started clicking toward the political handover.[37] Critics have commented how films from this decade have found a distinctively local voice that distinguishes itself from their predecessors.[38] As the economy continued to boom under a gloomy political climate, Cantonese became the basic tenor of this "voice" and an inherent quality of the local cinematic identity. This linguistic turn was a general trend in Hong Kong's film and popular music production (the latter's influence across the Chinese-speaking world is evidenced in the adoption of "Cantopop" as a standard reference to Hong Kong pop music). One can say that "Hong Kong cinema" and Cantopop presuppose a geo-linguistic sphere of cultural production that is coterminous with the city's quest for an identity that was not predetermined by either colonialism or nationalism. It is a kind of localism that bespeaks the city's middling position, an interstitial positionality that sits on the precarious balance between contending narratives of history, self, and nation. While patriotism had remained an official prerogative of the reconfigured left-wing film establishment, in actual practice Sil-Metropole was beginning to explore into new ways of engaging the local audience, who by now were displaying a more cosmopolitan outlook and more diversified tastes and preferences. The first sign of the left-wing's grasp of this trend in the cultural field was its collaboration with Allen Fong (Chapter 2), Ann Hui, and Yim Ho, arguably the most important New Wave directors of urban drama. The local and international success of these projects paved the way for Sil-Metropole's continuous involvement in arthouse film projects alongside mainstream genre films. The following discussion looks at the incubator's role of Sil-Metropole through its support to productions under independent labels, in particular the work of Jacob Cheung, whose filmmaking trajectory is insightful to an understanding of the new middle ground of the left-wing film network since the 1980s.

Jacob Cheung's "independent productions"

Having directed several award-winning films, Jacob Cheung has received scanty mention in critical literature on Hong Kong cinema. This is probably due to his in-betweenness as a young director whose career began after the New Wave had become an established phenomenon, and when the spotlight on the so-called "second wave" was focused on another cluster of newcomers to whom Cheung's work was somehow not affiliated. Beginning as an assistant producer at a local television station, Cheung made his debut, *Lai Shi: The Last Eunuch in China* (1988), with Golden Harvest before starting his next two award-winning films, *Beyond the Sunset* (1989) and *Cageman* (1990), at Sil-Metropole under the labels of two different companies (Dream Factory and Filmagica). In this way, Cheung's working relationship with Sil-Metropole exemplified a new model of collaboration. According to Cheung, political sensitivity was still a factor behind the use of alternative labels for distribution in Taiwan.[39] This could be the reason why Cheung's subsequent films with Sil-Metropole were released as independent labels. Between 1989 and 1999, he directed five feature films, all of which were Sil-Metropole-affiliated independent labels (Dream Factory, Filmagica and Midas). From the information available at the Hong Kong Film Archive's catalogue, Dream Factory and Midas probably were set up for a single production (respectively *Beyond the Sunset* and *The Kid*, 1999), while Filmagica is accredited with five titles.

The best-known films by Cheung, *Beyond the Sunset* was the winner of Best Film and Best Screenplay at the Hong Kong Film Awards in 1990, and *Cageman* added the Best Director award to these glories in 1992. As a work by a new director of just two feature films, *Beyond the Sunset* was a surprise win over a lineup of strong contenders, including John Woo's *The Killer* and Johnnie To's *All About Ah Long*. Timing could be a factor of the film's popularity among critics and panel judges. Unlike the fast-paced action vehicles of Woo and To, *Beyond the Sunset* is a family drama that touches on issues of parent-child relationship, the loneliness of old age, immigration, and cultural difference between the older and younger generations. Despite the sometimes overdrawn scenes about the schism between the young and the old, the local and the "foreign," and traditional and western values, the film has condensed some of the most pressing concerns shared by many Hong Kong people, who were yet to come to terms with the June 4th Incident (also known as the Tiananmen Square Massacre) in 1989. Released in July in the same year, the film could not have been conceived as a direct response to the tragedy, but a story of Hongkongers caught in a constant motion of (de)parting and the emotional challenges that result would find echoes among the local audience at a time when the society was struck by a massive wave of post-1989 emigration.

Cheung's next feature, *Cageman* (1992), is an unsparing exposé of the harsh living conditions inside a "bedspace apartment" (also known as "wired cage home" or "coffin cubicles"). A symptom of Hong Kong's chronic land shortage and hyper-density living space, coffin cubicles are probably a disgrace surpassing the rooming apartment portrayed in Lee Tit's classic, *In the Face of Demolition*, discussed in Chapter 3. In the 1990s, the property market was overheated by unchecked speculation activities, resulting in rocketing home prices and deteriorating living conditions among the lower income groups. As a "social problem" film, *Cageman* is stripped of sentimentalism and stylistic flourishes in its portrayal of low life inside the cage home, which is threatened by a removal order. Victims of a collusion between the government and property developers, the tenants begin as an inchoate mix of alienated individuals before they are awakened from self-abandonment to take concerted action to protect their "home." This pro-working class tale, however, does not offer any hope of empowerment as in the classical left-wing tradition. In *Cageman*, the idealism of collective struggle is bulldozed by the capitalist economic machine. The film's final scene further problematizes the image of the "cage" to allude to the society as a whole, when a chance encounter of ex-tenants in a zoo look at one another through a wired cage. The symbolism of the cage therefore destabilizes the class boundary between the "cage" and the outside world, which the film suggests might just be another form of imprisonment without an easy way out. In Cheung's words, "Life is about moving from one cage to another . . . We are all 'caged men.'"[40]

Cheung's profile became more diversified after the success of *Cageman*. As a producer and director, Cheung had been multi-tasking at different locations, working with partners in Hong Kong and China on film and television projects. He finally relocated to Beijing after making his first blockbuster-style costume drama, *A Battle of Wits* (2006), for which he won the Best Director title at the Hong Kong Film Awards and the Shanghai Golden Rooster Film Awards. After *The Kid*, his last film with Sil-Metropole, Cheung has been more focused on productions based in China, including a television drama in 2003. Although his later films were not able to outperform the critical impact of *Cageman*, Cheung's partnership with Sil-Metropole has laid the foundation for his later projects in Mainland China.[41]

In the 1980s and 1990s, Sil-Metropole continued to invest in film projects by new directors, among whom are familiar names associated with the local arthouse cinema, for instance, Mabel Cheung (*Beijing Rocks*, 2001), Stanley Kwan (*Full Moon in New York*), Lawrence Ah Mon (*Gangs*, 1988; *Queen of Temple Street*, 1990), and Herman Yau (*No Regret*, 1987). The youngest among them is an independent director, Carol Lai, whose second feature, *Floating Landscape* (2003), won the best cinematography award at the Hong Kong Film Awards in 2004 with several other local and international nominations. *Full Moon in New York* belongs to a cluster of films about immigration and the Chinese diaspora that came into vogue after the mid-1980s, when Hong Kong officially entered the historic countdown to 1997 and the local society was confronted by an unprecedented emigration wave. More intimate stories about the younger generation's excursions in Mainland China are found in *Beijing Rocks* and *Floating Landscape*. Stylistically and thematically diverse, in all three films, the chance encounters between migrant characters driven by unexpected circumstances are a common thread that connect people and places as the psychological drama of separation and dislocation unfolds. *Gangs*, *Queen of Temple Street*, and *No Regret*, on the other hand, explore the shadier side of urban life in stories about juvenile delinquency (*Gangs*), prostitutes (*Queen of Temple Street*), and the exploitation of women in the entertainment business (*No Regret*).

From the production information of these films gathered from various online sources and DVD credits,[42] *Beijing Rocks*, *Full Moon in New York*, *Floating Landscape*, and *Queen of Temple Street* were co-production films. Two little-known film companies, Shiobu (*Full Moon in New York*) and Filmway (*Queen of Temple Street*), were set up for the sake of a single project,[43] while *Floating Landscape* is a transnational co-production between Sil-Metropole, Filmko (Hong Kong), NHK (Japan), and Rosem Films (France). Listed as a Sil-Metropole production in the company's official filmography, *Beijing Rocks* is otherwise acknowledged as a Media Asia production.[44] These joint projects suggest a more diverse pattern of partnership and a departure from the "sub-unit" mode in the past. By the early 2000s, the left-wing film network was no longer a covert cultural broker in the service of an ideological mission. The experiments with a younger generation of homegrown filmmakers during the 1980s and 1990s can be seen as a conscious effort in localizing the left-wing cinema in Hong Kong. In this connection, cultivating a niche market production line had enhanced Sil-Metropole's standing as a label of "quality films" before the next phase of accelerated expansion and commercialization. This effort was paralleled by the company's investment in its arthouse screening venue, Cine-art, from 1988 to 2006.[45]

A key turning point occurred in 2003, when the Closer Economic Partnership Arrangement (CEPA) was signed between Beijing and Hong Kong as a measure to revitalize the local economy in the wake of the SARS epidemic.[46] Under the provisions of this agreement, films from Hong Kong could enjoy the status of "domestic films" as long as they fulfilled a percentage requirement of Mainland capital and personnel involvement. The implementation of CEPA brought about important structural changes in the Hong Kong film industry, as greater access to the China market through co-productions would become a dominant practice. Its commercial benefits aside, CEPA has been received with apprehension by critics, who have noted how filmmakers have to adapt to the regulatory and censorship practices in China as well as the tastes and viewing preferences of the Mainland audience, leading to a profusion of formulaic genre productions.[47] The implementation of CEPA marked the beginning of the latest phase of the left-wing film establishment's historical transformation. Since 2003, the company has been actively expanding its genre film collection, as evidenced in its collaboration with established names in Hong Kong action cinema, including Johnnie To (*Throw Down*, 2004), Gordon Chan and Rico Chung (*A1 Breaking News*, 2004), Andrew Lau and Alan Mak (*Confession of Pain*, 2007), Felix Chong (*Overheard*, 2009, with Alan Mak), and Dante Lam (*Beast Stalker*, 2008; *The Stool Pigeon*, 2010).

Conclusion

This chapter has sought to recover some of the missing links in the historical development of the left-wing cinema in Hong Kong. Beginning with the system of satellite studios set up as political alibi during the Cold War era, it traces the changing role and production strategies of smaller, and shorter-lived, studios that were directly or indirectly supported by the left-wing's core establishment. Using Hsia Moon and Bluebird as a case study, it has revealed how the company had served as a pathfinder under the helmsmanship of its resourceful and visionary producer, whose artistic principles, diplomatic skills, and risk-taking personality had been indispensable to the success of *Boat People* and *Homecoming*, two representative works by the Hong Kong New Wave still regarded as landmarks in Hong Kong cinema. The left-wing's incubator role is further delineated in the discussion of Sil-Metropole's collaboration with a younger generation of directors from the 1980s to the early 2000s. This phase saw the left-wing film network actively engaged in talent-grooming, a strategy to establish the company's credential as a locally based producer of "high quality" films. The implementation of CEPA in 2004 marked the latest phase of the left-wing cinema's transformation, characterized by accelerated commercialization and an increasing focus on mainstream genre films targeting the Mainland China market. As mentioned in Chapter 5, Sil-Metropole's dual mission as a state-owned cultural agency and a locally based film and media enterprise continues to steer its corporate direction today. The latest effort to bring Hong Kong films to Chinese screens is the "local content" project announced in 2017. Against the official impetus to achieve greater integration between Hong Kong and China, the incubator's role played by the left-wing film establishment since the 1980s sheds light on the post-Cold War version of the CCP's cultural front in Hong Kong. Since the change of sovereignty in 1997, the left-wing film establishment has gone far beyond its previous status as a covert cultural broker to a prominent industry player, and no less a torch bearer of the Chinese government's cultural policy toward Hong Kong. In retrospect, Mao's dictum of "making full use of Hong Kong in the interest of long-term planning" has been adaptively implemented throughout the second half of the twentieth century. Hong Kong's "use value" may not have gone up proportionally in time since the handover; hence its place in the state's long-term planning remains an open question in the on-going negotiations between city and nation in the foreseeable future.

Notes

1. One senior executive admits that Sil Metropole's performance was compromised by "internal issues." Sil-Metropole Organisation, *Sixty Years of Sil-Metropole*, 21.
2. For a discussion on the "interactive relationship" between television and filmmaking, see Cheuk, *Hong Kong New Wave Cinema*, Chapter 2.
3. The "New Hong Kong Cinema" came into being in the first half of the 1980s, when directors began to treat Hong Kong as a subject. Abbas, *Hong Kong: Culture and the Politics of Disappearance*, 23.
4. With a few exceptions that prove the norm, the aversion to politics has been a default reaction of Hong Kong filmmakers and celebrities when asked about their political views. Cf. n. 6.
5. These subsidiaries were founded by the creative personnel of the major studios to increase flexibility in financing and production schedules when their mother companies ran into operational deadlocks. Lo, "The Movies in Our Time," 132; Zhou, "Glory Be with Cantonese Films," 32–33.

6. It was very common among prominent film stars from the progressive camp to issue announcements in newspapers to deny allegations of political partisanship in local newspapers. Cf. Chapter 2. Up until today, this aversion to politics is still common among filmmakers and stars. Ann Hui, who is famous for tackling politically sensitive subjects since *Boat People* (1979, discussed in this chapter), routinely insists she has no interest in politics. Most recently, a daring minority who vocally supported the democratic movement in Hong Kong were subject to direct and indirect sanction in Hong Kong and China.

7. Lo, "The Movies in Our Time," 132.

8. The organizational structure of the major studios and the satellite studios is based on personal recollections and unofficial accounts from filmmakers' memoirs and oral history volumes referenced in this chapter.

9. Zhou, "Glory Be with Cantonese Films," 32–33.

10. Despite the caution of the moderate party leaders, the purge continued to the detriment of the CCP's principle of "making full use of Hong Kong in the interest of long-term planning." See Ching, *The Origins of the Hong Kong Riots*, 20–31.

11. Cf. n. 7.

12. Based on filmography and production details available from the Hong Kong Film Archive's (HKFA) online catalogue. Available at https:// ipac.hkfa.lcsd.gov.hk/ ipac/AS/AS-002–01_Tc.zul (last accessed 1 April 2019).

13. A regular screening venue in the United States for left-wing films was the World Theatre in San Francisco. Handbills of the World Theatre are in the HKFA's collection.

14. Ho, *Artistic Mission: An Exploration of Sun Luen Film Company*, 183.

15. The company suspended production in 1971. Cf. Chapter 2.

16. Sun Luen and Union's connection with Kong Ngee (established by Union director Chun Kim as the Hong Kong branch of its Singapore headquarters) added yet another variation to the left-wing film network. Cf. Chapter 2.

17. Liao, "Developing a Patriotic Cinema in Hong Kong," 553–556.

18. Hsia quit film acting shortly after the outbreak of the Cultural Revolution. After spending a few years in Canada with her husband, Hsia lived a low-profile life in Hong Kong until she was summoned back to filmmaking in 1978. See Yang, *The Life and Work of Hsia Moon*, 220–225.

19. Ibid., 237.

20. The third and last production by Bluebird is a martial arts film, *Little Heroes* (Zi gu yingxiong chu shaonian). It was less successful at the Hong Kong box office, but according to Hsia the film was popular among Chinese audiences as one of the first martial arts movies screened in China since the end of the Cultural Revolution. The use of children actors in leading roles in a martial arts film was also a pioneering attempt in Hong Kong cinema.

21. See, for example, Stringer, "Boat People: Second Thoughts on Text and Context," 15–22; and Yau, "Looking Back at Ann Hui's Cinema of the Political," 126–130.

22. China announced its withdrawal on 5 March 1979, which was soon dismissed by Vietnam as a "a smokescreen to cover further military action." Butterfield, "China Reports It Has Begun Withdrawal from Vietnam," *New York Times*, 6 March 1979. Border conflicts continued throughout the 1980s.

23. Yang, *The Life and Work of Hsia Moon*, 237.
24. Pardo, "The Film Producer as a Creative Force," 1–23.
25. The meeting marked the beginning of China's "Reform and Opening Up" policy under the leadership of Deng Xiaoping.
26. Yang, *The Life and Work of Hsia Moon*, 220–225.
27. Ibid., 230–233.
28. Kennedy, "Boat People," 41–47; Yang, *The Life and Work of Hsia Moon*, 243.
29. Box office figure based on the HKFA's online catalogue, available at https://www.filmarchive.gov.hk/en_US/web/hkfa/facilitiesandservices/rc/rc_cat.html (last accessed 1 April 2019).
30. Yau, "Looking back at Ann Hui's Cinema of the Political," 117.
31. Yang, *The Life and Work of Hsia Moon*, 238–239.
32. Shen, "Jin Yong's Dream Girl Hsia Moon."
33. Hsia talked about some missed opportunities much later, which included a film about Hong Kong's reunification with China and an adaptation of a novel by Zhang Ailing (1920–1995), a prominent Shanghai woman writer from the 1940s. See Yang, *The Life and Work of Hsia Moon*, 252–253. Hsia eventually sold the company to William Kong, founder of EDKO films and owner of the Broadway Cinema circuit.
34. Cf. n. 32.
35. Yang, *The Life and Work of Hsia Moon*, 243.
36. See "Filmography," in Sil-Metropole Organisation, *Sixty Years of Sil-Metropole*, 594–601.
37. Hong Kong's "pre-post-colonial" complex is captured in what Abbas calls a "culture of disappearance." See Abbas, *Hong Kong: Culture and the Politics of Disappearance*; Lee, *Hong Kong Cinema since 1997: The Post-Nostalgic Imagination*; and Lee, "Relocalising Hong Kong Cinema," 64–70.
38. See Abbas, *Hong Kong: Culture and the Politics of Disappearance*, 16–47; Teo, *Hong Kong Cinema: The Extra Dimensions*, 137–206; Cheuk, *Hong Kong New Wave Cinema*; and Lee, "The Hong Kong New Wave: A Critical Reappraisal."
39. Sil-Metropole Organisation, *Sixty Years of Sil-Metropole*, 400.
40. Wong, "Interview with Jacob Cheung."
41. Sil-Metropole Organisation, *Sixty Years of Sil-Metropole*, 547.
42. Information gathered from the Hong Kong Film Archive's online catalogue, Hong Kong Movie Database (HKMD), Internet Movie Data Base (IMDb), and production credits on DVDs.
43. Both Filmway and Shiobu have only one accredited film on the Hong Kong Film Archive's database.
44. The company information of Media Asia indicates ownership by the Lai Sun group of companies, a well-known business conglomerate in Hong Kong.
45. The cinema was reopened between 2009 to 2018 at another location as an affordable art film theater.
46. Under CEPA, Hong Kong productions will be exempt from foreign film import quota upon meeting certain requirements in Mainland personnel and capital involvement. Implemented at successive stages, the economic incentives under CEPA have prompted Hong Kong filmmakers to relocate their production bases to

China. The predominance of Hong Kong–China co-productions in the last fifteen years has aroused concerns over the marginalization of local-content films. See Teo, "Promise and Perhaps Love: Pan-Asian Production"; and Yau, "Watchful Partners, Hidden Currents," 17–50.

47. For a discussion on the "CEPA effect" and more recent trends, see Lee, "Relocalising Hong Kong Cinema," 64–70.

Epilogue

As a new world political order began to take shape in the wake of the Second World War, an intense interstate ideological battle was staged in Hong Kong, a British colony at the southern tip of the Chinese Mainland. Fought between two main protagonists, Nationalist Taiwan and Communist China, this battle would define the special character of the Cold War in this ex-colonial city. This book poses a set of questions that seek to unpack the meaning of "being on the left" in the cultural realm during the turbulent decades after the Second World War. Despite the fact that the terms "leftist" and "left-wing" in Hong Kong refer to a political identity founded upon one's support of the ruling regime in Mainland China, the concrete manifestations of the cultural left in Hong Kong was (and still is) more varied, ranging from being vocal party mouthpieces (such as *Ta Kung Pao* and *Wenhui Pao*) to progressive yet politically neutral or disinterested individuals. As such, "being on the left" of the filmmaking world encompasses not only political affiliation or conviction alone but also the processes of infrastructural and systemic construction that formed the basis of the production, distribution, and exhibition of left-wing films in and through Hong Kong. From this perspective, the inquiry into "being on the left" in the context of Hong Kong cinema in the Cold War era has sought to uncover the processes and the underlying causes and intentions (or the "how" and "why") behind overlapping lines of events and occurrences in reconstructing the history of the left-wing studios and their affiliated industry partners and collaborators. As such, this study has argued for a "middle ground" positioning of the cinematic left, and considers how this positioning has become deeply ingrained in the film industry, if not the field of cultural production, in Hong Kong up until today. Beginning with an overview of the macro- and micropolitics of interstate rivalry that made up the complex sociopolitical fabric of post-World War II Hong Kong, the analysis goes on to trace the historical footprints of the major left-wing studios and their official and unofficial collaborators and affiliates that occupied different positions in the local and regional film industries to obtain a more holistic view of the cinematic left as an organized film network, which came into being between 1949 and 1952.

As a member of the CCP's cultural brigade in Hong Kong, the left-wing film network carefully steered its course in the commercial film industry in carrying out their social and ideological mission. A close-knit community of progressive filmmakers with a patriotic and anti-imperialist outlook, the cinematic left perceived themselves more as cultural reformists than political revolutionaries, a self-perception encouraged by their CCP leaders as conducive to the party's long-term interest in Hong Kong. At the same time, their lofty ideals had to be translated into the popular medium of cinema and tested by the realities of the film market. The history of the left-wing studios in Hong Kong, therefore, is as much a story about art and politics—which has been the main rhythm of the critical discourse on the "classical" left-wing cinema of the 1950s and 1960s—as it is about the "making of" a popular left-wing cinema whose ideological mission had to be advanced by entrepreneurial finesse. These dual objectives of the popular left-wing in Hong Kong continued, albeit in a more sophisticated manner, in the post-Cold War, post-Cultural Revolution era. Without downplaying the ideological-political and ethical dimensions of the cinematic left, the preceding chapters have tried to reinterpret the cultural politics of the left-wing film establishment in Hong Kong through a closer scrutiny of its institutional affiliation and corporate practices, which nonetheless are inseparable from the CCP's cultural policy toward Hong Kong.

The historical mapping of the sociopolitical landscape of Hong Kong in light of the macropolitics of the Cold War and the micropolitics of the KMT-CCP rivalry offered in Chapter 1 has revealed the dilemmas of the British colonial administration to balance the conflicting interests of the "warring states." It has attempted to address an imbalance in the critical discourse (also noted in the Introduction) on the left-wing cinema, which has portrayed the left-wing as a patriotic and reformist community of filmmakers surviving under a hostile, pro-Taiwan/US colonial regime. While the exercise of political censorship and surveillance on the cinema has been well noted in writings on the left-wing cinema, historical scholarship on Cold War era Hong Kong and recent studies on film censorship have shed light on the colonial government's constant vigilance on the US intelligence service in Hong Kong, and its readiness to take tougher action, including arrests and deportation, against the KMT's aggressive activities.[1] Film censorship during this period, too, was not as exclusively hostile toward left-wing films as has been stated in some accounts.[2] Indeed, the contours of the localized Cold War in Hong Kong were more defined by the tacit understanding between the KMT, the CCP, and the British government that keeping Hong Kong a politically neutral zone would better serve the short- and longer-term interest of the KMT and the CCP. Such an understanding, in turn, opened up the cultural borders of Hong Kong to indirect forms of political interference and infiltration by the rivaling nation states. In this light, the left–right divide of the local film industry and the formation of the left-wing film network have to be weighed against the intentions and calculations of a wide spectrum of political and cultural agents in the context of Hong Kong's "mini-Cold war," and no less the numerous undercurrents occasioned less by political convictions than questions of personal, corporate, and institutional interests. These questions are pertinent to the discussion on the business models and corporate strategies of the cinematic left to establish a comprehensive line of operation in film production, distribution, and exhibition and their active cultivation of partnership with non-left-wing companies.

This understanding of the left-wing film network in Hong Kong has informed the analysis of the genre films of Sun Luen and Union, and the critique of modernity in the woman-centered films of Great Wall and Feng Huang. Apart from its much talked-about "literary and art film" (*wenyi pian*) classics, the left-wing's engagement with genre reveals its effort to reinvent commercial genre films as a vehicle to question the capitalist status quo without sacrificing cinema's capacity to delight. The comparison with the works of much later directors (Wong Kar-wai and Johnnie To) invites further reflection on the more enduring influence of the left-wing on Hong Kong cinema. The challenge to the right-wing's imagination of modernity is seen through the woman-centered films in which the conventional "modern girl" and "fallen woman" characters are given new interpretations as empowered individuals rather than projections of sexual and capitalist desire. The typical left-wing moral lessons embedded in these "strong woman" characters notwithstanding, attention is drawn to their alternative interpretations of modern womanhood through self-conscious citations of the right-wing's glossy prototypes. These woman-centered films, therefore, are insightful of the left-wing's conscious attempt to mount a meta-textual critique of the cinematic discourse of modernity popularized in right-wing films (such as *Mambo Girl, The Red, Red Rose,* and *Air Hostess*).

The nuanced legacies of the left-wing cinema can also be found in the careers of younger filmmakers who may have very different ideological and intellectual orientations. Patrick Lung Kong and Cecille Tang Shu-shuen stand out as critical transitions toward a local arthouse cinema represented by the Hong Kong New Wave. As China began to resume its modernization project in earnest, the left-wing film establishment in Hong Kong was also refashioned into a modern-style film and media conglomerate. Sil-Metropole, the new face of China's official film apparatus in Hong Kong, started to recruit younger filmmaking talents to develop its commercial and arthouse production streams. The story of the left-wing in Hong Kong cinema, therefore, continued in the post-Cultural Revolution era through the state's *reinvention of the cinematic left* as an institutionalized cultural broker in late colonial and postcolonial Hong Kong, one that would play a leading role in the integration of the film industries in Hong Kong and China.

Another characteristic of the reconfigured left-wing film network was the presence of smaller, and mostly short-lived, studios. While the existence of these satellite studios or sub-units has been noted by critics, their changing role as supporting units of the left-wing film network has been overlooked. Satellite studios in the past had served as political alibis and a means for maintaining a steady supply of films to fill up screen space. Beginning from the late 1970s, satellite studios took up a more proactive role as incubators of new talents. Hsia Moon's Bluebird, in this regard, was a pathfinder when the film industries in Hong Kong and China were looking for new directions in the post-Cultural Revolution era. Hsia's role as the studio's "star producer," too, has been a missing link in historical accounts of the left-wing cinema, which usually adopt a "boom and decline" framework to conclude at around the time of the Cultural Revolution. Hsia's brief sojourn as a film producer resulted in two internationally acclaimed films, *Boat People* and *Homecoming,* which became cornerstones of the Hong Kong New Wave cinema. Hsia's charismatic and risk-taking personality, in addition to her excellent public relations skills and superstar status, was indispensable to her success. Ironically, it was also a possible reason for her reluctance to continue in her new role after a third film, *Young Heroes* (1983), which catered more to the Mainland market.

The phasing out of Bluebird made way for the restructure and consolidation of Sun Luen, Great Wall, and Feng Huang into a modern film and media conglomerate. A product of the Reform and Opening Up era, Sil-Metropole represented the new economic policy under Deng Xiaoping and a continuation of the CCP's cultural policy of maintaining a local(ized) cultural presence in Hong Kong. The company has also invested in independent studios as incubators of more experimental projects that may not promise immediate market success (Jacob Cheung's Dream Factory and Filmagica are cases in point). Sil-Metropole's increasingly prominent role as a cultural broker between the Hong Kong and Mainland film industries resonates with Mao Zedong's dictum of "making full use of Hong Kong in the interest of long-term planning," even though Hong Kong's strategic value to the CCP seems to be wearing off faster in recent years than many might have expected.

Hong Kong officially entered the postcolonial era with the return of sovereignty to Mainland China on 1 July 1997. More than two decades have passed since the change of flag, and Hong Kong is increasingly making international headline news, not for the sake of its clichéd images as one of Asia's "little dragons" or the "Pearl of the Orient," but of its impeccably organized mass protests over human rights and political reforms, culminating in the Umbrella Movement in late 2014.[3] Alongside this unprecedented "Occupy" campaign was an active debate on the efficacy of the neoliberal economic system that was seen as the culprit of Hong Kong's worsening wealth gap, social inequality, and deteriorating living conditions. The general social and political atmosphere in Hong Kong in the last few years has, ironically, opened up a new space for cultural self-reflection and a rekindled interest in the concept of "left-wing" in academic and cultural arenas as a correction to the excess of neoliberal capitalism.[4]

Under the current political climate, more experimental and noncommercial independent films were making a moderate comeback, capturing the interest of a younger niche audience. A majority of these films take a highly critical look at the social and political malaise and injustice in present-day Hong Kong. In the past few years, a number of independent films have won applauses from local and overseas audiences and critics, from full-length feature films and mockumentaries to documentaries that cast fresh and critical looks at the city's crisis-stricken present. The more polemical works may even contain didactic criticism of the excesses of capitalism and the neoliberal state apparatus.[5] Allegedly, commercial theaters were reluctant to take up these "post-Umbrella Movement films" despite their popularity. Only *Ten Years* (2015), the first film of its kind, was shown at a limited number of venues. According to the film's producer Andrew Choi, *Ten Years* was made on a self-raised budget of 500,000 HKD (app. 70,000 USD), and its crews were basically unpaid. Originally conceived as a collection of shorts about Hong Kong in ten years' time, the film's production was interrupted by the Umbrella Movement, Hong Kong's first ever large-scale civil disobedience campaign. At an interview with the author, the directors said they felt compelled to alter the original stories after what they had witnessed on the occupied sites.[6] As a low-budget independent production by virtually unknown directors, *Ten Years* does not have the artistic finesse or even technical sophistication that would earn critical accolades. Surprisingly, it was the winner of the Best Film award at the 2016 Hong Kong Film Awards, and has been invited to over thirty international film festivals and special screenings overseas. By the end of 2018, the production crew had collaborated with filmmakers in Thailand, Taiwan, and Japan to produce their own *Ten Years*. Allegedly, the rejection of these "political" films by theater circuits and some institutional venues has renewed the public's uneasiness over covert censorship in present-day Hong Kong, despite the public statements made by event organizers to deny such claims.[7]

It seems that history is repeating itself with a plot twist. The question of what it means to be "on the left," too, is taking on a new shade when the traditional "left" has now become a privileged position occupied by a conservative and institutionalized circle of legislators, political parties, and their business sponsors that unambiguously supports the much begruntled status quo. At a time when the official, political "left" has become more regressive than progressive, what is left of the "left" in Hong Kong cinema, in the intellectual and philosophical senses, has to be sought in a minority community of noncommercial independent films (just as the most ferocious political criticism and lobbying campaigns are now reserved for a cyber subculture of anonymous "keyboard fighters") set against the backdrop of the city's collective struggle to liberate itself from an ideological and political cul-de-sac. It is hoped that the analysis of the left-wing studios and their network of cultural agents in Hong Kong during the Cold War era and their later transformations presented in this book has contributed toward an unpacking of the complex crossings between institutional, corporate, and individual agents caught in the capricious waters of colonial, national, and international politics. Their historical significance, as the previous chapters have argued, lies precisely in their contemporary relevance.

Notes

1. In the two collections of essays on left-wing studios published by the Hong Kong Film Archive, there is little mention of the incidents of the colonial administration's handling of KMT sabotages and aggressive US interference. Other book-length studies, including Zhang, *Studies on Hong Kong Leftist Films*; Mak, *Hong Kong Cinema and Singapore: A Cultural Ring between Two Cities*; and Su Tao, *Looking North from a Floating City*, also do not address the "multiple balancing" acts (Priscilla Roberts) of the Hong Kong government, a subject that has been repeatedly emphasized in historical research on the Cold War in Hong Kong, including the sources cited in this study.

2. One problematic aspect of these accounts is the lack of comparative empirical evidence. See Du, "Censorship, Regulations, and the Cinematic Cold War in Hong Kong," for an empirically based analysis of the Hong Kong government's film censorship practices from the 1940s to the 1970s.

3. Over 100,000 civilians, mostly students and young adults in their thirties, occupied the main roads of the city's busiest commercial districts for seventy-nine days in protest when hopes of a universal suffrage and genuine democratic reforms by 2017 were extinguished. The HKSAR's forced clearing of the occupied sites was followed by other isolated conflicts between protestors and police throughout 2015 and 2016. In September 2017, three student leaders of the 2014 protests were sentenced to serve a six-month jail term amid a wide public outcry.

4. The younger generation, most of whom were born in the 1990s, were particularly vocal in criticizing what they called the "fake left," referring to both the moderate (usually older) members of the pro-democracy camp and those whom they suspected to be infiltrators from the pro-establishment (pro-China) camp.

5. Lee, "Relocalising Hong Kong Cinema"; Fang, *Surveillance in Asian Cinema: Under Eastern Eyes*.

6. Author's interview with the *Ten Years* production team. Unpublished.

7. Lee, "Relocalising Hong Kong Cinema," 68–69.

Bibliography

Abbas, Ackbar. *Hong Kong: Culture and the Politics of Disappearance.* Hong Kong: Hong Kong University Press, 1997.

Anderson, Benedict. *Imagined Communities: Reflections on the Origin and Spread of Nationalism.* London: Verso, 1983.

"Archival Gems." Hong Kong Film Archive, 22 April 2014. https:// www.lcsd.gov.hk/ CE/CulturalService/HKFA/en_US/web/hkfa/facilitiesandservices/arcgem/ filmtitles/filmtitles02.html (last accessed 29 March 2019).

Berkeley Art Museum and Pacific Film Archive. "The Arch, Cecile Tang Shu Shuen Hong Kong/US, 1969." *Neighbour Posts,* 7 November 2013. https:// patch.com/ california/albany/the-arch-cecile-tang-shu-shuen-hong-kongus-1969 (last accessed 25 November 2018).

Biswas, Asit K., and Cecilia Tortajada. "China's Soft Power Is on the Rise." *China Daily,* 23 February 2018. http:// www.chinadaily.com.cn/a/201802/23/WS5a8f59a-9a3106e7dcc13d7b8.html (last accessed 20 January 2018).

Butterfield, Fox. "China Reports It Has Begun Withdrawal from Vietnam." *New York Times,* 6 March 1979. https:// www.nytimes.com/1979/03/06/archives/china-reports-it-has-begun-withdrawal-from-vietnam-china-announces.html (last accessed 5 April 2019).

Chan, Natalia Siu-hung. *Butterfly of Forbidden Colours: The Artistic Image of Leslie Cheung.* Hong Kong: Joint Publishing HK, 2008.

Chang, Jing Jing. *Screening Communities: Negotiating Narratives of Empire, Nation, and the Cold War in Hong Kong Cinema.* Hong Kong: Hong Kong University Press, 2019.

Chen, Edwin W. "Musical China, Classical Impressions: A Preliminary Study of Shaw's Huangmei Diao Film." In *The Shaw Screen: A Preliminary Study,* ed. Wong Ain-ling, 51–74. Hong Kong: Hong Kong Film Archive, 2003.

Cheuk, Pak Tong. *Hong Kong New Wave Cinema, 1978–2000.* Bristol: Intellect, 2008.

Cheung, Gary Ka-wai. *Hong Kong's Watershed: The 1967 Riots.* Hong Kong: Hong Kong University Press, 2009.

Ching, Cheong. *Xianggang liu qi bao dong shimo: jie du Wu Dizhou* [The Origins of the Hong Kong Riots: The Unpublished Notes of Wu Dizhou]. Hong Kong: Oxford University Press, 2018.

Chow, Vivienne. "Filmart: Sil-Metropole Sets Hong Kong Slate as Chinese Cinema's Saviour." *Variety*, 13 March 2017. https://variety.com/2017/film/asia/sil-metropol-hong-kong-movies-1202007551/(last accessed 18 January 2018).

Chu, Yingchi. *Hong Kong Cinema: Coloniser, Motherland, and Self.* London: Routledge, 2003.

Chung, Stephanie Po-Yin. "The Industrial Evolution of a Fraternal Enterprise: The Shaw Brothers and the Shaw Organisation." In *The Shaw Screen: A Preliminary Study*, ed. Wong Ain-ling, 1–18. Hong Kong: Hong Kong Film Archive, 2003.

Chung, Stephanie Po-Yin. "The Story of Kong Ngee: The Southeast Asian Cinema Circuit and Hong Kong's Cantonese Film Industry." In *The Glorious Modernity of Kong Ngee*, ed. Wong Ain-ling, 122–142. Hong Kong: Hong Kong Film Archive, 2006.

Chung, Stephanie Po-Yin. *Xianggang ying shi yi bai nian* [100 Years of the Hong Kong Film Industry]. Hong Kong: Joint Publishing HK, 2004.

Chung, Stephanie Po-Yin. "Xinlian gu shi: zhengzhi wenyi he yue yu ying ye" [The Story of Sun Luen: Politics, Art and the Cantonese Film Industry]. In *Wenyi renwu: Xinlian qiu suo* [Artistic Mission: An Exploration of Sun Luen Film Company], ed. Ho Sze-wing Sam, 35–52. Hong Kong: Hong Kong Film Archive, 2011.

Chung, Stephanie Po-Yin. "Zheng zhi jia feng zhong de dian ying ye: Zhang Shankun yu Yonghua, Changcheng ji Xinhua" [A Film Industry in between Two Political Powers: Zhang Shankun and Yong Hua, Great Wall and Xinhua]. In *Lengzhan yu Xianggang dianying* [Cold War and Hong Kong Cinema], ed. Wong Ain-ling and Lee Pui-tak, 175–187. Hong Kong: Hong Kong Film Archive, 2009.

Crowder, Michael. "Indirect Rule: French and British Style." *Africa: Journal of the International African Institute* 34, no. 3 (1964), 197–205.

Davis, Darrell William, and Yeh Yueh Yu Emilie. *East Asian Screen Industries.* London: British Film Institute, 2008.

Desser, David. "A New Orphan Island Paradise: Hong Kong Cinema and the Struggles of the Local, 1945–1965." In *Small Cinemas in Global Markets: Genre, Identities, Narratives*, ed. Lenuta Giukin, Janina Falkowska, and David Desser, 123–150. Lanham, MD: Lexington Books, 2014.

Du, Ying. "Censorship, Regulations, and the Cinematic Cold War in Hong Kong, 1947–1971." *The China Review* 17, no. 1 (2017), 117–151.

Dyer, Richard, *Stars.* London: British Film Institute, 1979.

Farquhar, Mary, and Zhang Yingjin, eds. *Chinese Film Stars.* London: Routledge, 2010.

Fang, Karen ed. *Surveillance in Asian Cinema: Under Eastern Eyes.* New York: Routledge, 2017.

Fauve, David. "Wo men zai liushi niandai zhang da de ren" [On growing up in the 1960s]. In *Xianggang dian ying zi liao guan* [Cold War and Hong Kong Cinema], ed. Wong Ain-ling and Lee Pui-tak, 13–20. Hong Kong: Hong Kong Film Archive, 2009.

Fong, Yuk Ping. "Ban bei shui, ban ge daoyan" [Half a Glass, Half a Director]. *Wen Wei Po*, 28 July 2009. http:// paper.wenweipo.com/2009/07/28/FA0907280001.htm (last accessed 18 January 2018).

Ford, Stacilee. "'Reels Sisters' and Other Diplomacy: Cathay Studios and Cold War Cultural Production." In *Hong Kong in the Cold War*, ed. Priscilla Roberts and John M. Carroll, 183–210. Hong Kong: Hong Kong University Press, 2016.

Fu, Poshek. *Between Shanghai and Hong Kong: The Politics of Chinese Cinemas*. Stanford: Stanford University Press, 2003.

Fu, Poshek. "The 1960s: Modernity, Youth Culture, and Cantonese Cinema." In *The Cinema of Hong Kong: History, Arts, Identity*, ed. Poshek Fu and David Desser, 71–89. Cambridge: Cambridge University Press, 2000.

Fu, Poshek. "Modernity, Cold War, and Hong Kong Mandarin Cinema." In *The Cathay Story*, ed. Wong Ain-ling, 24–33. Hong Kong: Hong Kong Film Archive, 2009.

Harris, Kristine. "The Goddess: Fallen Woman of Shanghai." In *Chinese Films in Focus II*, ed. Chris Berry, 111–119. London: British Film Institute, 2008.

Ho, Sze-wing Sam, ed. *Wenyi renwu: Xinlian qiu suo* [Artistic Mission: An Exploration of Sun Luen Film Company]. Hong Kong: Hong Kong Film Archive, 2011.

Ho, Sze-wing Sam, and Ernest Chan, eds. *The Cinema of Lee Tit*. Hong Kong: Hong Kong Film Archive, 2013.

Hong Kong International Film Festival. *China Factor in Hong Kong Cinema*. Hong Kong: Hong Kong Urban Council, 1997.

Hu, Jintao. "Report at the 17th National Congress of the Communist Party of China." *China Daily*, 15 October 2007. http:// www.chinadaily.com.cn/china/19thcpcnat ionalcongress/2010–09/07/content_29578561_6.htm (last accessed 20 January 2018).

Huang, Xiabo. *Xianggang xiy uan sou ji: sui yue gou chen* [Rediscovering the History of Hong Kong Movie Theaters]. Hong Kong: Chung Hwa Books Company, 2015.

Keane, Michael. *Creative Industries in China: Art, Design and Media*. Cambridge: Polity Press, 2013.

Kennedy, Harlan. "Boat People." *Film Comment* 19, no. 5 (September/October 1983), 41–47.

Law, Kar, and Frank Bren. *Hong Kong Cinema: A Cross-cultural View*. Lanham, MD: Scarecrow Press, 2004.

Law, Wing Sang. *Collaborative Colonial Power: The Making of the Hong Kong Chinese*. Hong Kong: Hong Kong University Press, 2009.

Leary, Charles. "The Most Careful Arrangements for a Careful Fiction: A Short History of Asia Pictures." *Inter-Asia Cultural Studies* 13, no. 4 (2012), 548–558.

Lee, Leo Ou-fan. *Shanghai Modern: The Flowering of a New Urban Culture in China, 1930–1945*. Cambridge, MA: Harvard University Press, 1999.

Lee, Pui-tak. "Zuo you ke yi feng yuan: Leng zhan shi qi de Xianggang dian ying jie" [The Best of Both Worlds: Hong Kong Film Industry during the Cold War Era]. In *Xianggang dian ying zi liao guan* [Cold War and Hong Kong Cinema], ed. Wong Ain-ling and Lee Pui-tak, 83–97. Hong Kong: Hong Kong Film Archive, 2009.

Lee, Vivian P. Y. *Hong Kong Cinema since 1997: The Post-Nostalgic Imagination*. Basingstoke: Palgrave Macmillan, 2009.

Lee, Vivian P. Y. "The Hong Kong New Wave: A Critical Reappraisal." In *The Chinese Cinema Book*, ed. Song Hwee Lim and Julian Ward. London: British Film Institute, 2011.

Lee, Vivian P. Y. "Relocalising Hong Kong cinema." *Wasafiri* 32, no. 3 (2017), 64–70. https:// doi.org/10.1080/02690055.2017.1322319.

Li, Xiang, and Si Ru. "'Jiuqi' hou zai teng fei: xin Yindu de zhuanxing yu fazhan" [Taking Off Again after 1997: The Transformation and Development of New Sil-Metropole]. In Sil-Metropole Organisation, ed., *Yindu liushi: 1950–2010* [Sixty Years of Sil-Metropole 1950–2010], 430–442. Hong Kong: Joint Publishing HK, 2010.

Liao, Chengzhi. "Fazhan Xianggang aiguo dianying shiye" [Developing a Patriotic Cinema in Hong Kong]. In *Liao Chengzhi wenji: Xia* [Liao Chengzhi: Selected Writings II], 553–556. Hong Kong: Joint Publishing HK, 1990 (31 January 1978). Excerpt also found in Ho Sze-wing Sam, ed., *Wenyi renwu: Xinlian qiu suo* [Artistic Mission: An Exploration of Sun Luen Film Company], 197–201. Hong Kong: Hong Kong Film Archive, 2011, and in Sil-Metropole Organisation, ed., *Yindu liushi: 1950–2010* [Sixty Years of Sil-Metropole 1950–2010], 317–319. Hong Kong: Joint Publishing HK, 2010.

Liao, Chengzhi. "Guanyu Xianggang de dianying gongzuo" [On the Work on Hong Kong Cinema]. In *Liao Chengzhi wenji: Shang* [Liao Chengzhi: Selected Writings I], 451–458. Hong Kong: Joint Publishing HK, 1990 (August 1964). Excerpt also found in Ho Sze-wing Sam, ed., *Wenyi renwu: Xinlian qiu suo* [Artistic Mission: An Exploration of Sun Luen Film Company], 189–195. Hong Kong: Hong Kong Film Archive, 2011.

Lin, Yusheng. *The Crisis of Chinese Consciousness: Radical Antitraditionalism in the May Fourth Era.* Madison: University of Wisconsin Press, 1979.

Lo, Duen. "Wo na shidai de yingxi" [The Movies in Our Time]. In *Oral History Series 1, Hong Kong Here I Come,* ed. Kwok Ching-ling. Hong Kong: Hong Kong Film Archive, 2000.

Lo, Wai-luk. "Cong Lu Dun de shijian kan zuopai dianying" [Reflections on the Left-wing cinema through Lo Duen's artistic practice]. In *Wenyi renwu: Xinlian qiu suo* [Artistic Mission: An Exploration of Sun Luen Film Company], ed. Ho Sze-wing Sa`m, 83–97. Hong Kong: Hong Kong Film Archive, 2011.

Lo, Wai-luk. "Shidai de qi yun: shuo 'Zhonglian' de qi yun" [Spirit of an Era: The Artistic Achievement of the Union Film Company]. In *One for All: The Union Film Spirit*, ed. Grace Ng, 62–75. Hong Kong: Hong Kong Film Archive, 2011.

Loh, Christine. *Underground Front: The Chinese Communist Party in Hong Kong.* Hong Kong University Press, 2018.

Lombardo, Johannes R. "A Mission of Espionage, Intelligence and Psychological Operations: The American Consulate in Hong Kong, 1949–64." *Intelligence and National Security* 14, no. 4 (1999), 64–81.

Lu, Xiaoning. "The Might of the People: Counter-espionage Films and Participatory Surveillance in the Early PRC." In *Surveillance in Asian Cinema: Under Eastern Eyes*, ed. Karen Fang, 13–32. New York: Routledge, 2017.

Lui, Tai Lok. *The Story of Hong Kong in the 1970s Retold.* Hong Kong: Chung Hwa Books, 2012.

Ma, Jean. *Sounding the Modern Woman: The Songstress in Chinese Cinema.* Durham, NC: Duke University Press, 2015.

Mak, Yan-yan Grace. *Xianggang dian ying yu Xinjiabo: Leng zhan shi dai xing gang 1950–1965* [Hong Kong Cinema and Singapore: A Cultural Ring between Two Cities, 1950–1965]. Hong Kong: Hong Kong University Press, 2018.

Marchetti, Gina. *From Tian'anmen to Times Square: Transnational China and the Chinese Diaspora on Global Screens, 1989–1997*. Philadelphia: Temple University Press, 2006.

Mark, Chi-kwan. *Hong Kong and the Cold War: Anglo-American Relations, 1949–1957*. Oxford: Oxford University Press, 2004.

Mazilli, Mary. "Desiring the Bodies of Ruan Lingyu and Linda Lin Dai." In *Transnational Chinese Cinema: Corporeality, Desire, and Ethics of Failure*, ed. Brian Bergen-Aurand, Mary Mazzilli, and Hee Wai-Siam, 69–94. Los Angeles: Bridge21 Publications, 2014.

Ng, Grace, ed. *One for All: The Union Film Spirit*. Hong Kong: Hong Kong Film Archive, 2011.

Ng, Kenny K.K. "Inhibition vs. Exhibition: Political Censorship of Chinese and Foreign Cinemas in Postwar Hong Kong." *Journal of Chinese Cinemas* 2, no. 1 (2008), 23–35.

Ng, May, ed. *Xianggang Chaoyu dianying xun ji* [Chaozhou-dialect Films in Hong Kong Cinema]. Hong Kong: Hong Kong Film Archive, 2013.

Ng, May ed. *Xianggang Xiayu dianying fang zong* [Amoy-dialect Films in Hong Kong Cinema]. Hong Kong: Hong Kong Film Archive, 2012.

Nye, Joseph S. "Soft Power." *Foreign Policy*, no. 80 (1990), 153–171, www.jstor.org/stable/1148580.

Pang, Laikwan, *Building a New China in Cinema: The Chinese Left-wing Cinema Movement, 1932–1937*. Lanham, MD: Rowman and Littlefield, 2002.

Pardo, Alejandro. "The Film Producer as a Creative Force." *Wide Screen* 22 (2010), 1–23.

Ramo, Joshua Cooper. *Brand China*. London: The Foreign Policy Centre, 2007.

Roberts, Priscilla. "Cold War Hong Kong: Juggling Opposing Forces and Identities." In *Hong Kong in the Cold War*, ed. Priscilla Roberts and John M. Carroll, 26–59. Hong Kong: Hong Kong University Press, 2016.

Roberts, Priscilla, and John M. Carroll, eds. *Hong Kong in the Cold War*. Hong Kong: Hong Kong University Press, 2016.

Schwarcz, Vera. *The Chinese Enlightenment: Intellectuals and the Legacy of the May Fourth Movement of 1919*. Berkeley: University of California Press, 1986.

Shen, Yin. "Duihua Jin Yong 'meng zhong qingren': wo de yuanze shi 'jian hao jiu shou'" [Jin Yong's Dream Girl Hsia Moon: My Principle Is One Should Know When to Stop Winning]. *Wai Tan*, 18 December 2014. http:// www.bundpic.com/posts/post/54927d5e97ea0b32a23fd452 (last accessed 1 April 2019).

Shing, Angel, and Lau Yam, ed. *Oral History Series 6: Director Lung Kong*. Hong Kong: Hong Kong Film Archive, 2010.

Sil-Metropole Organisation. "Qiye jianjie" [Background]. n.d. http:// www.sil-metropole.com/m/infopages.aspx?mid=1000001 (last accessed 18 January 2018).

Sil-Metropole Organisation, ed. *Yindu liushi: 1950–2010* [Sixty Years of Sil-Metropole 1950–2010]. Hong Kong: Joint Publishing HK, 2010.

Staiger, Janet. "Hybrid or Inbred? The Purity Hypothesis and Hollywood Genre History." In *Film Genre Reader III*, ed. Barry Keith Grant, 185–200. Austin: University of Texas Press, 2003.

Stokes, Lisa Odham. *Historical Dictionary of Hong Kong Cinema*. Lanham, MD: Scarecrow Press, 2007.

Stringer, Julian. "Boat People: Second Thoughts on Text and Context." In *Chinese Films in Focus II*, ed. Chris Berry, 15–22. London: British Film Institute, 2008.

Su, Tao. *Fu cheng bei wang: chong hui zhanhou Xianggang dianying* [Looking North from a Floating City: Remapping Post-war Hong Kong Cinema]. Beijing: Peking University Press, 2014.

Teo, Stephen. *Director in Action: Johnnie To and the Hong Kong Action Film*. Hong Kong: Hong Kong University Press, 2007.

Teo, Stephen. *Hong Kong Cinema: The Extra Dimensions*. London: British Film Institute, 1997.

Teo, Stephen. "Promise and Perhaps Love: Pan–Asian Production and the Hong Kong–China interrelationship." *Inter–Asia Cultural Studies* 9, no. 3 (2008), 341–358. DOI: 10.1080/14649370802184429.

Teo, Stephen. *Wong Kar-Wai: Auteur of Time*. London: British Film Institute, 2005.

Tsang, Steve. "Strategy for Survival: The Cold War and Hong Kong's Policy Towards Kuomintang and Chinese Communist Activities in the 1950s." *Journal of Imperial and Commonwealth History* 25, no. 2 (1997), 294–317.

Tsang, Steve Yui-Sang. *A Modern History of Hong Kong*. London: I.B. Tauris, 2004.

Tsang, Steve Yui-Sang. "Target Zhou Enlai: The 'Kashmir Princess' Incident of 1955." *China Quarterly* 139 (September 1994), 766–782.

Van den Troost, Kristof. "Under Western Eyes? Colonial Bureaucracy, Surveillance, and the Birth of the Hong Kong Crime Film." In *Surveillance in Asian Cinema: Under Eastern Eyes*, ed. Karen Fang, 89–112. New York: Routledge, 2017.

Wang, Gungwu. *Anglo-Chinese Encounters since 1800: War, Trade, Science and Governance*. Cambridge: Cambridge University Press, 2003.

Wing-Fai, Leung. *Multimedia Stardom in Hong Kong: Image, Performance and Identity*. London: Routledge, 2014.

Wong, Ain-ling, ed. *The Cathay Story*. Hong Kong: Hong Kong Film Archive, 2009.

Wong, Ain-ling, ed. *The Glorious Modernity of Kong Ngee*. Hong Kong: Hong Kong Film Archive, 2006.

Wong, Ain-ling, ed. *Oral History Series 2: An Age of Idealism: Great Wall and Feng Huang Days*. Hong Kong: Hong Kong Film Archive, 2001.

Wong, Ain-ling, ed. *The Shaw Screen: A Preliminary Study*. Hong Kong: Hong Kong Film Archive, 2003.

Wong, Ain-ling, ed. *Yue gang dianying yin yuan* [The Hong Kong–Guangdong Film Connection]. Hong Kong: Hong Kong Film Archive, 2005.

Wong, Ain-ling, and Lee Pui-tak, eds. *Lengzhan yu Xianggang dianying* [Cold War and Hong Kong Cinema]. Hong Kong: Hong Kong Film Archive, 2009.

Wong, Cindy Hing-yuk. *Film Festivals: Culture, People, and Power on the Global Screen*. New Brunswick, NJ: Rutgers University Press, 2011.

Wong, Nga-ting. "'Nongmin' daoyan Zhang Zhiliang: Xianggang jiu xiang yi ge long" [Interview with Jacob Cheung, Director of "Cageman": Hong Kong is Like a Cage]. *HK01*, 20 August 2018. https:// www.hk01.com/%E5%91%A8%E5% A0%B1/225002/%E5%B0%8E%E6%BC%94%E8%AB%87%E5%9C%9F%E5% 9C%B0-%E7%B1%A0%E6%B0%91-%E5%B0%8E%E6%BC%94%E5%BC%B5 %E4%B9%8B%E4%BA%AE-%E9%A6%99%E6%B8%AF%E5%B0%B1%E5%83 %8F%E4%B8%80%E5%80%8B%E7%B1%A0 (last accessed 8 April 2019).

Wong, Wai Lun Max. *Yue du zhi min di* [Reading the Colony]. TOM Cup Magazine Pub. Ltd., 2005.

Xu, Dunle. "Er shi shiji wu liu shi nian dai shehui zhuyi he ziben zhuyi yishi xingtai de douzheng zai Xianggang dianying de suo ying" [The Projection of Socialist vs. Capitalist Ideological Struggle in Hong Kong Cinema in the 1950s and 1960s]. In *Lengzhan yu Xianggang dianying* [Cold War and Hong Kong Cinema], ed. Wong Ain-ling and Lee Pui-tak, 263–270. Hong Kong: Hong Kong Film Archive, 2009.

Xu, Dunle. *Ken guang tuo ying* [Light and Shadow]. Hong Kong: MCCM Creations, 2005.

Yang, Ziyu. *Meng hui zhong xia: Xia Meng de dianying he rensheng* [The Life and Work of Hsia Moon]. Hong Kong: Open Page, 2017.

Yau, Ching. *Filming Margins: Tang Shu Shuen, a Forgotten Hong Kong Woman Director.* Hong Kong: Hong Kong University Press, 2004.

Yau, Esther C. M. "Watchful Partners, Hidden Currents." In *A Companion to Hong Kong Cinema*, ed. Esther M. K. Cheung, Gina Marchetti, and Esther C. M. Yau, 17–50. West Sussex: Wiley Blackwell, 2015.

Yau, Ka-Fai. "Looking Back at Ann Hui's Cinema of the Political." *Modern Chinese Literature and Culture* 19, no. 2 (2007), 117–150. www.jstor.org/stable/41490983.

Yeh, Yueh Yu Emilie. "A Small History of Wenyi." In *The Oxford Handbook of Chinese Cinemas*, ed. Carlos Rojas and Eileen Cheng-yin Chow, 225–249. Oxford: Oxford University Press, 2013.

Yi, Yiwen. *Xie shi yu shu qing: cong yueyupian dao xinlangchao* [Realism and Lyricism: Cantonese Cinema and the Hong Kong New Wave]. Hong Kong: Joint Publishing HK, 2015.

Yip, Man-Fung. "Closely Watched Films: Surveillance and Postwar Hong Kong Leftist Cinema." In *Surveillance in Asian Cinema: Under Eastern Eyes*, ed. Karen Fang, 33–59. New York: Routledge, 2017.

Yu, Mo-wan. *Xianggang dian ying shi hua er: san shi nian dai* [The History of Hong Kong Cinema II, 1930s]. Hong Kong: Subculture Ltd., 1997.

Zarrow, Peter. *China in War and Revolution, 1895–1949*. London: Routledge, 2005.

Zhang, Yan. *Studies on Hong Kong Leftist Films*. Beijing: Peking University Press, 2010.

Zhang, Yan. "'Wenge' shi nian de ying xiang yu zhong chuang" [The Cultural Revolution's Impact and Damage]. In *Yindu liushi: 1950–2010* [Sixty Years of Sil-Metropole 1950–2010], ed. Sil-Metropole Organisation, 216–225. Hong Kong: Joint Publishing HK, 2010.

Zhang, Yingjin. *Chinese National Cinema*. New York and London: Routledge, 2004.

Zhou, Chengren. "Glory Be with Cantonese films: Ng Cho-fan and Union Film." In *One for All: The Union Film Spirit*, ed. Grace Ng, 26–35. Hong Kong: Hong Kong Film Archive, 2011.

Zhou, Chengren. "Lengzhan beijing xia de Xianggang zuopai dianying" [Hong Kong's Leftist Cinema during the Cold War Era]. In *Lengzhan yu Xianggang dianying* [Cold War and Hong Kong Cinema], ed. Wong Ain-ling and Lee Pui-tak, 21–34. Hong Kong: Hong Kong Film Archive, 2009.

Zhou, Chengren. "Zhi you yueyu pian cai neng zai Xianggang sheng gen shi shuo Xinlian cheng li bei jing" [Only Cantonese Films Can Rake Roots in Hong Kong: On the Establishment of Sun Luen]. In *Wenyi renwu: Xinlian qiu suo* [Artistic Mission:

An Exploration of Sun Luen Film Company], ed. Ho Sze-wing Sam, 53–68. Hong Kong: Hong Kong Film Archive, 2011.

Zhou, Chengren, and Li Yizhuang. *Zaoqi Xianggang dianying shi 1897–1945* [The Early History of Hong Kong Cinema, 1897–1945]. Shanghai: Shanghai People Publishing, 2009.

Zuo, Guifang. "Zi you zong hui jian jie yu da shi ji" [The Free Association: Introduction and Chronology of Key Events]. In *Lengzhan yu Xianggang dianying* [Cold War and Hong Kong Cinema], ed. Wong Ain-ling and Lee Pui-tak, 271–289. Hong Kong: Hong Kong Film Archive, 2009.

Filmography

Film Title	Director(s)
A Battle of Wits/ Mo gong 墨攻 (2006)	Jacob Cheung Chi-leung 張之亮
A Better Tomorrow 英雄本色 (1986)	John Woo Yu-sen 吳宇森
A Chinese Ghost Story I/ Qian nü you hun 倩女幽魂 (1987)	Ching Siu-tung 程小東
A Chinese Ghost Story II/ Qian nü you hun er: ren jian dao 倩女幽魂二之人間道 (1990)	Ching Siu-tung 程小東
A Chinese Ghost Story III/ Qian nü you hun san: dao dao dao 倩女幽魂三之道道道 (1987)	Ching Siu-tung 程小東
A Home of a Million Gold/ Qian wan renjia 千萬人家 (1953)	Chu Kea 珠璣
A Simple Life/ Tao jie 桃姐 (2012)	Ann Hui On-wah 許鞍華
A Widow's Tears/ Xin gua 新寡 (1956)	Zhu Shilin, Chan Ching-po, Long Ling 朱石麟, 陳靜波, 龍凌
A World Without Thieves/ Tianxia wu zei 天下無賊 (2004)	Feng Xiaogang 馮小剛
A1 Breaking News, A1 Tou tiao A1 頭條 (2004)	Gordon Chan Kar-seung, Chung Kai-cheong Rico 陳嘉上, 鍾繼昌
Ah Ying/ Ban bian ren 半邊人 (1983)	Allen Fong Yuk-ping 方育平
Air Hostess/ Kong zhong xiaojie 空中小姐 (1959)	Evan Yang 易文
All About Ah Long/ A lang de gushi 阿郎的故事 (1989)	Johnnie To Kei-fung 杜琪峯
An Orphan's Tragedy/ Gu xing xie lei 孤星血淚 (1955)	Chu Kea 珠璣
An Unmarried Mother/ Wei chu jia de mama 未出嫁的媽媽 (1958)	Zhu Shilin, Wen Yimin 朱石麟, 文逸民
Assembly/ Ji jie hao 集結號 (2007)	Feng Xiaogang 馮小剛
Autumn/ Qiu 秋 (1954)	Chun Kim 秦劍
Back to 1942/ Yi jiu si er 一九四二 (2012)	Feng Xiaogang 馮小剛
Beast Stalker/ Zheng ren 証人 (2008)	Dante Lam Chiu-yin 林超賢
Beijing Rocks/ Beijing le yu lu 北京樂與路 (2001)	Mabel Cheung Yuen-ting 張婉婷
Beyond the Sunset/ Fei yue huanghun 飛越黃昏 (1989)	Jacob Cheung Chi-leung 張之亮
Blood and Gold/ Xie ran huangjin 血染黃金 (1957)	Chu Kea 珠璣

Blossom Time/ Ge lü qing chao 歌侶情潮 (1933)   Chiu Shu-sun (aka Joseph Sunn Jue), Kwan Man-ching 趙樹燊, 關文清

Boat People/ Tou ben nu hai 投奔怒海 (1982)   Ann Hui On-wah 許鞍華

Broken Spring Dreams/ Chun can meng duan 春殘夢斷 (1955)   Lee Sun-fung 李晨風

Butterfly Murders/ Die bian 蝶變 (1979)   Tsui Hark 徐克

Cageman/ Long min 籠民 (1992)   Jacob Cheung Chi-leung 張之亮

Cell Phone/ Shou ji 手機 (2005)   Feng Xiaogang 馮小剛

Centre Stage/ Ruan Lingyu 阮玲玉 (1990)   Stanley Kwan Kam-pang 關錦鵬

China Behind/ Zai jian Zhongguo 再見中國 (1974)   Cecile Tang Shu-shuen 唐書璇

Confession of Pain/ Shang cheng 傷城 (2007)   Alan Mak Siu-fai, Andrew Lau Wai-keung 麥兆輝, 劉偉強

Crouching Tiger, Hidden Dragon/ Wohu Canglung 臥虎藏龍 (2000)   Ang Lee 李安

Exiled/ Fang zu 放·逐 (2006)   Johnnie To Kei-fung 杜琪峯

Extra/ Jia li fei 茄哩啡 (1978)   Yim Ho 嚴浩

Family/ Jia 家 (1953)   Ng Wui 吳回

Father and Son/ Fu yu zi 父與子 (1954)   Ng Wui 吳回

Father and Son/ Fu zi qing 父子情 (1981)   Allen Fong Yuk-ping 方育平

Floating Landscape/ Lian zhi fengjing 戀之風景 (2003)   Carol Lai Miu-suet 黎妙雪

Full Moon in New York/ Ren zai Niuyue 人在紐約 (1989)   Stanley Kwan Kam-pang 關錦鵬

Gangs/ Tong dang 童黨 (1988)   Lawrence Ah Mon 劉國昌

Girl on the Front Page/ Xinwen Renwu 新聞人物 (1960)   Li Pingqian 李萍倩

Green Swan Nightclub/ Lü tian'e yezhonghui 綠天鵝夜總會 (1958)   Li Pingqian 李萍倩

Hero/ Ying xiong 英雄 (2002)   Zhang Yimou 張藝謀

Hiroshima 28/ Guangdao 28 廣島廿八 (1974)   Patrick Lung Kong 龍剛

Homecoming/ Si shui liu nian 似水流年 (1984)   Yim Ho 嚴浩

In the Face of Demolition/Wei lou chun xiao 危樓春曉 (1953)   Lee Tit 李鐵

In the Mood for Love/ Hua yang nian hua 花樣年華 (2000)   Wong Kar-wai 王家衛

Joyce and Deli / Zi mei qu 姊妹曲 (1954)   Zhu Shilin 朱石麟

Just Like Weather/ Meiguo xin 美國心 (1986)   Allen Fong Yuk-ping 方育平

Kung Fu Hustle/ Gong fu 功夫 (2004)   Stephen Chow 周星馳

Kung Fu Panda/ Gongfu xiongmao 功夫熊貓 (2008)   Mark Osborne, John Stevenson

Lai Shi: the Last Eunuch in China/ Zhongguo zui hou yi ge tai jian 中國最後一個太監 (1988)   Jacob Cheung Chi-leung 張之亮

Life without Principle/ Duo ming jin 奪命金 (2011)   Johnnie To Kei-fung 杜琪峯

Linger/ Hu die fei 蝴蝶飛 (2008)   Johnnie To Kei-fung 杜琪峯

Loving Father, Faithful Son/ Fu ci zi xiao 父慈子孝 (1954)   Tso Kea 左几

Lust Caution/ Se jie 色，戒 (2007)   Ang Lee 李安

Mad World/ Yi nian wu ming 一念無明 (2016)   Wong Chun 黃進

Mama Sings a Song/ Fu chang fu sui 婦唱夫隨 (1957) — Zhu Shilin, Chan Ching-po, Ren Yizhi 朱石麟, 陳靜波, 任意之

Mambo Girl/ Manbo nülang 曼波女郎 (1957) — Evan Yang 易文

Money/ Qian 錢 (1959) — Ng Wui 吳回

Mr. Cinema/ Lao gang zheng zhuan 老港正傳 (2007) — Samson Chiu Liang-ching 趙良駿

Mulan/ Hua Mulan 花木蘭 (1998) — Barry Cook, Tony Bancroft

Neighbours All/ Jia jia hu hu 家家戶戶 (1954) — Chun Kim 秦劍

No Regret/Liang mei zheng zhuan 靚妹正傳 (1987) — Herman Yau Lai-to 邱禮濤

Overheard/ Qie ting feng yun (2009) 竊聽風雲 — Felix Chong Man-keung, Alan Mak Siu-fai 莊文強, 麥兆輝

Parents' Hearts/ Fumu xin 父母心 (1955) — Chun Kim 秦劍

Prince of Broadcasters/ Bo yin wang zi 播音王子 (1966) — Patrick Lung Kong 龍剛

Queen of Temple Street/ Miao jie huang hou 廟街皇后 (1990) — Lawrence Ah Mon 劉國昌

Rendezvous/ Jiaren you yue 佳人有約 (1960) — Li Pingqian 李萍倩

Sap Sam Bup Dup/ Shi San Bu Da 十三不搭 (1975) — Cecile Tang Shu-shuen 唐書璇

Seven Swords/ Qi jian 七劍 (2005) — Tsui Hark 徐克

Shaolin Temple/ Shaolin si 少林寺 (1982) — Cheung Sing-yim 張鑫炎

Spring/ Chun (1954) 春 — Lee Sun-fung 李晨風

Spring in a Small Town / Xiao cheng zhi Chun 小城之春 (1947) — Fei Mu 費穆

Story of a Discharged Prisoner/ Ying xiong ben se 英雄本色 (1967) — Patrick Lung Kong 龍剛

Sunrise/ Ri chu 日出 (1956) — Hu Siaofung, Su Chengsho 胡小峰, 蘇誠壽

Suspicion/ Zhuo gui ji 捉鬼記 (1957) — Huang Yu 黃域

Sworn Sisters/ Jin lan zi mei 金蘭姊妹 (1954) — Ng Wui 吳回

Teddy Girls/ Fei nü zheng zhuan 飛女正傳 (1968) — Patrick Lung Kong 龍剛

Ten Years/ Shi nian 十年 (2015) — Jevons Au, Ng Ka-leung, Kwok Zune, Chow Kwun-wai Wong Fei-pang 歐文傑, 伍嘉良, 郭臻, 周冠威, 黃飛鵬

The Arch/ Dong fu ren 董夫人 (1969) — Cecile Tang Shu-shuen 唐書璇

The Bloody Paper Man/ Xue zhi ren 血紙人 (1964) — Lee Tit 李鐵

The Boy from Vietnam/ Shizishan xia zhi lai ke 獅子山下之來客 (1978) [Television drama] — Ann Hui On-wah 許鞍華

The Burning of the Imperial Palace/ Huo shao Yuanmingyuan 火燒圓明園 (1983) — Li Han-hsiang 李翰祥

The Butterfly Lovers/ Liang Shanbo yu Zhu Yingtai 梁山伯與祝英台 (1954) — Sang Hu, Huang Sha 桑弧, 黃沙

The Cruel Husband/ Du zhangfu 毒丈夫 (1959) — Ng Wui 吳回

The Enigmatic Case/ Bi shui han shan duo ming jin 碧水寒山奪命金 (1980) — Johnnie To Kei-fung 杜琪峯

The Eye /Jian gui 見鬼 (2002) — Pang Brothers 彭氏兄弟

The Eye 2/ Jian gui er 見鬼 2 (2004) — Pang Brothers 彭氏兄弟

The Grandmaster/ Yi dai zong shi 一代宗師 (2013) — Wong Kar-wai 王家衛

The Hong Kong Tycoon/ Bao fa hu 暴發戶 (1979)

Cecile Tang Shu-shuen 唐書璇

The House of 72 Tenants/ Qi shi er jia fang ke 七十二家房客 (1963)

Wong Wai-yat 王為一

The House of 72 Tenants/ Qi shi er jia fang ke 七十二家房客 (1973)

Chor Yuen 楚原

The Idiot's Wedding Night/ Sha zai dong fang 傻仔洞房 (1933)

Lai Bak-hoi 黎北海

The Kid/ Liu xing yu 流星語 (1999)

Jacob Cheung Chi-leung 張之亮

The Killer/ Die xue shuang xiong 喋血雙雄 (1989)

John Woo Yu-sen 吳宇森

The Love Eterne/ Liang Shanbo yu Zhu Yingtai 梁山伯與祝英台 (1963)

Richard Li Han Hsiang 李翰祥

The Orphan/ Ren hai gu hong 人海孤鴻 (1960)

Lee Sun-fung 李晨風

The Prodigal Son/ Bai jia zai 敗家仔 (1952)

Ng Wui 吳回

The Secret/ Feng jie 瘋劫 (1979)

Ann Hui On-wah 許鞍華

The Stool Pigeon/ Xian ren 綫人 (2010)

Dante Lam Chiu-yin 林超賢

The Story of Woo Viet/ Hu yue de gushi 胡越的故事 (1981)

Ann Hui On-wah 許鞍華

The Wedding Night/ Xin hun di yi ye 新婚第一夜 (1956)

Zhu Shilin, Jiang Ming, Wen Yimin 朱石麟, 姜明, 文逸民

The Window/ Chuang 窗 (1969)

Patrick Lung Kong 龍剛

Throw Down/ Rou dao long hu bang 柔道龍虎榜 (2004)

Johnnie To Kei-fung 杜琪峯

Typhoon Signal No. 10/ Shi hao feng bo 十號風波 (1959)

Lo Duen 盧敦

Vanished Archives/ Xiao shi de dang'an 消失的檔案 (2017)

Connie Lo Yan-wai 羅恩惠

White Gold Dragon/ Bai jin long 白金龍 (1933)

Tang Xiaodan 湯曉丹

Wild, Wild Rose/ Ye meigui zhi lian 野玫瑰之戀 (1960)

Wong Tin-lam 王天林

Yesterday, Today, Tomorrow/ Zuo tian, jin tian, ming tian 昨天今天明天 (1970)

Patrick Lung Kong 龍剛

Young Heroes/ Zi gu ying xiong chu shao nian 自古英雄出少年 (1983)

Mou Tun Fei 牟敦芾

Zhuangzi Tests His Wife/ Zhuangzi shi qi 莊子試妻 (1913)

Lai Bak-hoi 黎北海

72 Tenants of Prosperity/ Qi shi er jia zu ke 七十二家租客 (2010)

Eric Tsang Chi-wai, Chung Shu-kai, Patrick Kong 曾志偉, 鍾澍佳, 葉念琛

Index